MW00617774

Following Their Footsteps

Following Their Footsteps

A Travel Guide & History of the 1775 Secret Expedition to Capture Quebec

with canoeing and hiking guides
& maps of the entire route

by Stephen Clark

Steve Clark

Jan 2006

Photography by Stephen and Sherri Clark

Cover by Lisa Biasin of Lisart Gallery and Framing, Wells, Maine

Produced by Lance Tapley and Asa Tapley

Designed by Jeffrey Haste

Printed in Canada

ISBN:0-9741677-0-3

Dedication

There can be only one possible dedication of this book:
to the men of the Expedition to Quebec and their leader.
There were 1,105 known men who began the expedition.
Some became sick or injured and had to turn back.
Some turned back because the hardships were too great.
Some were buried along the way.
Some died, were wounded, or were captured before Quebec.
Many were truly courageous, others much less so.
Each, in his own way, contributed to this great endeavor,
a beginning of the effort to build a country
dedicated to its citizens' inalienable rights.

Table of Contents

Canoe Trips

Appendices

Maps

Author's Preface: About Benedict Arnold and Courage

Benedict Arnold was thirty-four when he was given command of the Expedition to Quebec. At that time, he had only limited military experience. It did not include commanding a large expeditionary force through a little-known wilderness to capture the most heavily fortified city in North America. He had gained some experience in the local militia in his home state of Connecticut. Soon after the outbreak of hostilities at Lexington and Concord, he proposed attacking, and was sent to capture, Fort Ticonderoga on Lake Champlain. This was accomplished in a surprise attack in cooperation with Ethan Allen and his Green Mountain Boys on May 10, 1775.

This action gave the rebel cause the only heavy cannons available in America at that time. They were laboriously sledded across the Berkshire Mountains and used to break the siege of Boston, driving out the British. Arnold also used several small sloops captured at Ticonderoga to ravage and destroy British military supplies and vessels at St. John near the northern end of Lake Champlain. However, the command of a large body of men such as the expedition against Quebec was quite another thing. It should be pointed out that very few officers in the fledgling American army had much experience.

Yet Arnold performed brilliantly during the march. For the participants, the expedition proved to be a crucible of extreme hardship and danger, from which Arnold emerged as an outstanding leader of soldiers and, as later events unfolded, possibly the finest field general of the Revolutionary War on either side. And, though he was on the losing side in the attack on Quebec, the serious wound in his leg attested to his valor.

During the American retreat from Canada, he had the foresight and energy to plan and oversee the building of a small fleet of ships on Lake Champlain during the summer of 1776. This strategy delayed a huge, onrushing British army, forcing it to build its own fleet of ships to counter Arnold's. This development led to the naval battle at Valcour Island near Plattsburgh, New York, in October of 1776. A vastly superior fleet manned by veteran British seamen soundly defeated Arnold's tiny flotilla. But the summer-long holding action caused General John Burgoyne to delay an advance of his crack British army until the spring of 1777. This gave the Americans a year to gather forces to oppose this threat from the north.

The climax of the northern campaign for both armies occurred at Saratoga in October of 1777. The bumbling and incompetent American commander, General Horatio Gates, hated Arnold and denied him direct command of any of the forces there. When the first shots of the final battle sounded, Arnold could wait no longer, leaped to his horse, and galloped to the front of the lines. He led the American forces, many of whom had been with him at Quebec, against the British right. He charged from one part of the battlefield to another, through a hail of lead balls, constantly exhorting his men forward against entrenched British positions. His reckless bravery in the face of heavy fire was breathtaking and inspiring to the men of both sides.

Near the end of the day, forces led by Arnold overran several key British positions and soundly defeated Burgoyne's best troops. Arnold lay wounded again. His horse had been shot out from under him and had crushed his leg in the fall, the same leg wounded at Quebec. He was carried from the field, but this battle had been won.

General Burgoyne, now cut off from supplies and deep in enemy territory, with no hope of breaking through to Albany or retreating to Canada, surrendered several days later with his entire army of 6,000 soldiers. General Gates, who had never ventured forth from the safety of his headquarters during the entire battle, got credit for the glorious victory, but the men who fought the battle knew who had led them.

All this makes Arnold's later treachery and treason at West Point unfathomable. Many historians have tried to make sense of so great a contradiction. Even today, it is difficult to understand. It is outside the scope of this book to delve into such a complex investigation, to gain understanding of why Arnold chose such a contradictory path, which led him to become a traitor to the cause for which he had fought so valiantly. This book's bibliography suggests several fine biographies of Benedict Arnold that attempt to explain these events. The Maine State Library in Augusta has almost fifty volumes devoted all or in part to his life.

In this book, the reader may note the lack of focus on the person of Benedict Arnold. The author does not use the terms "the Arnold Expedition to Quebec" or "the Arnold Trail" to characterize the expedition's route. These labels are very commonly used, but tend to place too much attention on the expedition's leader, de-emphasizing the *collective* bravery and accomplishments of all the men who survived the wilderness and eventually fought before the gates of Quebec.

All of the approximately 675 soldiers who emerged from the wilderness had proven their courage. That courage was further tested by fire during the wild night attack upon Quebec on December 31, 1775. They paid a terrible price. More than two-thirds of the soldiers were wounded, died, or were taken prisoner during the attack.

The bravery of these soldiers is unquestioned. It is that bravery we honor in writing *Following Their Footsteps*. Those footsteps track through the black mud of the Maine wilderness and the red-tinted snow under the walls of Quebec. Those tracks lead farther, all the way to our own twenty-first century, to our similar need for courage as we face the multitude of crises confronting our own age.

Benedict Arnold, 1741-1801
This engraving is from a painting in 1777. Arnold was later promoted to general before his treason at West Point.

Acknowledgments

In a way, every book is the sum total of an author's ancestry and life experiences. I think of the high-school English teacher who taught me really how to read; the grandfather who shared with me his experiences in the Maine woods; my reading of the great Maine historical novelist, Kenneth Roberts, whose *Arundel* inspired my imagination, as it has for so many others.

As is the case with most authors, I owe special thanks to several people for their important contributions in shaping this book: Duluth Wing of Eustis, who shares my deep interest in the Quebec expedition and who has discovered piles of lead musket balls along the Dead River; Jay Adams of Old Fort Western, who has advised me on many technical aspects of the expedition; my wife, Sherri, who took many of the pictures in the book and has supported me throughout my long work on it; my daughter, Lisa Biasin, who did such a great job on the cover painting; W. Elery Keene and Elaine Campbell, who have spent many hours double-checking the book and making many suggestions on how to improve it; and Daniel Warren, ancestor of Reuben Colburn and an officer of the Arnold Expedition Historical Society.

I also wish to thank those many people who have offered small but important suggestions and clues that fill in the chinks and add quality to any effort. And thanks to the inventors of the computer spell-checker, who have saved me from innumerable embarrassments.

Most of all, the author is in debt to the approximately fifty journal writers of the expedition, who in their own vivid words have revealed to us that they were men who believed and men who risked all. Their inspiring courage has not only enriched the author but all who follow in their footsteps.

Stephen Clark
Shapleigh, Maine

Following Their Footsteps

Chapter One

History Prologue

In the creation of a new nation, 1775 was a very tumultuous year. It began with Boston's occupation by redcoated troops sent there to quell unrest in a rebellious, defiant local populace. Emotions in the city and surrounding towns were like tinder, ready to explode into bloodshed at the smallest spark. The British generals had obtained intelligence that powder and arms had been collected and stored in nearby Concord. In April, they decided to send a military force to confiscate the munitions. This action was the first in a long series of errors in British judgment that eventually led to the loss of their American colonies.

On April 19, 1775, seventy local militia and several hundred British regulars nervously faced each other on Lexington Green. A shot was fired, and the Revolution was on. Later that day, the British soldiers faced a much larger force of minutemen at Concord Bridge, and many more shots were fired and men died. This was much more resistance than the British commander had anticipated. Realizing his precarious plight, he ordered a retreat to the safety of Boston. Colonial snipers hidden behind stone walls and trees killed and wounded many redcoats on their long march back to Boston. Blood had been spilled; there was no going back. The Revolutionary War would last eight long years.

The electrifying news of these monumental events traveled with great speed, for that time, to all parts of the American colonies, to London, and beyond. Local militias from throughout the colonies formed up and marched to join the rebels, forming a ring around the British troops in Boston. Their numbers rapidly grew to 15,000 loosely organized, sometimes unruly men.

In June, the colonial troops decided to preempt an anticipated British attack by occupying and fortifying the heights of Bunker and Breed's Hills near Charlestown, just across the Charles River from Boston. On June 16, militia regiments under Prescott and Warren marched at night to occupy Breed's Hill. In the morning, the surprised and enraged British leaders and all of Boston could easily see the new entrenchment and breastworks thrown up on the hills above Charlestown. These works threatened the entire harbor and city and could not be tolerated. Action had to be taken.

On June 17, General Gage, the British commander,

Introduction

We live in an age of profound change, adapting as best we can to radical new technologies, ideas, and ways of living. The year 1775 was in many ways in a similar period of upheaval. European Americans were striking out into a vast new continent. They were in the beginning stages of moving from an agrarian society to the Industrial Age. They were forcibly throwing off the yoke of a king and a way of rule no longer respected nor accepted. They were beginning to form a new country with a very different kind of government. Our understanding of what our ancestors did ten generations ago may help us cope with our own rapidly changing world. There was a favorite song of that age, "The World Turned Upside Down." That could well be a hit tune today.

Our connection with the past is often characterized as "shared memories," and they are revered by every civilization. Indeed, some cultures have built their religions and social structures around such reverence. This book seeks to invoke that reverence through the medium of understanding what our ancestors did. A way to gain that understanding is to retrace the great events of the birth of our country. One of these events took place in the first tumultuous year of the Revolutionary War. This is the Expedition to Quebec of 1775.

Some historians have compared the expedition, led by Colonel Benedict Arnold, to Hannibal and his Carthaginians crossing the Alps into northern Italy in 218 B.C., during the Punic Wars with Rome. As with Hannibal, the attack on Quebec ended in defeat for the young American army of the north. But, as is sometimes the case in military history (though not with Hannibal), defeat in a given battle may eventually lead to winning the war. This was exactly the case with the men who were defeated at Quebec. Besides being one of the great adventure stories of our country's military history, the Expedition to Quebec was of great importance to the outcome of the war.

When United States history is taught in high schools, many, maybe most, students find textbooks uninteresting and of little relevance to their lives. Oh those names, dates, and places! It is a rare history teacher indeed who is able to stimulate excitement in his or her students and lead them to the discovery of the richness of our shared memories. Even many adults have a hard time hitting the History Channel's button.

An alternative way to enliven an interest in history is to learn within the context of an experience. In addition to reading novels and histories about the Quebec expedition, we can understand and enjoy this saga by converting our automobile into a time machine.

This book's title, Following Their Footsteps, suggests the reader undertake his or her own expedition, retracing the American army's epic journey over the entire distance from Cambridge to Quebec. This adventure allows one to visit the same buildings, walk the same portage trails, canoe the same rivers, and even see the same dungeons in Quebec that the expedition's men experienced. The route described in this book approximates, as closely as possible, the expedition's route more than 225 years ago. Parking lots, roads, buildings, dams, and other modern developments in some places have covered or altered the exact route. However, much of it remains the same, if you know where to look.

To prepare yourself for our journey, consider reading Kenneth Roberts's great novel Arundel. It comes about as close as possible to transforming the story of the expedition into a live event. Roberts's meticulous research, wonderful characters, and vivid style ensure that his book is a joy to read. We strongly recommend that you read his book as a primer to the expedition's experience.

Combining the Guide and the History

It is difficult to read a book that is a travel guide and weave into it an extensive historical narrative. That approach makes the reading choppy and hard to follow. To avoid such a hodgepodge, we have put two separate books under one cover. One book presents a modern traveler's guide, describing in detail how to follow the route, generally using a car, from Massachusetts to Quebec. A second book contains an historical narrative of the events that took place in 1775. The two books are connected as closely as possible. A chapter of the Travel Guide is matched with an historical chapter that describes the events that occurred in the places covered by the guide. This format allows readers some flexibility in deciding how much history they wish to digest as they travel along the route.

There also are five suggested canoe trips along the route, and several hiking trips are described within the Travel Guide chapters.

Planning the Trip

To comfortably follow the expedition's footsteps in a single trip, covering the entire distance by auto, you will need a bare-bones minimum of five to seven days. If you elect to stop at most of the many points of interest, as we recommend, this will require additional days. If you choose to undertake some of

decided to teach a lesson to the arrogant rabble on the hills and possibly end this rebellion then and there. He ferried boatload after boatload of troops to Charlestown and began forming ranks. Supported by heavy cannon fire from British warships in the harbor, they began a slow, methodical climb to the beat of drums, solid rank by solid rank, up through the farm fields toward the men who lay waiting in their trenches at the brow of the hill. People watched from the rooftops of Beacon Hill to view the anticipated rout. As the perfectly straight lines of red-coated soldiers neared the top of the hill, the colonials in the trenches fired hundreds of musket balls into the massed lines of British soldiers. The front ranks melted under the deadly hail of lead balls.

The battle went on for hours. The British made three separate frontal assaults. Only when the rebels ran short of powder and ball did they retreat, leaving the bloody heights to the enemy. Driving the rebels off cost the British dearly, more than a thousand brave men. For the colonials, it proved that red coats did not make the British invincible. After the battle, a long siege of Boston commenced. It would last until the following spring.

During the winter, the colonials laboriously sledded heavy, long-range cannons, captured at Fort Ticonderoga on Lake Champlain, across the Berkshire Mountains to the siege lines around Boston. When these cannons were mounted on Dorchester Heights, within range of Boston and the vital harbor, the British hastily evacuated. They loaded all they could on their ships and sailed to Halifax, Nova Scotia, never to return.

Even before the battle of Bunker Hill, the newly formed Continental Congress in Philadelphia had recognized the need to appoint a leader for this fledgling army. A commander was needed who possessed experience, stature, and who could begin the process of organizing the hodgepodge of militias around Boston into a cohesive military force. The Congress almost immediately recognized George Washington of Virginia as the right man, and he was appointed commander-in-chief. Directed to proceed posthaste to take command of the troops besieging Boston, he arrived in Cambridge, just west of Boston, on July 2.

In a ceremony held on Cambridge Common in front of 9,000 of the assembled troops billeted in the area, Washington officially took command on July 4, 1775, coincidently exactly one year prior to the signing of the Declaration of Independence. He established his headquarters in Cambridge at the Vassal House, now the

Longfellow House. Immediately, he began the monumental task of molding a new army out of independent militia companies paid by colonial and local governments. The terms of enlistment for the men usually were quite short, six months or less. Often, companies headed home whenever they felt like it.

A number of colonial leaders advised Washington to expand the war against the British. A strategic campaign against a British-held but lightly defended Canada was one suggestion. Such a campaign appeared tempting because of the ease with which Benedict Arnold of Connecticut and Ethan Allen of Vermont had captured the small British garrison at Fort Ticonderoga in a surprise attack earlier in the year. Arnold had also ravaged British installations and shipping on the north end of Lake Champlain, leaving Canada open to an invasion. General Schuyler in Albany concurred that a campaign against Canada could succeed.

In 1775, the British hold on Canada was tenuous. The predominantly French Catholic population of Quebec seethed with resentment against their relatively recent conquest by the Protestant British. The ceding of all of Canada to England after the humiliating French defeat at Quebec in 1759 and 1760 was still very fresh in French-Canadian minds. If the small British garrison in Canada could be swiftly overcome, the French might rise up and join the colonial cause in order to gain their own independence. The British had only a small number of troops spread out through the vastness of Canada, mainly at Quebec, at Montreal, and at smaller garrisons in the Great Lakes. Washington and his officers saw a Canadian campaign as a golden opportunity to gain allies, while dividing the British forces in North America.

So a campaign to conquer all of Canada and bring the French Canadians into the rebellion was discussed in July and agreed upon during early August, 1775. The historic route of invasion of Canada for most of the eighteenth century had been along the waterways of the Hudson and Champlain Valleys, via Lake George and Lake Champlain, past Ticonderoga and Crown Point, and then into Canada. The route led down the Richelieu River near Montreal, then down the St. Lawrence River to Quebec. At that time, Quebec was Canada's capital and principal city. This was an all-water route. Such water routes were needed to move troops and supplies through the roadless wilderness of the Champlain Valley. The Americans already held the lake, thanks to Arnold's foresight. An invading American army was to be

the hikes or canoe trips suggested, this will require still more time. Exploring and thoroughly enjoying Quebec City require at least three days. Wow! This means you will need to dedicate a couple of weeks of your hard-earned vacation time to complete this adventure. It's worth it!

Of course, if you live in or near New England or the province of Quebec—within a reasonable driving time of the route—it may work best to follow the trail in successive sections, perhaps a weekend at a time. This may be wise, too, if you bring youngsters, who may need to digest such an adventure in small doses.

The best time of year to head out on this expedition is May through mid-October. June has the drawback of being black fly and mosquito season in Maine and Canada. These critters can be voracious and mean during that month. Illiterate bugs that can't read the tourist brochures may even be present in July and early August.

Where should one begin? We recommend at the same place the expedition did, on the Common in Cambridge, Massachusetts. Then explore the route northward to Quebec, 350 miles away, in the same sequence as Arnold's men did. You could cover the entire distance to Quebec in about eight hours of steady Interstate and high-speed highway driving, but you would entirely miss the essence of what the expedition experienced. The trip should be savored. Allow time to explore the beautiful country and interesting towns along the route. Swim in the streams and ponds, pick wild raspberries, climb Bigelow Mountain, canoe a section of the route, and hike over the Great Carrying Place or the Height of Land. These experiences make the trip fun for all. Also, camp at some of the many fine campsites along the route, some of which are those the expedition used. Visit the historical sites and museums. Be sure to finish your trip with a visit to the friendly people in Quebec, one of the finest cities in North America.

The Route

The 1775 route was a mixture of land and water travel. The section from Cambridge to Newburyport was a march overland. The army sailed on small ships from Newburyport to Fort Western (now Augusta, Maine). Wooden boats called bateaux were used to ascend the Kennebec and Dead Rivers from Fort Western to the Height of Land at the Canadian border. The remaining distance, through Canada to Quebec City, was accomplished mainly on foot. Small boats and canoes carried the men the short distance across the St. Lawrence River to Quebec.

While retracing the route of the expedition, you will need to use auto roads that closely approximate the original route. In places, you will be required to bypass sections of the route because of obstructions not present in 1775 or because of the lack of roads. The most significant example of these obstructions is Flagstaff Lake, a man-made impoundment that covers the middle section of the Dead River—the expedition's pathway—for more than twenty miles. In Quebec province, a wild, roadless section along the Chaudière River from Lake Megantic to St-Gédéon, will require you to swing away from the original route for more than twenty miles. Dams on all the rivers have inundated portions of the original course. This is especially true on the Kennebec River in Maine. There are seven dams on this river's section of our route, forming pools behind each that cover the original features. Many of these dams are built on falls where portages occurred. Towns and their related developments along the banks of the rivers also have contributed to alter the route. On some of the land route, modern graded and asphalted roads cover the old rutted wagon paths present in 1775.

However, even with all of these changes, the route basically can still be followed. It will give the traveler a clear view of what the army encountered. There are still many sections that are wild, with a minimum of change since 1775. This is particularly true of the Great Carrying Place, the Upper Dead River, and the Chain of Ponds.

Route Description

The route description is in two formats. The route from Cambridge to Newburyport and from Lake Megantic to Lévis is in narrative form. The route from the mouth of the Kennebec River to Lake Megantic is in a cumulative mileage format. The mileage format is used because of the greater descriptive detail given along those sections. The cumulative mileage method will use your auto's odometer. There always will be some degree of discrepancy between the odometer readings given in this book and those observed in a given car. To minimize these discrepancies, which tend to accumulate, each new section will begin with a zero odometer setting. These new zero settings are prominently announced in the Travel Guide.

Side Trips

Along the route of travel are a number of possible side trips from the main highway. In some places, the highway bears well away from the army's route and a side trip is needed to reach an important

assembled in Albany and led by the able General Richard Montgomery. He would proceed north over this route during the late summer and fall of 1775.

The American leaders believed that most of the available British troops and their allies among the French would be concentrated against Montgomery's main advancing force near Montreal, leaving Quebec City with a light garrison. It was decided to send a second, "secret" expedition to capture Quebec by a more direct route, catching the British between two armies in a classic pincer movement. Since there was an excess of troops around Boston, the best of these were to be dedicated to this enterprise. The route Benedict Arnold and others suggested was by way of the Kennebec River in the Province of Maine, then down the Chaudière River, which empties into the St. Lawrence just six miles above Quebec City. This was an old Indian route. It had been explored and partially mapped in 1761 by Lieutenant John Montresor, a British officer. Washington possessed a copy of his map and journal. After much debate—information about the route was thin—Washington and the senior officers decided that the Kennebec-Chaudière route was feasible for the surprise attack on Quebec.

The final decision to undertake this expedition was not made until August of 1775, only a month after Washington had taken command. This left little time to organize the army and send it on its way before winter. Preparations commenced immediately, but the challenge of transporting an army and its tons of supplies through a little-known wilderness presented many daunting problems.

Captain Reuben Colburn, owner of a small shipyard and sawmill on the Kennebec in Gardinerstown—present-day Pittston, Maine—was summoned to Cambridge and asked if he and his men could construct boats sufficient to transport an army of 1,100 men up the river. After assuring Washington that he could, he was given orders to commence construction. Colburn immediately returned to his shipyard to begin the hectic construction of the boats. Other preparations were well under way by late August. Supplies and arms were gathered. Volunteers for the expedition signed up. Arrangements for transports up the coast and into the Kennebec were made in Newburyport, Massachusetts.

All that was left to decide was who would lead the expedition. Washington recognized Colonel Arnold's daring and energetic qualities and knowledge of Canada, Quebec in particular. He had visited the city several times in his business travels. Command of the expedition was a much sought-after plum, and many officers vied for the assignment. Washington pondered this decision for some time. In early September, it was made. It would be Benedict Arnold. There was some grumbling, as several more senior and experienced officers had been bypassed. Arnold had no previous experience in leading a force of this size. But his knowledge of Canada, his success on Lake Champlain, and Washington's instincts about Arnold's leadership qualities had led the commander-in-chief to believe that he was the best choice.

The stage was now set for one of the greatest military campaigns in American history, the March to Quebec.

Toasting Arnold and his officers in Newburyport
Courtesy, Library of Congress

point the expedition passed. Although side trips may slow down your overall progress, they will provide variety to the adventure, including opportunities to stretch your legs and see the world outside of your car. Follow as many as you can.

Points of Interest

These may be historic buildings, museums, scenic overlooks, or historical markers. For each, its relevance to the expedition is explained. We encourage you to visit as many of them as time and energy allow. They will add much fun and quality to your experience.

Canoe Trips

Much of the expedition's route used rivers and remote ponds. You will be unable to duplicate this experience cruising in an air-conditioned car. If you can navigate a canoe, then we highly recommend traveling on parts of the route by water. This will be the closest you will come to hearing the men of the expedition shouting on the rivers as they toiled upstream against the current. If you can canoe some of these sections, it will be the high point of your adventure.

We have selected five trips, one an overnight, on various sections of the expedition's route. Available time will be a critical factor in your decision to weave in one or more canoe trips. None of the five recommended trips is technical in the skill required, although there are fast water and easy Class I rapids on three of them. If you do not have a canoe, places where you can rent one are noted in the book.

Where to Stay Overnight

There is an abundance of motels and inns along the route—too many to cite. We do cite several establishments that have some significance to the expedition, such as the Benedict Arnold Motel near St-Georges in Canada and the Evergreens Campground in Solon, Maine.

If you tent or use a recreational vehicle, there are excellent accommodations along the route. Four in particular have special relevance to the expedition—in Phippsburg, Solon, Eustis, and at the Chain of Ponds, all in Maine. They are described in this Travel Guide.

Maps

Included with this book is a series of maps to provide helpful detail on the route. Some of the roadways you will follow using these maps you would not be able to find on a regular highway map because those maps are on a larger scale. Included with each map are notes indicating specific points of interest.

In addition to these maps, you should obtain highway maps for Massachusetts, Maine, and the province of Quebec. A detailed map of Quebec City will also be helpful.

Travel in Canada

Because part of the expedition's route is in Canada, you will be required to pass through customs when you cross the border from one country to another. You should have little trouble because no passport is required as long as you are an American or Canadian citizen. A driver's license and other normal identification will suffice. If you are not a citizen of the United States or Canada, you will have to take along your passport. There are some restrictions on what you can take over the border in each direction. Firearms are always forbidden. Enforcement of drug and alcohol laws in Quebec is quite strict. Because of recent events, entry into the U.S. has been considerably tightened, and delays may occur.

So with all these minor planning details out of the way, pile into your car and let's get started!

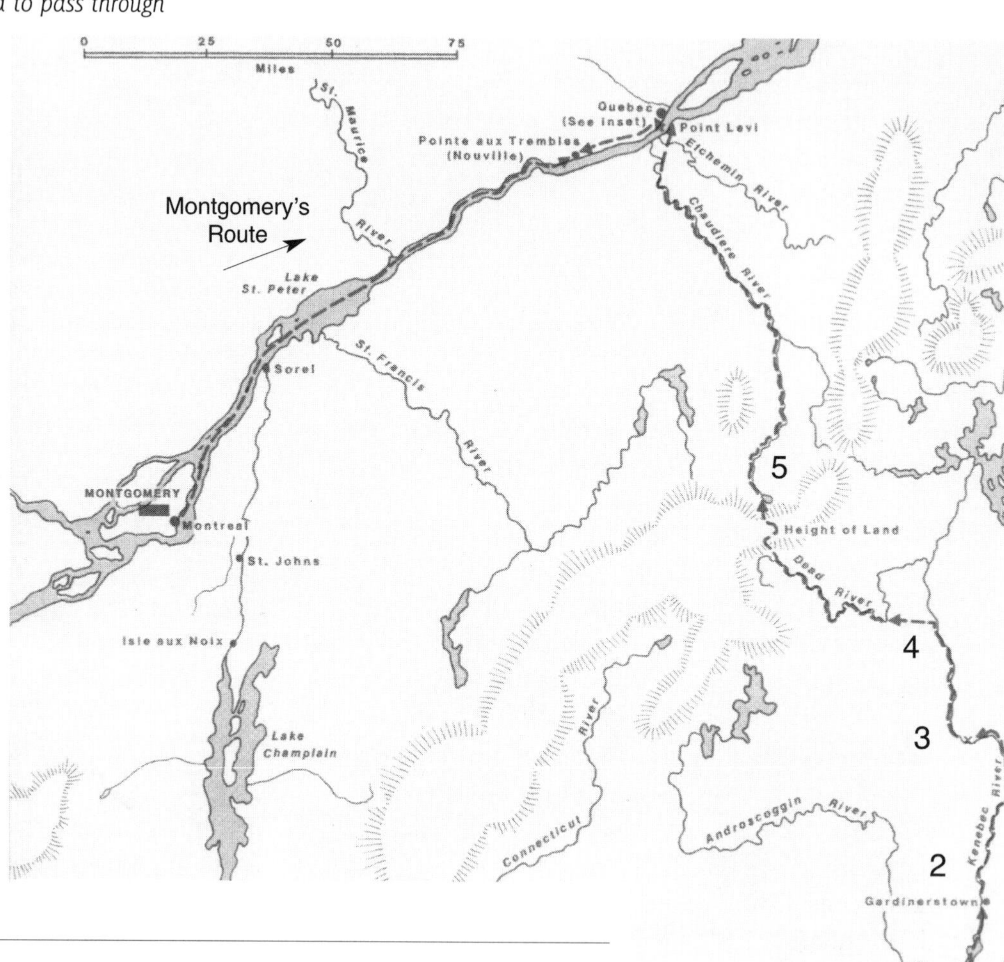

Campaign Routes during the 1775 Invasion of Canada

1. Expedition embarks on eleven small schooners and sloops for the trip up the coast into the Kennebec River.
2. Expedition receives bateaux at Colburn Shipyard and moves to Fort Western for assembly.
3. Norridgewock Falls, where expedition repaired their bateaux and portaged around falls.
4. The Great Carrying Place, a thirteen-mile portage between the Kennebec and Dead Rivers.
5. The eight-mile portage over the Height of Land into Canada and the swamps of Lake Megantic.

Courtesy of *Encyclopedia of the Revolutionary War*

Chapter Two

Cambridge to Newburyport

The Expedition to Quebec began to assemble its companies at Cambridge Common on Sept. 8, 1775. Some of the companies joined the expedition intact. Others were mixtures of men who signed on independently or groups that were from county or state militias. Soldiers in these companies, for the most part, were trained for local defense and had little experience in actual warfare. They had a wide variety of terms of enlistment with their sponsoring local governments, not with the new central American command. Allegiance to the new Continental Congress and a unified command would come later in the war. This hodgepodge of companies and their divided allegiances meant that they would have to learn to be a cohesive army as the expedition progressed. They did not begin as a unified, trained force.

The small army consisted of thirteen companies: three rifle companies and ten equipped with less-accurate muskets. Colonial military companies varied greatly in size, seventy to ninety men being average. The total number of soldiers comprising the expedition varied throughout the two months required to reach Quebec, but the most accurate estimates place the starting figure at eighty-four soldiers and officers per company. The total roster of officers and men, therefore, was approximately 1,100. This figure changed considerably along the route, as some men enthusiastically joined as the army passed, but sickness, injury, death, and faint hearts considerably reduced the force before it reached its destination.

Beginning on Sept. 8, the quartermaster issued each company whatever uniform parts, blankets, arms, powder, and lead that were available. Food supplies, tents, and other equipment would be picked up in Newburyport.

Colonel Arnold immediately initiated the process of becoming familiar with his men and officers. He reviewed his new command, company by company, as they trained on the common. As the expedition progressed, he would gradually gain from his men the loyalty and confidence that are critical to the success of a dangerous journey into hostile, unknown country.

Cambridge to Newburyport

We follow the first steps of our journey north to Quebec on the front porch of Washington's headquarters at the Longfellow House on Brattle Street in Cambridge, Massachusetts. This was the exact spot where Washington and Arnold stood when they shook hands as Arnold departed for Quebec. The building is a magnificent Colonial mansion in the center of historic Cambridge, not far from Harvard Square.

The date was Sept. 15, 1775. After General Washington wished them godspeed, Arnold and his adjutant, Captain Ebenezer Oswald, strode to their waiting horses, mounted, and left no grass growing under their horses' hooves as they galloped off to Newburyport to catch up with their troops, who had marched from Cambridge Common on Sept. 11 and 12.

After the battles of nearby Lexington and Concord in April of 1775, prominent Tories, people who remained loyal to the English crown, hastily vacated their homes and fled to the safety of the British enclave in Boston. This mansion's owner was a wealthy merchant and landowner, Major John Vassell, who had built his home in 1759. The local Revolutionary Committee of Safety confiscated the house. It became Washington's headquarters when he arrived to take command of the troops around Boston on July 4, 1775. His wife Martha later joined him there. They made it their home until the British were forced out of Boston in the spring of 1776.

After the war, it had several owners until it was purchased for the Maine-born poet Henry Wadsworth Longfellow in 1843 as a wedding dowry

for his new wife, Fanny Appleton. They lived in the house for forty-five years. He was a professor of modern languages at Harvard College. He wrote many of his great poems there. The Longfellow House is now a National Historic Site operated by the National Park Service and is open to the public. The house has recently been completely refurbished and contains period furnishings emphasizing Longfellow's life there as well as Washington's occupancy. For more information, contact:

Longfellow National Historic Site
National Park Service
105 Brattle St.
Cambridge, MA 02138
(617) 876-4492
www.nps.gov/long

We recommend traveling to Harvard Square in downtown Cambridge by using the subway on the Blue Line from nearby Boston. This is because of the tight parking in and around the square adjacent to Harvard University. Not having to worry about parking will allow you to freely visit many other historic sites in Cambridge, which are within easy walking distance. Plan to spend a half a day or more to adequately view the many sites around the square and at Harvard. You may wish to expand your Cambridge exploration with visits to the Boston area's other famous historic sites such as the Bunker Hill Monument, the USS Constitution, the Old North Church, and many others. Boston is, after all, the "cradle of the American Revolution."

Nearby, historic Cambridge Common is also

Cambridge Common

Moving armies in the 1700s was no small task. There was no such thing as lightweight equipment. All food and supplies had to be packed in fifty-, one-hundred-, or two-hundred-pound wooden barrels or boxes. Once the soldiers entered the wilds, they had to have with them everything they would need to survive. They could not hope to obtain more food until they reached the French settlements near Quebec City. Some additional supplies were to be picked up at Newburyport, at Colburn's shipyard, and at Fort Western on the Kennebec River.

The American colonial army's main object was driving the British out of Boston. Consequently, most of its limited resources and energy went to that purpose. It is remarkable that the Quebec expedition was planned and organized as quickly as it was. Detailed planning had begun only six weeks after Washington had arrived in Massachusetts. It was well understood by all, from General Washington on down, that it was late in the season to launch a major campaign toward the north. Winter came early in that country, and the waterways would be frozen by December.

There was also the difficult issue of coordination of the attack with General Montgomery's force, which was to advance up the Champlain Valley. Once the expedition left Cambridge, the two claws of the pincer would be hundreds of miles apart and essentially out of communication until they met near Quebec.

By Sept. 11, the first companies were ready to move. The first leg northward was a forty-mile march to Newburyport, at the mouth of the Merrimack River. The roads in the Province of Maine north of nearby Portsmouth, New Hampshire, were very poor and soon petered out into wooded paths. Travel between Massachusetts and Maine was usually by ship. Accordingly, the expedition would use small coastal fishing schooners and sloops to go from Newburyport to the head of navigation on the Kennebec at Fort Western, present-day Augusta. Since the powerful British fleet controlled Boston Harbor and the seacoast northward, Newburyport was the safest place to assemble the transporting ships for the trip north.

The first three companies of riflemen under Captain Daniel Morgan left Cambridge on Sept. 11. Morgan's own company was a tough group of backcountry Virginian Indian fighters. After leaving Virginia to join the fray around Boston, they covered the 600 miles, evidently mounted, in a phenomenal twenty-one days, without losing a man. Joining Morgan's men were two other strong rifle companies from Pennsylvania led by Captains Hendricks and Smith. The three companies totaled about 250 men. Arnold intended to use them to spearhead the expedition, as light infantry, for most of the distance to Quebec.

All companies did not use the same route to reach Newburyport. Most marched north from Cambridge to Medford in order to avoid the wider part of the Mystic River, then traveled east over the Salem Road through Malden, then under the cliffs of what is now Saugus, skirting the Revere marshes and on to the common in the center of Lynn. There, they picked up the main coastal road and followed it northeast to Salem.

From Salem, the road went north through the towns of Beverly, Wenham, Ipswich, and Rowley, finally reaching Newburyport. Some companies swung farther north through Danvers. The route was along rutted, dirt roads that were lined by high stone walls and fine farms. People in each village came out to see and cheer the troops as they proudly marched past.

Morgan's three companies camped the first night at Neale's Tavern in Medford, spent the second at Mr. Bucknam's church, and arrived in Newburyport on the thirteenth, camping on the upper common about a mile from the center of town.

The second contingent to leave Cambridge was a full battalion of five companies under the command of Lieutenant Colonel Christopher Greene and Major Timothy Bigelow. Captains Ward, Thayer, Topham, McCobb, and Hubbard commanded the five companies. They left on the morning of Sept. 13 and spent the first night in Malden, the second in Beverly, and arrived in Newburyport on the fifteenth. They spread out through the town to find accommodations wherever they could. Some stayed in the huge ropewalks—rope manufacturing buildings, common in seafaring towns—along the waterfront.

The third and final contingent was also battalion-sized. It was under the command of Lieutenant Colonel Roger Enos and Major Return Meigs, and it consisted of five companies of musketmen. These were captained by Williams, Dearborn, Hanchet (the spelling varies; this spelling is to be used throughout the book), Goodrich, and Scott. Most of the Maine men were in Goodrich's company. They got a late start on the thirteenth and were only able to cover five miles to Medford before nightfall. They reached Salem and Danvers the second night, Ipswich and Rowley the third

significant to our journey. This was where many of the expedition's men were billeted prior to beginning their march to Newburyport It is two blocks east of the Longfellow House. The common is a traditional New England "green" or central park, with monuments, cannon, and historic markers throughout.

The expedition's route of march from Cambridge was north to Medford, across the Mystic River, then east through Malden, Saugus, and onto the coast road at Lynn, then on to Salem. In 1775, these were small villages clustered around their own common greens. From historic Salem, the soldiers marched northward to Beverly, Wenham, Ipswich, Rowley, and ended this first leg of their journey at Newburyport.

The small villages and picturesque country roads and lanes used by the soldiers are, of course, long gone. The entire route from Cambridge to Salem is now a continuous suburb of Boston bearing no resemblance to what the soldiers saw in 1775. Trying faithfully to follow the expedition's historic route over this stretch will not be much fun until you reach Salem. There is little to see except traffic lights, heavy traffic, and suburbia. We recomend that, upon leaving Cambridge, you drive by the easiest route on your road map to Salem and pick up the expedition's trail there.

Purists who wish to follow the exact route as closely as possible through present-day city streets may wish to use the following route to Salem.

From Cambridge Common various contingents of the army followed different roads, but they all converged on the bridge over the Mystic River in Medford. The army had to swing north to where the Mystic River narrowed. To reach the river crossing, follow Routes 2A and 16 from Cambridge. After crossing the river in Medford, turn right onto Salem Street, which bears easterly. Follow Salem Street as closely as possible through Malden and into Saugus. In Saugus, Salem Street becomes Lincoln Avenue. Follow it into the next town, Lynn. Drive to the Lynn Common in the center of the community. Just beyond the common, pick up US Route 1A and follow this to Salem. Present-day US Route 1A is the approximate line of march used by the expedition all the way to Newburyport

Salem is a marvelous place to visit. Plan to spend at least a day exploring the many historic sites here. Its location on a fine harbor accounts for its early settlement—in the 1630s. It is a very historic city because of its long maritime history and, of course, the events surrounding the infamous Salem Witch Trials of 1692. Even a full day will only scratch the surface of all there is here. There are a few tourist-trap places playing up the witch theme, but you should be able to easily recognize and avoid them. To get oriented, start at the National Park Service's Regional Visitor Center. There you can obtain all the information and local maps you will need to navigate. It is located in the center of town at the corner of Brown and New Liberty Streets. The famous Peabody Essex Museum is located on both sides of the visitor center. For more information, contact:

National Park Service Regional Visitor Center
2 New Liberty St.
Salem, MA 01970
(978) 740-1650
www.nps.gov/sama

We recommend these sites as highlights.

• ***The Peabody Essex Museum**. This is a world-class museum, most certainly one of the best in the northeastern United States. It has eight sections containing exhibits of rare china, paintings, ship's models, tapestries, and other exhibits. (www.pem.org)*

• *On the waterfront is the **Salem National Maritime Historic Site**. (www.nps.gov/sama)*

• ***The House of the Seven Gables,** made famous by the classic novel of that title by Nathaniel Hawthorne. (www.7gables.org).*

• *A one-hour walking tour of the **McIntire Historic District,** containing more than 300 significant architectural and historic structures. (www.essexheritage.org)*

Continuing our journey, we will follow US Route 1A the remaining distance to Newburyport. It took the men three days to march the approximately forty miles from Cambridge to Newburyport.

Pass by beautiful Salem Common and drive north on US Route 1A. It is twenty-two miles from Salem to Newburyport You will pass through a series of towns of great pastoral and "old village" beauty. Hamilton and Ipswich are particularly handsome. As you arrive in the center of Ipswich, you will notice a visitor center on the right where you can obtain information about the historic town and its many Colonial houses. The best is a pamphlet entitled "A Walking Tour of Old Ipswich." North of Ipswich, the highway nears the coast and huge salt marshes begin to appear.

In Newburyport, the expedition embarked on eleven small coastal schooners and sloops on the Merrimack River to go by sea to the mouth of the Kennebec River in the Province of Maine, then part of Massachusetts. Therefore, the waterfront on the river should be the focus of your visit in Newburyport When you reach the common in Newburyport, leave US Route 1A and turn right, taking a street that leads to the center of town,

day, and arrived in Newburyport on the morning of the sixteenth, spreading around town to find lodging or sites to set up tents.

On the morning of Sept. 15, General Washington, Colonel Arnold, and Arnold's aide Captain Ebenezer Oswald strode out onto the broad, columned front entry of the beautiful Vassal Mansion on Brattle Street, Washington's headquarters, two blocks from Cambridge Common. A sentry held the reins of two saddled horses. Arnold had received his last-minute instructions from the commander-in-chief; only farewells were left. Both men knew that great danger lay ahead.

Washington shook hands with Arnold and Oswald. They mounted their horses and galloped off to catch up with their troops. They rode rapidly over the same roads their men had taken. They reached Salem in time to dine at noon and then continued northward. They arrived in Newburyport that evening and were the honored guests at the home of Nathaniel Tracy, the wealthy merchant who had organized the shipping to transport the army to the Kennebec. Arnold used the home as his headquarters for the next several days. The first leg of the journey, the easiest, had been completed without incident.

In Newburyport

Newburyport in 1775 was a thriving, small seaport in northeastern Massachusetts. The Merrimack River was a vital artery of commerce, reaching far inland to the White Mountains, allowing huge logs to be floated right to the port's sawmills. The town boasted several large shipyards, wharfs, ropewalks, a commercial center for the region, and two thousand inhabitants. It was located on the south bank of the river about three miles from its mouth and the open sea. Newburyport had already established a rich trading tradition with other ports on both sides of the Atlantic.

With the expedition's 1,100 hungry and very thirsty men in town, with many small ships in the river assembled to transport them, and with tons of supplies piled high on the docks, the community was a hive of activity. Many men lodged in private homes. They filled the small inns and crammed into the town's two ropewalks and the Town House. One company lodged in the Presbyterian Meeting House. The three rifle companies set up tents near Rolfe's Lane, now Green Street, in nearby Newbury. Late-arriving companies had to set up tents wherever they could on the common or in open fields around the town. The local inns and taverns near the waterfront did a brisk business quenching the soldiers' thirst. More than twenty men from Newburyport had enlisted in Ward's company of musketmen, so the residents considered the army to be their own and did all they could to accommodate this relatively large force. Nothing like this had ever happened before in the small town.

Nathaniel Tracy had a beautiful, three-story, Federal brick home a few blocks from the waterfront. Arnold and his chief officers made this house their headquarters. In mid-August, General Washington and Arnold had conferred with Tracy, who had assured them that he could find the ships needed for the next leg of the journey, which would go along the coast and into the Kennebec River. They had given him orders to proceed with haste. The ships had to be small so as to negotiate the shallows and shoals of the Kennebec, which had to be ascended far upstream to Gardinerstown, where the bateaux that were being constructed would be waiting.

Washington also charged Tracy with supplying most of the stores of food. He was able to scour the coast as far

which is located on the shore of the river. It is three miles east to the mouth of the river and the ocean. There are several large parking areas on the riverfront.

Newburyport, like Salem, has a rich maritime history. Its fine Federal houses and historic sites reflect that heritage. There are only a few buildings still standing that were there in 1775 because the town suffered a devastating fire in 1811, wiping out most of the wooden structures near the waterfront. Among those that escaped the fire is the Nathaniel Tracy House, in which Arnold and several of his officers lodged on the nights of Sept. 15 to 18. Tracy was a prominent shipbuilder and merchant. Washington and Arnold had asked him to make arrangements for the transports from Newburyport to Fort Western on the Kennebec. The Tracy House is now part of the Newburyport Public Library at 94 State St. Plan to stop here for a visit. Several of the original rooms have been preserved, and in one there is a very fine oil painting of Nathaniel Tracy.

The expedition's ships were tied up or anchored near Tracy Wharf, which at the time was located along the present Boardwalk. The troops were housed all over town in private homes and buildings or in tents erected on some of the local commons. On Sept. 17, many of the men attended services at the Old South Church (Presbyterian), which stands today.

While you visit Newburyport, we recommend that you visit the following places that have relevance to the expedition's stay in town. The pamphlet "The Official Walking Tour of the Downtown Area" may be obtained at the information building near the waterfront. It will include information on these sites:

- ***The Nathaniel Tracy House,*** *built 1771 (now the library), 94 State St.*
- ***The Old South Church,*** *built 1756, on Federal Street.*
- ***The Custom House Maritime Museum,*** *built 1835, 25 Water St.*
- ***The Cushing House Museum,*** *housing the Historical Society of Old Newbury, at 98 High St.*
- ***The Boardwalk,*** *on the waterfront, where the expedition embarked.*

For more information about Newburyport and the surrounding area, contact:

Greater Newburyport Chamber of Commerce
29 State St.
Newburyport, MA 01950
(508) 462-6680
www.seacoast.com/chamber

While strolling on the Boardwalk, try to imagine the eleven small, one- and two-masted sailing ships packed with soldiers as they broke out sail to begin their journey up the coast. The soldiers somberly wondered if they would ever see their homes and loved ones again. Some would not. More than twenty men of the expedition came from Newburyport. The crowd of townspeople that lined the wharves and shoreline cheered loudly and waved handkerchiefs as the ships moved downstream. Drums and fifes played on board the ships. Many of the soldiers had never been at sea, could not swim, and may have begun to feel queasy as the Atlantic swells rolled in to meet them when they left the river's mouth.

It is not practical for most people to follow the Quebec expedition out to sea, so we recommend that you drive up the coast into Maine to the point where the army entered the mouth of the Kennebec River. We will pick up the route of the expedition's ships there. To reach that point, drive west from Newburyport about four miles to Interstate 95 northbound. Follow I-95 to Brunswick, Maine. There, take US Route 1 north for eleven miles to Bath. It will take you about two and a half hours of steady driving to reach Bath from Newburyport. At Bath, we will leave US Route 1 and head south on Route 209 to reach the point where the Kennebec meets the sea at Popham Village.

The Nathaniel Tracy House. Courtesy, Newburyport Public Library.

away as Beverly and Salem to obtain the ships and supplies. The powerful British fleet was in control of Boston Harbor and the sea approaches to it, so there was great danger if the British got wind of a gathering of ships in Newburyport for a military operation. Secrecy was essential, especially with so many Tory eyes watching.

Tracy had done his work well, collecting eleven unarmed sloops and schooners, which were ready and waiting at his wharf. These were small fishing or cargo vessels that could hug the coast and dart into shallow harbors if a British man-of-war was sighted. The trip up the coast and into the uncharted Kennebec would have many dangers, both man-made and natural.

By Saturday, Sept. 16, the last of the troops had arrived in Newburyport. Down at the waterfront, men worked steadily loading supplies and military stores into the holds of the vessels. Arnold wisely dispatched three small ships with orders to scout up the coast to check for British warships snooping around. Also, the winds were against an immediate start.

On Sunday, the troops were drilled and paraded in front of cheering local crowds. Most of the day, the men were busy with preparations for embarkation. Many did take time to crowd into services at the First Presbyterian Meeting House, now the Old South Church, which still stands. The army's young chaplain, the Reverend Samuel Spring, delivered the sermon. The local parishioners evidently liked the sermon. In 1777, they hired him to be their church's minister. Arnold, impatient to be off, awaited the return of the scout vessels with their critical information.

The weather improved on Monday, and at midday the first of the scout vessels returned with the good news that the coast was clear. Arnold immediately sent messages to all company commanders. He ordered them to collect their troops and begin the process of boarding their men. The activity and noise at the waterfront must have been impressive. Guards were posted to prevent men from wandering away from the loaded vessels. By nightfall, the army was ready to sail at a moment's notice. The men slept uncomfortably aboard the crowded ships. Many complained of the putrid, fishy smell. Most chose to sleep on the open decks rather than in the smelly, stifling cargo space below.

Early on the morning of Sept. 19, Arnold and his chief officers walked briskly down to the Tracy wharf and boarded the *Broad Bay*. This was to be the flagship of the small fleet. Captain Clarkson, the ship's master, was also to be the sailing master for the fleet, since he was familiar with the Kennebec up to Fort Western. Signals had been issued the night before to each of the ship's captains and key officers. The names of nine of the vessels are known: *Abigail, Admiral, Broad Bay, Britannia, Conway, Eagle, Houghton, Hanna,* and the *Swallow*. Each carried about 100 men, crammed in with their arms and supplies.

As the morning tide ebbed, shortly after nine o'clock the fleet of ships moved away from the docks, hoisted sail, and, with a brisk, favorable wind, sliced down the broad Merrimack River. The entire town had come to see them off. Crowds lined the docks and shores, shouting and waving goodbye. Fife and drums on board added to the pageantry.

It is about three miles downriver to the mouth of the Merrimack. As the ships approached the mouth's bar, the *Swallow* ran aground on a shoal. It was an unlucky start. All the ships hove to while efforts to free the grounded ship were made. As the tide dropped, the heavily loaded vessel would not budge. Arnold decided to distribute most of the men on board the *Swallow* among the remaining ten ships, which crowded their decks even more. Arnold ordered the captain of the *Swallow* to follow as soon as possible at the next high tide. The ship had important supplies in her hole. The other ten ships finally were able to leave the river's mouth and move out into the open sea. They sailed away to the northeast along the coast toward the Kennebec, ninety miles away.

Sloop

Schooner

Courtesy, Custom House Maritime Museum, Newburyport

No British ships were sighted, so rapid progress was made along the coast. Night fell long before they reached the mouth of the Kennebec.

One of the fleet's ships anchored in the Kennebec River near Hallowell
Courtesy, Old Fort Western Museum

Chapter Four

Mouth of the Kennebec to Fort Western

It was an easy run down east from the Merrimack River. The ten small vessels of the fleet swiftly passed the Isle of Shoals off Portsmouth, then Casco Bay, reaching the mouth of the Kennebec River before midnight of Sept. 19. Luckily, they had not encountered any British men-of-war patrolling the coast. Fear of the British was well founded. Only a month later, on Oct. 17, Captain Henry Mowat, leading a squadron of five ships, would sail into the harbor of Falmouth, now Portland. The ships proceeded to bombard and burn the undefended town to the ground, destroying more than 400 buildings.

Arnold's fleet hove to for the night off Wood Island just outside the entrance to the Kennebec. An attempt to enter the river in the dark would have been foolhardy. The lower river is a labyrinth of heads, bays, inlets, and islands that would confuse an experienced navigator. At dawn, the fleet made sail and headed north into the mouth of the river. In the morning mist and fog, not all of the fleet's vessels were in sight of each other. As they passed Honeywell Head, now the location of Fort Popham, local militia hailed them. They were guarding the river's entrance. Here, Arnold's flagship, the *Broad*

Fort Popham

Bay, took on an experienced pilot.

The ships sailed with the tide about six miles to Parker Flats, a small cove near the present village of Parker Head. They anchored and waited for the scattered ships to join the main body. As the morning wore on, only eight

Popham to Augusta

Our journey up the Kennebec River begins in the town of Phippsburg, another "cradle" of American history. It was here, in 1607, thirteen years before the Pilgrims landed at Plymouth, that an English colony was established. It was located at the river's entrance to the sea near present Popham Beach. The colony managed to construct a number of rough-hewn buildings, a small fort, and launched the first ship ever constructed in North America, the Virginia. But the small colony survived only a year. These brave souls, numbering fewer than a hundred men, found that the winter in what was to become Maine was quite harsh. The surrounding Native Americans became understandably hostile with these strange intruders. Discouraged, the colonists abandoned Popham the next year and sailed home to England.

To reach the beginning of our upriver journey, we must travel south from Bath via Route 209. This small city is the site of the huge Bath Iron Works, a large shipyard producing frigates and destroyers for the navy. Drive south for seventeen miles to the tiny resort village of Popham Beach. It is located on a long peninsula where the highway ends at the mouth of the Kennebec at Fort Popham. Here the expedition's ships entered the river after their journey up the coast.

Fort Popham is a massive granite structure constructed in the 1830s to prevent enemy ships from marauding up the river. Built on the prominent headland of Honeywell's Point, it occupies the site of earlier fortifications present when the expedition passed. The fort was manned by troops during the Civil War, the Spanish-American War, and World War I. It was never attacked and never fired an angry shot. It is built as a two-tier cannon platform. The upper level is supported by massive arches

bearing the tremendous weight of large-caliber cannons. Shaped as a half moon, the fort commands the entire mouth of the river and is one of thirteen forts that were located at various sites during three centuries along the Lower Kennebec. The state's Bureau of Parks and Lands operates it as an historic site.

(From the mouth of the Kennebec to Lake Megantic in Canada, you should use your auto's odometer readings to help you identify points cited along the route. Most likely, there will be small discrepancies caused by mechanical differences in odometers from one car to another. Beginning at the rotary parking area at the main entrance to Fort Popham, set your odometer to zero. Mileage within this book is abbreviated "mi." Let us commence the journey up the Kennebec River.)

0.0mi. *From Fort Popham, follow the main road (Route 209) through the village of Popham Beach, with the harbor to the right.*

0.4mi. *On the right is the Fort Baldwin Road, which leads along the edge of the harbor 0.2mi. to a small park and parking area. (Side road distances are not calculated into the route mileage.) The trail to Fort Baldwin begins directly across the road from the parking area. The Popham Colony's remains are located under the park's turf and the parking-lot asphalt.*

Hike to Fort Baldwin

This is a short hike of a fifth of a mile uphill to an overlook of the river and the coast. The fort is a series of seven naval gun emplacements positioned to protect the river. It was used during World Wars I and II. The batteries have concrete mounting platforms, hidden magazines, barracks, and a fifty-foot-high observation tower. The guns have been removed. The observation tower provides great views along the coast. This hike is highly recommended. The actual hiking time is ten minutes of easy uphill walking. We now return to the regular route.

1.5mi. *We reach the entrance to* ***Popham Beach State Park****. It includes a beautiful mile-long sand beach affording cool but outstanding swimming, beach walking, and picnic facilities. There are no overnight state camping facilities here, but there are commercial campgrounds nearby. We recommend Hermit Island (275 sites) on the ocean near the end of nearby Route 216. It is six miles from the state park. Contact:*

Hermit Island

of the ten vessels joined Arnold. He waited impatiently for six hours, finally deciding that the fleet could wait no longer. The eight ships broke out sail and headed upriver, battling currents that can reach six to eight knots as the tide ebbs. The land along the river was settled, and the men of the expedition commented favorably on some of the well-kept villages they passed such as Georgetown and Phippsburg.

When the *Broad Bay* reached what is now Bath, all on board were surprised to see the two missing ships emerging into the river from a narrow gut on the east shore. They had overshot the Kennebec and entered the parallel Sheepscot River to the east. Luckily, they were able to use a series of narrow passages to weave their way over from the Sheepscot and reenter the Kennebec just above Arrowsic Island. In the fading light, the ten ships anchored in the river for the night. A few men went on shore to the settlement of Georgetown for a decent meal. At dawn on Sept. 21, the fleet again began to move upriver, passing through the very narrow, tricky Chopps and entered broad Merrymeeting Bay. At this point, the vessels of the fleet gradually became separated, as it was impossible as a body to navigate the narrowing river with all its twists and turns. The Chopps is so narrow, and the current so swift, that the ships were required to pass through the channel in single file.

Much of Merrymeeting Bay is quite shallow. The deep main channel was, at that time, not generally known or marked. Arnold, with a local pilot on board the lead ship, the *Broad Bay*, was able to progress rapidly upriver to Swan Island, at the bay's northern tip. In colonial times, an Indian village was located near Maxwell Cove on the lower end of the three-and-a-half-mile-long island.

Just north of the island, the Kennebec again took on the character of a narrow river. Some of the men on board Dearborn's ship saw the ruins of Fort Richmond on the west shore. Two miles above Swan Island, they passed the Pownalborough Courthouse. At one time it was surrounded by a palisade and was named Fort Shirley. Once again, the men were impressed to see well-kept farms along the river's shore, as they believed all of the Province of Maine to be a virtual wilderness.

By the end of the day, the fleet was strung out and the ships out of sight of each other. Arnold's ship ran out of tide and wind and had to anchor short of its goal, which was the Colburn shipyard in Gardinerstown.

Arnold transferred to a ship's boat and was rowed the

remaining few miles to the yard. He arrived there in the early evening of Sept. 21. Captain Colburn invited him to stay in his house, which overlooked the yard and river. Arnold used the house as his headquarters for the next two days.

Meanwhile, Dearborn's ship ran aground near the upper end of Swan Island. While awaiting high tide to float her off, he and some of his officers, including young Aaron Burr, went ashore on the island to obtain a home-cooked meal and sleep more comfortably than on a packed, smelly, small ship.

On Sept. 22, the expedition's ships trickled into Colburn's shipyard where the bateaux had been built. Arnold ordered each arriving company to come ashore to be assigned its bateaux and equipment. Many of the heavily laden ships were unable to progress farther up the shallowing river. Consequently, their supplies were offloaded into the newly assigned bateaux. Although several of the ships were able to ascend the river as far as Hallowell, most of the men traversed the twelve miles upstream to Fort Western in the bateaux. The *Swallow*, which had extricated itself from the shoals of the Merrimack, finally caught up with the fleet and arrived at the Colburn shipyard with the bad news that now the *Eagle* and *Houghton* were grounded on mud flats and shoals in the bay. After offloading its supplies, Arnold ordered the *Swallow* back downstream to transfer enough men and cargo from the grounded ships to free them from the shallows.

Colonel Arnold was not satisfied with the newly constructed bateaux. He was particularly concerned with their capacity, as many of them were smaller than he had specified. He ordered an additional twenty bateaux to be built immediately. He spent Sept. 22 and 23 greeting the arriving ships and men and working tirelessly with the company commanders to assign bateaux, equipment, and supplies, then hurry them upriver to Fort Western. The fort was to be the final staging point for the journey into Canada.

The shipyard was full of frantic activity, increasing with the arrival of each ship. Completed bateaux, oars, paddles, and poles were stacked on the shore, while new boats were hurriedly being built in the yard. Many of the men had never handled a bateau before. This added to the confusion. The last of the ships that had been hung up in the river arrived on Sept. 23. Late in the day, Arnold wrote dispatches to Washington in Cambridge, entrusting them to Captain Clarkson of the *Broad Bay*.

Small Point, ME 04562
(207) 443-2101
www.hermitisland.com
Email: info@hermitisland.com

3.1mi. *We turn right at a "T" intersection onto the Parker Head Road. This follows the river more closely, providing better views as we progress north than does the main road, Route 209. A short distance will bring us to the small hamlet of Parker Head. Arnold anchored his fleet at nearby Parker Flats while waiting for his scattered ships to reassemble. Note the interesting eel weirs in the river. This was once known as Eels Cove. Proceed north, with outstanding views of the river and its many heads, islands, and coves. Try to visualize the expedition's small schooners and sloops with their white sails working their way upriver, battling the tricky tides, currents, and winds.*

8.1mi. *We pass through picturesque Phippsburg Village, marked by its old captain's houses. Some of these were present when the expedition's ships passed by. Beyond the village we rejoin Route 209, turning right (north).*

13.1mi. *As you approach Bath, turn right onto Webber Avenue, which later becomes Washington Street. This will take us closer to the river than the main road.*

13.6mi. *Here is a public boat-launching site on the river.*

Point of Interest

14.0mi. *On the right is the* ***Maine Maritime Museum****. This is an outstanding institution consisting of ten buildings demonstrating different phases of the shipbuilding for which Bath is famous. The museum includes an art gallery, a nineteenth-century shipyard, lobstering exhibits, a child's area, and interactive displays. Boat excursions on the Kennebec originate here. One building houses a variety of small boats. One of these is an old bateau used for log drives on the Dead River in the early part of the twentieth century. It is about forty feet long, much larger than those used by the expedition, but its design is similar. In the same building is a dugout canoe called a pirogue. This is one of the few examples in existence. On the first day of the ascent of the river from Fort Western, Arnold's birch-bark canoe leaked so badly that he traded it for a pirogue in Vassalboro. The museum is interesting even for children. Allow at least half a day to fully view all the fine exhibits. For more information, contact:*

Maine Maritime Museum
243 Washington St.
Bath, ME 04530
(207) 443-1316

maritime@bathmaine.com

15.2mi. *After passing the huge Bath Iron Works, we reach US Route 1 in the center of town. There are several excellent restaurants in Bath. The community has many historic houses.*

To continue on the expedition's route, turn right onto US Route 1 (northbound) and immediately cross the broad Kennebec on the new Sagadahoc Bridge, with good views of the shipyard and the big ships under construction. On the east side of the river, in Woolwich, we will turn left onto Route 127, about 0.2mi. beyond the bridge.

Set your auto's odometer back to zero to begin the next section.

0.0mi. *At the junction of US Route 1 and Route 127 in Woolwich, turn left and proceed northbound.*

1.9mi. *Turn left onto Route 128, the Days Ferry Road. This will lead to better views of the river and Merrymeeting Bay.*

2.6mi. *We reach Days Ferry, a quaint village on the east shore of the river. During the early 1800s, here was located the main ferry to cross the river for traffic moving up and down the coast. Park on a side road to the right, the Old Stage Road. Parking on the narrow main road at this point is dangerous. Walk down the road to the old ferry-landing pier, which has great views of the big river, especially south toward Bath and its prominent bridge. The ships of the expedition sailed past this point on the third day out of Newburyport, heading to Colburn's shipyard and Fort Western. Opposite the Days Ferry Road, the Old Stage Road leads east toward Wiscasset.*

6.9mi. *Pass the Chopps Point Road on our left.*

Side Trip

The Chopps *is a narrow passage in the river about two hundred yards wide. The entire volume of the Kennebec, Androscoggin, and six other smaller rivers emptying into Merrymeeting Bay has to flow through this constriction in its journey to the sea. The bay is a wide, shallow "inland sea." It has extensive salt marshes, making it a waterfowl heaven, especially during the migratory periods in spring and fall. Geese and ducks by the thousands rest and feed here. At the change of tide, the flow of water through the Chopps reverses and causes very powerful currents, eddies, and whirlpools. When a breeze picks up, the Chopps really earns its name.*

To reach a viewing point, travel down the gravel Chopps Point Road for two miles. The point is occupied by a private children's camp, so you will

He bade goodbye to his hosts, Captain and Mrs. Colburn, and then he struck out for Fort Western by river, arriving there before dark. Most of the army was there, although some supplies and men were still to be brought up from Colburn's. Now came the arduous task of organizing the army for the trip into the wild country above Fort Western.

Bateaux at the Colburn House, Pittston

At the Colburn House

Large bateau at Fort Western

Chapter Five

The Bateaux

The army was to proceed by water up the little-known Kennebec River, then down the unknown Chaudière River. There were only rudimentary, rutted roads, little more than pathways, above Fort Western, and none at all above Fort Halifax. The only way to proceed through the wilderness was by water. When the army left Fort Western, it had to transport food, arms, and equipment that are estimated by the author to be slightly more than 100 tons. It could not go to Quebec by sea. The powerful British navy would have made that choice foolhardy.

The type of craft they chose to construct were small wooden boats called bateaux—also spelled bateau or battoe. (In this book, bateau is used as singular, bateaux as plural, following the French usage. The word means boat in French.) The choice of this type of craft, the timing of the expedition, and the quality of construction all were critical in the outcome of events at Quebec City.

The bateau is a cousin to the common dory. There were several different types that evolved during the colonial period. The "lake" bateau was quite large, weighing up to a ton or more, capable of carrying heavy loads of twenty or more fully equipped soldiers. This type of boat was not intended to negotiate rocky, shallow rivers such as the Kennebec. Rather, they were chiefly used in Canada's lake country and along large rivers. They were easily distinguished from other types of bateaux by their size, weight, and the almost vertical arrangement of their bow and stern posts. A good example of this type of bateau is on display at Old Fort Western in Augusta.

The "river" bateau was smaller, of lighter construction, about twenty-two to thirty feet in length, and it had an extended, overhanging bow and stern to better maneuver in swift, rocky rivers. The low-angled bow also allowed the craft to slide over rocks more easily. Collisions with rocks in fast, shallow water were inevitable. Both types of bateaux were flat-bottomed and without a full keel. The sides of river bateaux were flared more to provide stability when heavily loaded, as well as to provide more carrying capacity. A bateau was easily constructed from sawed boards, and a minimum of inside ribbing was required. It could be made from pine, spruce, or fir, but pine was the most common wood used, as it was lightest and easiest to mill and shape. Ribbing was of the more solid oak, if available. Unfortunately, the

need to ask permission to cross a grassy lawn to the river's edge. The powerful currents are an awesome sight at tide change or at high water in the spring. The ships of the expedition had to wait for a flood tide to move through the Chopps into the bay to continue their journey.

Return to Route 128 and proceed north.

10.9mi. *Open farm fields provide views of Merrymeeting Bay to the west. Some of the extensive salt marshes can be seen in the distance. The shallow bay is where several of the expedition's ships ran aground.*

11.2mi. *Cross the Eastern River, one of eight rivers that feed fresh water into the brackish bay.*

13.5mi. *Cross Route 197. To the left, it is a short distance to the Richmond Bridge over the Kennebec, which will take you to the town of Richmond. Our path continues straight ahead on Route 128.*

Point of Interest / Side Trip

We highly recommend a side trip to Richmond in order to reach Swan Island in the Kennebec. First because of the island's sheer beauty, and second because of its historical relationship to the expedition. As the ships ascended the river, some anchored for the night next to the island. Captain Henry Dearborn and several of his officers, including Aaron Burr, the future vice president of the United States, came ashore and accepted the hospitality of the island's inhabitants.

There is a legend that Burr met an Indian maiden named Jacquetta and both fell instantly in love. The legend goes on to tell that she accompanied Burr and the expedition much of the way to Quebec before reality set in and they parted. There is no written record of this occurring, and English Americans did not accept consorting with Indian women at that time. If it did happen, that inhibition may account for the lack of any of the many journal writers mentioning such an interesting event.

Swan Island is four and one-half miles long and a half to three-quarters of a mile wide. The state Department of Inland Fisheries and Wildlife manages it as a wildlife preserve and historic site. The island was the home of Abenaki Indians for centuries; a small village was located on the southeast side near Maxwell Cove. Europeans settled it in the early 1700s. More than ten buildings were present in 1775, some of them quite prominent farmsteads. Several of these buildings have been preserved, and many old foundations can be identified. The island abounds with all kinds of wildlife, including deer and many species of birds. There are campsites halfway down the island's east shore, with log lean-tos providing opportunities for overnight stays.

We recommend at least a day to explore the island's wonders. An overnight camping trip would be even better. Private autos are not allowed on the island, so walking is the mode of transport. A state-operated ferry reaches the island across a narrow river channel. The island is open May 1 through Labor Day by reservation, then on a day-by-day basis to Sept. 30.

To reach the ferry, drive to the picturesque town of Richmond and its riverfront park, two miles from Route 128. (Richmond, long off the main roads, in the early twentieth century became a colony for Russian and Ukrainian refugees.) The ferry is boarded at the dock. Nearby is the site of Fort Richmond, the remains of which were mentioned in several of the expedition's journals. There are no structures of the fort remaining today.

For further information about Swan Island, its facilities, and the ferry, contact:

Swan Island Reservations
IF&W Regional Office
270 Lyons Rd.
Sidney, ME 04330
(207) 547-5322

To continue the route description, return to Route 128.

14.8mi. *Turn left onto Court House Road, leading a short distance to the Pownalborough Court House.*

Point of Interest

The ***Pownalborough Court House*** *in present-day Dresden is beautifully situated on the east shore*

of the Kennebec. It was built in 1761, serving as a courthouse for the area until 1794. It has been restored and is operated by the Lincoln County

exact design and size of the expedition's bateaux are unknown. No plans or dimensional details have been found.

The design of bateaux had been brought to the New World by the French, who needed a sturdy, utilitarian craft to ply the waterways of the St. Lawrence, Great Lakes basin, and beyond. It could carry heavy loads and was relatively stable in rapids, rocky streams, or on the huge waves encountered in the Great Lakes. In the French and Indian Wars, their enemy, the English, copied the design and used these boats for most of the military operations they conducted along the Hudson and Mohawk Rivers. When huge English armies were thrown against the French and Indians on Lake George, Ticonderoga, and Fort Niagara farther west, thousands of these craft were constructed and used.

During the 1750s, English generals combed the Atlantic coast, paying huge bonuses to entice carpenters and shipwrights to Albany (near the junction of the Mohawk and Hudson Rivers) to construct bateaux for use in military campaigns. These carpenters carried knowledge and skills about bateau construction back to their hometowns. The use of the bateau, especially for military transport, was widely known.

In early August, 1775, when the decision to attack Quebec was made, the choice of bateaux as the watercraft was obvious. Birch-bark canoes, although much lighter, faster, and easier to portage, took too long to construct and could not have carried the huge weight of supplies and men. Birch-bark canoes also require much more skill to maneuver in rapid water without puncturing the very frail bark skin. Bateaux could be built to any size, from a small eighteen- to twenty-footer weighing 200 to 300 pounds to a much larger lake bateau of forty feet, weighing more than a ton.

The proposed bateaux to be used on the Quebec expedition were specified to carry six to seven men along with their supplies. Arnold listed these specifications for the bateaux in a letter to Captain (later Major) Reuben Colburn on Aug. 21, 1775:

> His Excellency, General Washington Desires you will Inform your self how soon, there can be procured or built, at Kennebec, Two hundred light Bateaux Capable of Carrying Six or Seven men each, with their Provisions & Baggage (say 100 wt.

to each man) the Boats to be
furnished four Oars two Paddles
& two setting Poles.

Several pieces of evidence indicate that the bateaux were constructed smaller than these stated specifications. First, when Arnold arrived at Colburn's shipyard in Gardinerstown, he immediately perceived that the bateaux were smaller than they should be and ordered an additional twenty to be built. Second, when Colburn and his heirs solicited Congress to be paid for their construction, they cited only 230 pairs of oars, enough for one pair per bateau, plus a few spares for breakage, rather than the two pairs specified in Arnold's letter. A third piece of evidence is that numerous expedition journal writers observed that many men were required to walk along the banks of the river, rather than ride in the boats, presumably because there was not enough room for all of them in the heavily laden bateaux.

In addition to size, the quality of construction of the bateaux has always been a source of controversy among historians. It was even more so for the men who had to use them. The vehement comments made in their journals attest to the anger the men felt toward the builders of these heavy, leaky craft. The bateaux's hasty and poor construction led to their literally falling apart during the ascent of the Kennebec. Water entered the boats through poorly caulked seams between the boards, as well as over the sides in rapid water.

It was necessary to constantly bail water out of the boats, a persistent inconvenience. More important, water in the boats penetrated the barrels of precious food. Flour, hard bread, Indian corn, salted meats, and other food items were all stored in wooden barrels. By the time the expedition reached Norridgewock Falls, sixty-five miles upriver from Fort Western, the men already were throwing out spoiled food sorely needed for the journey. This food loss from leaky bateaux was the critical factor in the decision of Lieutenant Colonel Enos's division (more than a quarter of the men) to abandon the expedition.

In defense of the boatbuilder and his men, it should be pointed out that after having traveled to Cambridge to confer with Washington and Arnold, Colburn did not receive his final construction orders until Sept. 3, 1775. Allowing a minimum of three days for him to reach his shipyard in Gardinerstown, he could not have started the final assembly of construction crews, lumber, and hardware until Sept. 6. This gave him only fifteen days

Small bateau at Lac-Mégantic

Historical Association. Master builder Gershom Flagg constructed it for the Proprietors of the Kennebec Purchase, the Massachusetts businessmen who developed the area. He was also overseer of the construction of Fort Western. The courthouse was built within the parade grounds of the earlier Fort Shirley. It is a three-story masterpiece of pre-revolutionary Colonial architecture, with simple but strikingly elegant lines. A number of the expedition's journal writers mentioned observing it as they sailed upriver.

It also served as a tavern, a post office, and a town meeting house—and, at times, as a home for several families. The historical association acquired it in 1954. Its restoration has been as authentic as possible. Its two huge central fireplaces are marvels of masonry work. The courtroom is located on the second floor, along with the judge's chambers. John Adams and other prominent jurists practiced here.

Allow about two hours to visit this wonderful building. A small fee is charged. It is open 10 a.m. to 4 p.m. during the summer or by appointment otherwise. For further information, write to:

Lincoln County Historical Association
P.O. Box 61
Wiscasset, ME 04578

We continue on Route 128, which soon turns more easterly and bears away from the river.

***17.4mi.** Reach the junction with Route 27 and turn left (north). Route 27 actually goes all the way to the Chain of Ponds. After leaving it in Augusta, we will rejoin it when we reach Stratton.*

***22.1mi.** Watch for an obscure secondary road on the left (west). This is the Arnold Road, named*

after the expedition's leader. Turn left and soon parallel the river quite closely.

22.4mi. *Pass the Riverside Cemetery on the right. Toward the center front, a large monument marks the graves of Major Reuben Colburn and his wife. Colburn was the builder of the expedition's bateaux.*

22.6mi. *On the left is the* ***Major Reuben Colburn House****, on a hill overlooking the Kennebec, and it is now the home of the Arnold Expedition Historical Society. There is a bronze plaque on a rock next to the road indicating that Arnold used this building as his headquarters Sept. 21 to 23, 1775.*

Point of Interest

The task of building the boats for the army was given to then-Captain Colburn. He operated a small shipyard and sawmill next to the river below his home. This is where most of the army disembarked to transfer their provisions and arms to the 220 bateaux, which waited in stacks along the shore. The shipyard is long gone, and several private residences now occupy the location. The historical society moved into the Colburn house in the 1970s and, with the help of the state Bureau of Parks and Lands, maintains it as an historic site. It consists of the main house, a barn, and a carriage house. In the barn are several replicas of bateaux, some of which are approximately the same dimensions and design as those used on the expedition. A stop here is highly recommended. It is open to the public on Saturday and Sunday during July and August or by appointment.

For more information, write to:
Arnold Expedition Historical Society
RR 4, Box 6895
Gardiner, ME 04345

We continue on the Arnold Road for a hundred yards and then rejoin Route 27, turning left, northbound.

25.3mi. *At a traffic light in Randolph, turn left onto a bridge over the Kennebec. The size of the river at this point is about the same as it was in 1775. At the end of the bridge, turn right toward Augusta on US Route 201 and parallel the river.*

29.0mi. *At a turnout near the river's shore are historical information panels relating to the expedition. There are fine views upriver here, including the dome of the State Capitol Building.*

29.4mi. *We reach the small "city" of Hallowell and a public boat landing to the right. This is a good picnic spot. From this point northward, the river flows through a deep valley for the next twenty-five miles. Hallowell is a lively and historic town*

to gather the men and materials and construct 200 bateaux, 460 oars, 480 paddles, and 400 setting poles. Colburn had traveled to Cambridge twice in early August to discuss construction of the boats. Undoubtedly, he had already begun the process of gathering men and materials, but the very narrow fifteen-day window from the receipt of his final orders caused, of necessity, very hurried construction, resulting in shoddily built bateaux.

The compressed construction period also affected the eventual net weight of the boats. Best estimates are that each weighed somewhere between 350 and 500 pounds. Most of the lumber to build them would have had to be sawed from newly cut, green logs. Luckily, there were several sawmills nearby to supply Colburn with the boards for the boats and wood to mill paddles, oars, and setting poles. No small shipyard of that day could have been expected to have on hand enough seasoned and dry lumber to fulfill an order of that size. The green, wet, pine wood added many pounds to each bateau's weight. The men of the expedition railed and raged about this weight during their first and subsequent portages. The shrinking of the green lumber as it dried probably contributed to the rapidity with which the bateaux sprung leaks and fell apart.

Other factors also contributed to the rapid rate of destruction of the bateaux. One was the shallowness of the Kennebec at that time of year. Dennis Getchell, a scout sent upriver by Colburn several weeks before the expedition arrived at Fort Western, stated in a report to Arnold that the river was "quite shallow." Maine rivers were and are at their lowest flow rates in September and October. Also, in 1775 there were no upriver reservoirs and dams to maintain a more even and higher flow rate, as is the case today. The heavy bateaux were undoubtedly scraping and hitting rocks from the day they left Fort Western. The journal writers observed that the men frequently waded in cold water, dragging bateaux over rocky, shallow spots and through rapids.

How heavily loaded was each bateau? This question would have a great bearing on how low they sat in the water and how often they collided with rocks. The expedition's journals give us no clues regarding this critical issue. We must make a very rough estimate.

We know 220 bateaux were built. We know that Arnold planned to carry food provisions for forty-five days. The probable weight of food per man, per day, including an allowance for the containers—usually wooden barrels and boxes—would be approximately three pounds per day per man. This estimate is based on an average of rations issued to colonial soldiers of the day, taken from military records of the time.

Multiplying 1,100 men with food for forty-five days would calculate to seventy-five tons of food at the start at Fort Western or an average of about 675 pounds per bateau. Each man would be taking about fifty pounds of personal items: tents, blankets, cooking gear, arms, powder, and ball. An average of five men were assigned per bateau (1,100 men divided by 220 bateaux). This adds another 250 pounds of personal weight, totaling 925 pounds per bateau. This estimate is on the conservative side. The total cargo weight could have been as high as 1,000 pounds.

Add to this the weight of four men to operate the bateau, with one or more walking on shore, then include the weight of oars, paddles and poles, and the gross weight might be about 1,500 pounds. Jay Adams, director of the Old Fort Western Museum in Augusta, believes this figure may be too low. In any case, it was a very heavy load indeed. It would imply that the bateaux departing Fort Western were literally "loaded to the gunnels," drawing at least a foot or more of water. Boats loaded that heavily would frequently strike against the bottom of the shallow river.

Another issue was the bateau-handling ability of the men themselves. Washington, in his orders, called for recruiting experienced boatmen. Instead, the expedition's soldiers were mostly farmers, deep-water sailors, or tradesmen. Their inexperience undoubtedly played a part in the rapid deterioration of the boats. Four or five men pushing, pulling, paddling, or poling a bateau that sits a foot deep in the water requires a high degree of experience and coordination. For many, maybe most, of the expedition's men, this was a first-time, hands-on learning experience.

Another determinant in the fate of the bateaux was the high degree of technical ability needed to load and trim a heavy, small craft—with 100- to 200-pound barrels of food and supplies—in order to properly maneuver these unfamiliar boats against a swift current while "reading" the best channels to avoid the many rocks. An experienced canoeist knows that such skills take time to learn. The men of the expedition had no such time.

A final issue in the use of the bateau was the elevation to be overcome along the route. Most historians have overlooked this vital matter. No information was available to Washington or Arnold at that time citing or

with many old houses, antique shops, and fine restaurants (Slate's is especially good). Locally, there are many interesting hiking trails to explore. Information on them can be obtained at Fort Western in Augusta or at Hallowell City Hall.

RATION FOR THE MILITARY FORCES
OF THE PROVINCE OF MASSACHUSETTS
APRIL, 1755

One Pound of Pork per Day	One Pound of Flour per Week
One Pound of Bread per Day	One Pint of Indian Meal per week
One Gill of Rum per Day	Four Ounces of Butter per Week
One-Half Pint Peafe per Day	One Pint Molaffes per Week
Two Ounces of Ginger per Week	One-Half Pound Sugar per Week

W Shirley

Governor of Maffachufetts and Captain-General of His Majefty's Forces

Courtesy, Old Fort Western

In the center of town on the river side of the main street, marked on a granite corner post, is a column showing the height of the river at floods that have been recorded over the past century and a half. You won't believe these marks, but they are true!

29.7mi. *On the right, next to the river, at a point where the stores start petering out, there is a small park and picnic area. The park has good views for some distance up and down the river.*

Here, too, begins a recently constructed two-mile-long walking, running, and bicycling trail that runs right next to the river. It is one of the best walks to see the river as Arnold's men saw it because much of the eastern shore is undeveloped. This path is known as the Rail Trail because it also parallels railroad tracks that are, at this writing, unused. It will take you all the way to downtown Augusta and, across a short bridge, to Fort Western.

By car, we continue north on US Route 201 toward Augusta.

31.2mi. *Pass the State Capitol (or State House, as it is usually called in Maine) on the left. Spacious Capitol Park is to the right. On the south side of the Capitol complex is a building housing the state library, museum, and archives. The museum is well worth a visit, as is the State House itself.*

Point of Interest

The ***Maine State Museum*** *is a fine facility containing displays of Maine life, industries, and crafts; a logging locomotive and a Lombard Log Hauler; a complete woodworking factory; and natural history and many other excellent exhibits. It is one of the best museums in the state.*

31.5mi. *We arrive at a tricky traffic rotary. Enter and take the second turn out. Continue straight ahead, passing a fire station on the right, and descend a hill onto the main street of Augusta (Water Street), which parallels the river.*

32.1mi. *In the center of town, approach a traffic light. Stay in the right-hand lane and turn right across a bridge. Old Fort Western is on the east bank of the river.*

32.2mi. *Turn right into the parking area for the fort and Augusta City Hall.*

Point of Interest

In September of 1775 the Expedition to Quebec used ***Fort Western*** *as the embarkation point for the journey into the wilds. In the 1600s, this place was known as Cushnoc, and it was a Pilgrim trading post at the head of navigation and tide on the Kennebec. Today, the original main barracks and commissary building remains intact. In 1754, it was one of two frontier forts built on the Kennebec River. Later, it was used as a store and home. The present corner block houses, watch boxes, and stockade fence have been rebuilt as a part of the fort's restoration by the City of Augusta and the Trustees of Old Fort Western. The fort was constructed to be a supply facility for Fort Halifax, eighteen miles upriver in present-day Winslow. With the capture of Quebec by the British in 1759, military threats from the north were finally ended, and the frontier forts were no longer needed. It was a trading post in 1775.*

Today, Fort Western is an outstanding frontier fort museum and educational facility. It has interactive displays of eighteenth-century life on the frontier. The displays of cannon, muskets, carts, and implements of frontier life are presented in such a way as to be interesting to all ages. Historical interpreters in period dress demonstrate weaving, cooking, the firing of muskets, and many other activities.

Of special interest is a beautiful replica of a lake bateau with its almost vertical bow and stern posts. Its construction was based on the remains of a boat found on the bottom of Lake George in New York. The dimensions of this replica are similar to those used to shuttle supplies and men between Fort Western and Fort Halifax. This bateau would have been too heavy to be used during the Quebec expedition's many portages and on the shallow waterways and rocky rapids of the Kennebec above Fort Halifax.

The barracks building was used by some of the expedition's men as a place to sleep while they prepared their bateaux for the trip ahead. When you

even estimating the elevation that needed to be ascended via the Kennebec-Chaudière route through the Appalachians. The bateaux had to be dragged, pushed, poled, paddled, and carried on men's backs to an elevation of more than 1,400 feet above sea level at the Height of Land on the present American-Canadian border.

This effort added greatly to the hardships encountered and the time lost. If Arnold, Washington, and other planners of the expedition had known about the huge elevation gain, their estimates of the time and effort needed to reach Quebec might have been different. This not-so-gradual elevation gain contributed to slow the army to a crawl and drain its very strength.

Most of the bateaux surviving the ascent of the Kennebec and Dead Rivers were abandoned between the Chain of Ponds and Arnold Pond. Only a few were carried over the Height of Land into Canada. Some were used to transport the retreating Fourth Division back to Fort Western.

All these issues, complex as they are, revolve around the bateaux used by the expedition. The wonder of it is that many soldiers survived and reached Quebec at all. Some did not. The bateau represents a symbol of all the hardship and suffering experienced by the men of the expedition. Only men who had great courage, perseverance, and belief in their cause could have overcome what lay before them as they ascended the Kennebec and Dead Rivers in their bateaux.

"Our men are as yet in very good spirits, considering they have to wade half the time, and our boats so villainously constructed, and leaking so much that they are always wet. I would heartily wish the infamous constructors, who, to satisfy their avaricious temper, and fill their purses with the spoils of their country, may be obliged to trust to the mercy of others more treacherous than themselves, that they might judge the fear and undergo the just reward of their villainy."

—Thayer's journal

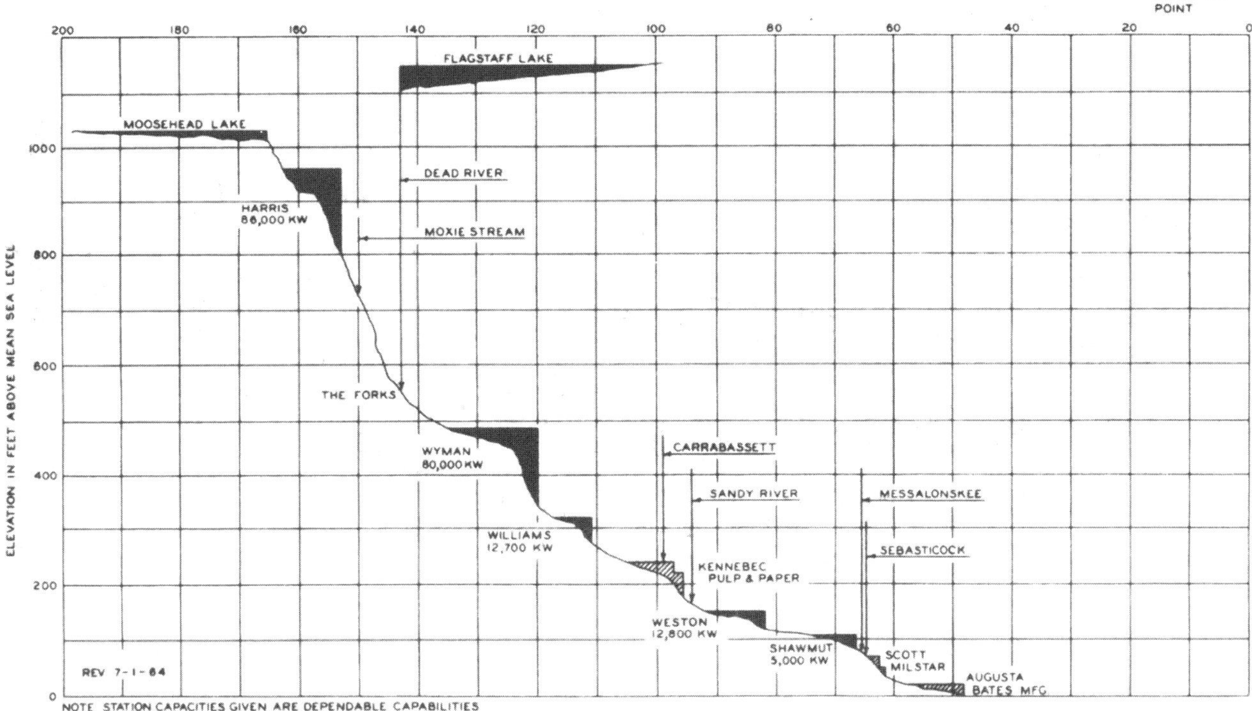

Profile of the Kennebec River Elevations & Dams

This profile illustrates the great difficulties the expedition encountered during the ascent of the river. No information about elevations was available to Arnold in 1775.

Start at the lower right at sea level (Fort Western) and trace the features.

First, the Bates Mfg.(Edwards) Dam was removed in 1999. The river ascends gradually to the first portage.

Second, the Milstar Dam is located at Ticonic Falls. The first portage of the expedition occurred here. From that point, the river ascends steeply as far as the Shawmut Dam. This section was known as the Five Mile Rips.

Third, the Weston Dam is located at Skowhegan Falls, the second portage for the expedition.

Fourth, the Kennebec Pulp and Paper Dam at Madison is located at Norridgewock Falls, site of the third and longest portage on the Kennebec main stem.

Fifth, the Williams Dam at Solon is located on the site of Caratunk (Devil's) Falls, the next portage on the river.

Sixth, the river ascends steeply through the site of the present Wyman Dam. At the upper end of the pool formed by the dam is the point where the expedition left the Kennebec to traverse the Great Carrying Place. The river and its west branch, the Dead River, ascend very steeply beyond this point. Harris Station and Moosehead Lake are on the east branch of the Kennebec.

Seventh, the Great Carrying Place ascended from the point on the river previously cited to the Dead River, at present Flagstaff Lake. On this profile, that would calculate to more than a phenomenal 600-foot ascent. It was actually 300 feet more for the men, as they had several high ridges to overcome to reach the Dead River.

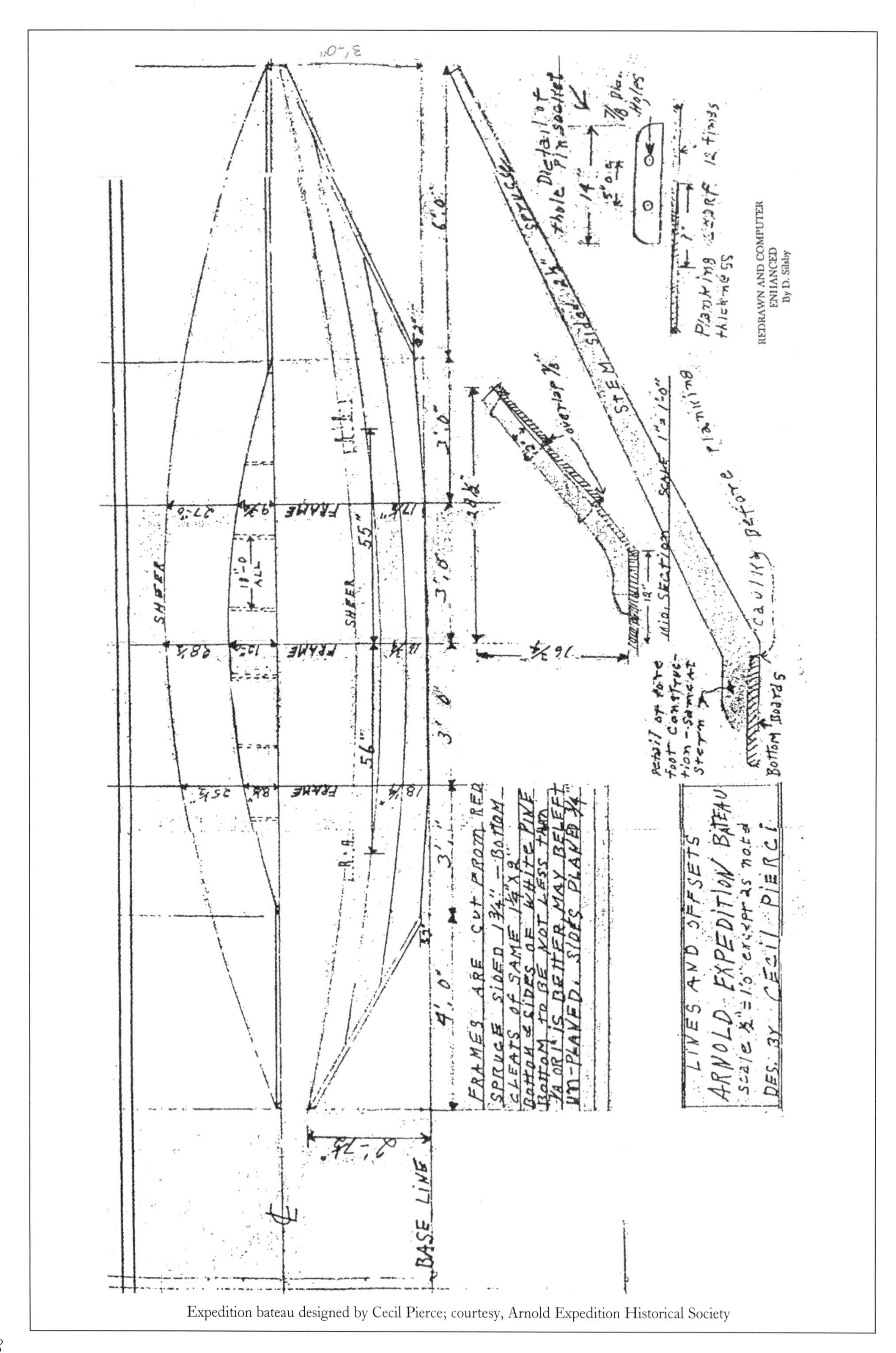

Expedition bateau designed by Cecil Pierce; courtesy, Arnold Expedition Historical Society

At Fort Western

From the perspective of a high-flying eagle, the twelve-mile stretch of the Kennebec River between Colburn's shipyard and Fort Western must have appeared to be full of water bugs. But these "bugs" were heavily laden bateaux with oars being rowed and paddled by sweating men, stubbornly battling the river's currents as they crawled upstream. The smart ones had waited for the incoming tide. Those who were not so savvy fought the currents and swore. Some of the fleet's ships that drew less water also moved slowly upriver to help transport the expedition's cargo to Fort Western. Upon reaching what is now Hallowell, four miles below the fort, the ships were stopped by shallow water and mud flats. The crews had to offload their cargos into the passing flotilla of bateaux or wait for empties to come down from the fort.

Arnold arrived at the fort during the late afternoon of Sept. 23, and he was greeted by the sight of hundreds of bateaux hauled up or stacked up on the landing just south of the fort. Men were drawing supplies from the quartermaster and trying to figure how to fit all the heavy barrels, casks, and sundry other items, along with their personal gear and arms, into their newly acquired craft. Arnold dived into this wild activity and began dealing with the multitude of critical details of trying to outfit thirteen companies of men for a journey into the

look down over the steep bank to the valley to the south, you will be able to visualize the bateaux packed tightly on the shore below.

It is highly recommended that you stop here to see what the Quebec-bound men saw. Nowhere else along the entire course of the expedition will you encounter a human site that is nearly the same as it was in 1775. Although there were a few scattered farms north of Fort Western, this was the jumping-off point from civilization to wilderness.

The tour through the facility will take about two hours. It is open daily from May 1 through Labor Day, then weekends through Columbus Day. Hours vary, so you may need to check ahead. A small fee is charged, except for Augusta residents. Many special programs and events are scheduled during the year. Fort Western is a National Historic Landmark.

There is a play and picnic area adjoining the fort. A brief, tree-shaded walk will take you downriver to the city's main boat-launching facility, which is a part of another small park. This park is where many of the bateaux were launched for the upriver journey. A fine riverside walking trail continues south for about a mile.

For further information, contact:
Old Fort Western
16 Cony St.
Augusta, ME 04330
(207) 626-2385
www.oldfortwestern.org

A bird's-eye view of the fort. Courtesy, Old Fort Western.

Views of Fort Western today

wilderness and enemy-held country.

Fort Western had been built in 1754 as part of a defensive system of fortifications to protect the Kennebec and the Maine coastal settlements from marauding French and Indian war parties, which had a history of swooping down the river from Canada. It was meant as a supply depot at the head of tide to support Fort Halifax, eighteen miles farther upriver. The wooden fort consisted of a large two-and-a-half-story barracks, 100 by 32 feet, which included a commissary and magazine for the storage of military supplies and arms. It was surrounded by a stockade, with two-story blockhouses at the northeast and southwest corners, and two small watch boxes at the other two corners. The fort was perched on a high bank on the east shore of the river. It had been built at the site of an earlier Plymouth Company trading post, Cushnoc, established in the 1620s. The area near the fort on both sides of the river was already dotted with newly built farms. In 1759, the British army had soundly defeated the French at Quebec, and in 1763 all of Canada had been ceded to England, thus ending the long, bloody French and Indian Wars. Since there was no further threat from the north, both Fort Halifax and Fort Western had been decommissioned.

During wartime, a small force of colonial soldiers, commanded by Captain James Howard, had garrisoned the fort. At the war's end, the enterprising Howard was able to purchase the fort and establish it as a major trading post for the rapidly growing settlements along the river valley and its tributaries. When Arnold arrived, Howard greeted the commander and invited him to stay at his nearby large home. It served as Arnold's headquarters for the next several days.

Tents had sprung up on any flat ground available around the fort. Some men, whose tents and equipment had not yet come up the river, improvised by building crude board huts. Some lucky men found lodging in the far more comfortable main barracks or in nearby private homes. Campfires spewed smoke all around the fort and the smell of cooking food filled the air during the day. At night, many roaring campfires lit the area. Groups of talking, laughing soldiers ringed the fires. They warmed themselves as they discussed the dangerous journey ahead. The din of an army of 1,100 excited men must have been unforgettable to the local inhabitants. Officers growling orders strove to sort their men out and bring order to seeming chaos. With time, the companies began to take on a more orderly appearance.

After conferring with his officers, Arnold decided to divide the army into four divisions of three or four companies, each division consisting of about 250 to 300 men. This separation, he believed, would prevent bottlenecks on the narrow portage trails and not overload the small campsites along the route.

The lead division consisted of the three rifle companies under the command of Captain Morgan. A natural leader, he was one of the few officers with previous military experience, and he was well suited to command this important lead contingent of, essentially, light infantry. Later in the war, he extracted a terrible price from the British at Saratoga and, as a general in the southern campaign, at the battle of Cowpens.

Lieutenant Colonel Christopher Greene from Rhode Island led the Second Division. Major Timothy Bigelow from Worcester, Massachusetts, assisted him. This division consisted of three musket companies led by Captains Thayer, Topham, and Hubbard.

The Third Division, led by Major Return Meigs, consisted of four musket companies under Captains Dearborn, Ward, Hanchet, and Goodrich. Captain Henry Dearborn from New Hampshire was later to rise to fame, becoming General of the Army during the early 1800s.

Lieutenant Colonel Roger Enos led the Fourth Division. It included three musket companies under Captains Williams, McCobb, and Scott. Captain Reuben Colburn, builder of the bateaux, led a partial company of carpenters and shipwrights who traveled with this division. Their function was to try to keep the bateaux repaired and afloat.

Arnold's first task was to organize two scouting parties, and he immediately sent them upriver. The first was under the command of Lieutenant Steele from Smith's company. He led a party of six men and a guide, using two large birch-bark canoes, with orders to reconnoiter the route all the way to Chaudière Pond (Lake Megantic), including a route across the long portage over the Height of Land. Steele was also ordered to try to capture the Indian Natanis at his camp on the Dead River. Arnold had faulty intelligence that Natanis was a spy in the pay of the British governor of Canada, Guy Carleton.

The second advance party was led by Lieutenant Church. It had six men, a guide, and a surveyor, young Jonathan Pierce. They were to proceed upriver to the Great Carrying Place, where the route left the Kennebec

General Henry Dearborn

Colonel Christopher Greene

Captain Daniel Morgan

Young officers on the expedition who later became famous: Dearborn as Jefferson's Secretary of War, Greene in a heroic death at Croton Bridge, and Morgan as a general at Cowpens. Courtesy of the Arnold Expedition Historical Society.

Colonel Samuel Ward

Colonel Return J. Meigs

Fort Western from the river

River. They were to survey and mark the portage, then move farther up the Dead River to survey and mark the many portages along that river's course. Both advance parties struck off upriver on Sept. 24.

There is no official, complete roster of all the men who comprised the army as it departed from Fort Western. A substantial number had joined as it progressed along the route from Cambridge to Fort Western. The expedition also included four women. It was not unusual then for women to accompany their husbands during military service.

It is also unknown how many bateaux were assigned to each company. Simple math would suggest that each bateau would have five men assigned to it, and 1,100 men divided by 220 bateaux would produce an average of five men per bateaux. However, not all the bateaux were the same size and capacity. Each company was probably assigned approximately sixteen bateaux to carry its men and supplies.

On Sept. 25, Arnold went down to the landing south of the fort to see off Morgan and his division. He shook Morgan's hand, and the forty-five to forty-eight bateaux accommodating the three companies of riflemen pushed off into the swift current. Large groups of men lined the shore and cheered as the lead division finally got underway toward their goal, a city 250 miles to the north. Arnold had also ordered Morgan to begin cutting and widening the portage trail across the Great Carrying Place. To allow this lead division to move faster, they were not encumbered by their full complement of food and supplies. They presumably would draw on the other divisions' reserves later.

Arnold had calculated the time necessary to reach the French Canadian settlements along the Chaudière River. He planned to obtain additional food there. He ordered the commissary to issue provisions to each company for forty-five days. This estimate of time proved to be right on the nose. The expedition arrived on the shore of the St. Lawrence on Nov. 8, after forty-four days of travel from Fort Western.

At noon of the next day, Arnold bid goodbye to the Second Division under Lieutenant Colonel Greene, with his three companies. On the twenty-seventh, late in the afternoon, Major Meigs and his four companies, comprising the Third Division, launched their roughly sixty bateaux and splashed upstream and out of sight of the fort.

On the twenty-eighth, Arnold was impatient to be off

as well. Lieutenant Colonel Enos, leader of the Fourth Division, had not yet made his appearance. He was still at Colburn's waiting for the completion of the oars and paddles to outfit the remaining bateaux. Arnold could wait no longer. The lead units of his army were now as much as three days ahead of him. He ordered the men of the three remaining companies, who were ready, to start up the river.

Arnold gathered his personal effects, sword, and writing desk and climbed into a birch-bark canoe. James Howard, proprietor of Fort Western, was there to see him off. He wished Arnold well on his precarious journey. Arnold sat in the middle of the bark canoe, and his two Indian paddlers pushed off, beginning one of the great adventures of American military history. Fort Western now returned to its usual tranquility. Never again would it see a military campaign at its gates.

"At 12 o'clock, set out again for Squhegan Falls; the stream is very swift, which makes it difficult, and our Batteaux leaky, besides the place being very shallow, which obliges our men to go into the river and haul Batteaux after them, which generally occupies three or four men, two of whom are at her head and one or two at her stern, which occasioned a slow progress. To-night we encamped within three miles of the falls, the water still continues to run very rapid."
—Thayer's journal

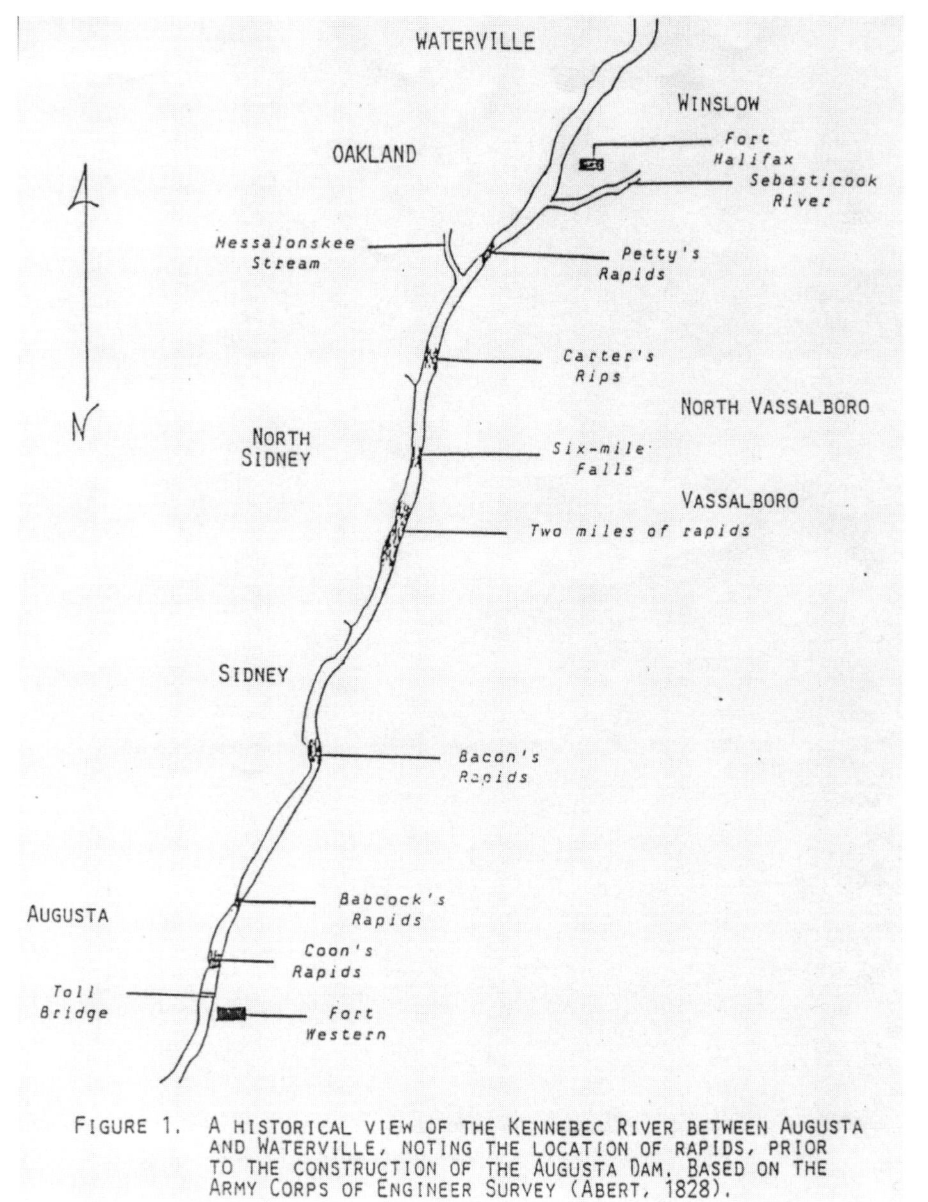

FIGURE 1. A HISTORICAL VIEW OF THE KENNEBEC RIVER BETWEEN AUGUSTA AND WATERVILLE, NOTING THE LOCATION OF RAPIDS, PRIOR TO THE CONSTRUCTION OF THE AUGUSTA DAM. BASED ON THE ARMY CORPS OF ENGINEER SURVEY (ABERT, 1828).

The river the expedition faced before the dams. It is much the same today.

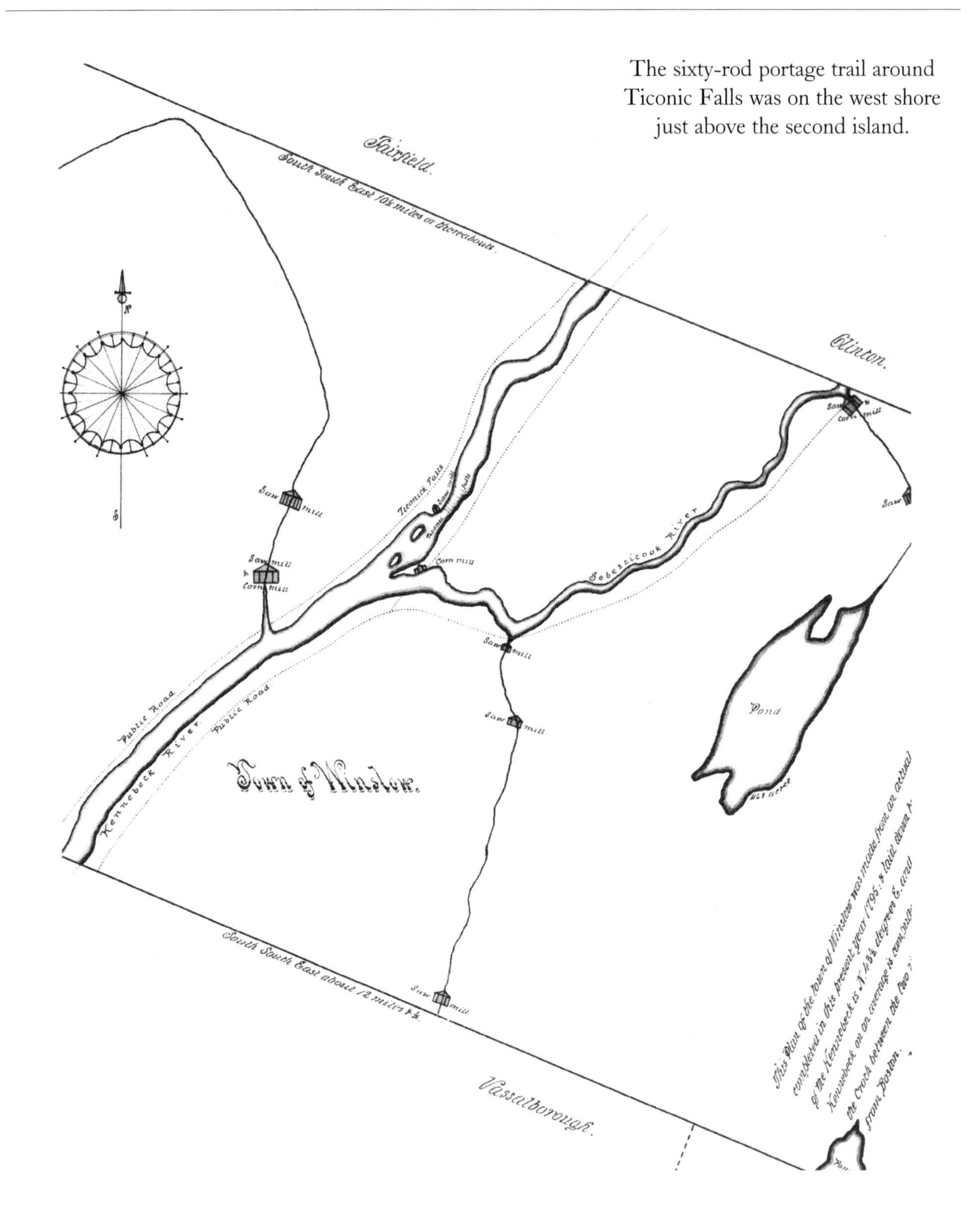

The sixty-rod portage trail around Ticonic Falls was on the west shore just above the second island.

1790s map of Winslow. Courtesy, Maine State Archives.

"The dry codfish lying loose in the bottom of the bateaux were wet constantly. The bread casks admitted the water in plenty . . . swelled the bread and burst the casks . . . The same fate attended the fine casks of peas."
—Dr. Isaac Senter

Chapter Seven

Fort Western to Norridgewock Falls

At noon on Sept. 29, the birch-bark canoe carrying Arnold and his two Indian paddlers left Fort Western and moved rapidly up the Kennebec. The first impression that Arnold recorded of this leg of the journey was that the seat of his pants became quite wet. Seams in birch-bark canoes were notorious for their leakage unless constantly recaulked with pitch or spruce gum. He tolerated this only eight miles upriver to the settlement of Vassalboro, where he went ashore and bought a pirogue, a dugout canoe. To his satisfaction, it proved to be considerably dryer than the birch-bark.

The companies led by Captains McCobb and Scott had left Fort Western at about 10 a.m. Arnold overtook them soon after leaving Vassalboro. The bateaux were making slow headway against the swift current. And there were five fast rips between Fort Western and Fort Halifax. The men who were not able to find space in the loaded bateaux were crashing through the brush along the shore. Some followed an old, rough road that connected the two forts. This was located on higher ground, some distance to the east of the river, avoiding the dense brush, trees, and uneven ground along the river's shore. Over thousands of years, the river had cut a deep valley. This entrenchment extended all the way to Fort Halifax and Ticonic Falls. The river itself was approximately 150 yards wide, with high, forested banks on both shores. There were a few farms sprinkled along its edge in both Vassalboro on the east bank and what is now Sidney on the west. The water level in the river was quite low, so the bateaux, sitting deep, were scraping against rocks much of the way.

Arnold rapidly passed the approximately thirty bateaux of McCobb's and Scott's companies. The pirogue was considerably lighter and faster; it was paddled and poled upstream by the two strong, river-wise Indian guides. The eighteen-mile stretch between Fort Western and Fort Halifax is almost continuous swift current. Arnold was able to ascend it that day as far as Six Mile Falls—actually, a short Class 2 rapid—before he camped for the night. As the name implies, it is located approximately six miles below Ticonic Falls.

Early in the morning of Sept. 30, Arnold and his party

Augusta to Skowhegan

From Augusta northward to Winslow, the Kennebec River is deeply entrenched, so you won't see much of it unless you elect to canoe this section. From Winslow to Skowhegan, you will see the river often as it emerges from the deep part of the valley.

In 1999, the Kennebec saw a profound change. For the previous 134 years, the Edwards Dam, located about a half-mile above Fort Western in Augusta, had covered the natural river above it with a seventeen-mile-long pool, hiding what the expedition's men beheld. The dam had been built to provide power for sawmills, woolen mills, and other industrial enterprises, and eventually to generate electric power. The original dam included a lock to lift steamships and other shallow-draft vessels above the dam, allowing them to travel as far upstream as Waterville. A regular steamship route used the Kennebec between Waterville and Boston during the mid-1800s, but it was soon displaced by the railroads. The lock was ruined by a flood and never replaced.

In 1999, after a long legal and political battle, agreement was reached between fishermen, environmentalists, state and federal authorities, and the company still operating the dam to eliminate it and return the river to its natural condition. The huge dam was breached and removed completely so that the river could run free, allowing sea-run fish to go up the river. This was the first major dam in the United States to be removed for environmental reasons, and its breaching made national news. The river still is in the process of recovery, but already millions of sea-run fish have returned as far as Ticonic Falls between Waterville and Winslow. The dam's removal also has exposed many rocky rips and shoals that the men of the expedition had to laboriously surmount.

The expedition faced no portages, however, until it reached Ticonic Falls. Above the falls was a five-mile stretch of fast, shoaly current that required the men to pull their bateaux while wading up to their waists in cold water. Above these rips, the river was less rapid until Skowhegan Falls was reached.

We begin this travel section at Fort Western. Drive east and uphill a short distance to a traffic rotary. Exit the circle onto US Route 201 northbound, which we will follow to Winslow.

Set your odometer to zero as you exit the rotary.

0.0mi. *After the rotary on the east side of the river, we proceed north on US Route 201. The highway parallels the river at a distance of a* *quarter- to a half-mile through farmland.*

17.2mi. *At the bottom of a hill, turn left onto Lithgow Street in Winslow and immediately cross a set of railroad tracks. At this point, the road passes close to the river's east shore.*

17.5mi. *On the left, just across from the Winslow Congregational Church, we see a Daughters of the American Revolution bronze plaque on a rock, indicating that the men of the expedition camped on this intervale after ascending the river from Fort Western.*

17.8mi. *At a traffic light, we rejoin US Route 201 by turning left and immediately crossing the Sebasticook River, a large tributary of the Kennebec. Near the end of the bridge turn left into a parking area next to* ***Fort Halifax Park.***

Point of Interest

Here is the one remaining original wooden blockhouse of Fort Halifax. The fort was constructed in 1754 on this strategic point of land to prevent hostile Indians or French troops from passage along either the Kennebec or Sebasticook water routes. When built, the fort consisted of a large barracks building, two large blockhouses, and a smaller watch house at each of the corners. A stockade fence connected the buildings at the corners to

broke camp and pushed through two swift rips, covering the five miles to Fort Halifax by 10 a.m. Located on the river's east shore on a point of land at the confluence of the Kennebec and Sebasticook Rivers, the fort was in poor condition, not having been occupied by troops for more than twelve years. It was of wooden construction similar in design to Fort Western, with a barracks house and large blockhouses at two corners. An additional blockhouse had been built on a hill overlooking the fort. A local family had taken over the barracks for their home. The advance divisions of the expedition had camped on an intervale to the south of the fort. Arnold did not tarry here long. He continued upstream a short distance to the first major portage at nearby Ticonic Falls.

The portage trail around the falls began at a small cove on the west shore of the river. Captain Dearborn's and Captain Goodrich's companies had just finished getting their boats and equipment over this portage and were preparing to launch into the river above the falls. Arnold estimated the portage to be sixty rods (a rod is sixteen and a half feet). Some of the local inhabitants had brought their oxen down to the river and were using sledges to assist the men in hauling bateaux and equipment over the portage.

Conducting a Portage

Ticonic Falls was the first of many portages to be encountered on the route up to the Height of Land at the Canadian border. The four falls on the Kennebec were well known and marked in 1775. Beyond the Kennebec, most portages were poorly marked and uncleared, little more than a vague path through the woods. Indian hunting parties used these portage routes but spent little time on their upkeep. Often they were marked with almost indiscernible knife cuts on a tree. All these portages had to be cleared and widened, once the route around the falls or rapids was located.

The crews would haul their boats on shore, then offload the 800 to 1,000 pounds of cargo, paddles, oars, and poles. The walkers who had been following their company's bateaux along the shore would join the boat crew in the laborious task. Dr. Senter, the expedition's physician, who kept a journal, states that a bateau weighed "no less than 400 pounds." Some may have considerably exceeded this weight.

One way to carry a boat over the uneven ground was to line four or six men along both sides, grab it by the gunwales, lift it a few inches off the ground, and walk with it along the trail. This technique was best used over relatively short or well-cleared trails, with a pathway eight to ten feet wide. Such trails existed for the four Kennebec River portages. Beyond the Kennebec, particularly over the horrors of the thirteen-mile Great Carrying Place, the portage trails had to be cleared, so stumps and rocks were encountered every few feet and had to be stepped over.

Another method to carry a bateau under these conditions was to flip it over and slide two or three poles under it. Four to six men would then lift the 400-plus-pound bateau to arm height and walk it along the trail. This method had the advantage of lifting the boat high over the newly cut stumps and numerous rocks. A third method was to flip the bateau over and raise the gunwales onto the men's shoulders. The men would then carry the bateau at shoulder height along the trail until a rest was needed. Most of the portage trails were uphill and over uneven ground, and these difficulties added to the misery of the work.

After the boat had been carried over the portage, the task of retrieving the cargo began. It included barrels of flour, salted pork or beef; casks of lead to make musket balls, powder, guns, other weapons, tents, blankets, personal effects, cooking equipment, oars, paddles, and setting poles. A bateau's crew had to make three or more trips across the portage trail to carry across all this cargo. A mile-long portage might mean eight to ten miles of walking, half of the time carrying very heavy loads.

Complicating this picture was the fact that different crews portaged their bateaux and equipment over the same trail at the same time, the faster crews shouting at the slower crews to get out of the way. Adding to this mix of toil and frustration was the fact that the men were often wet, cold, and very tired. Several days of hard labor were

enclose the grounds. It is believed that this is the oldest remaining original wooden blockhouse in the United States. As each division of the expedition reached this point, they camped overnight at the fort or nearby.

In the great flood of April, 1987, the blockhouse was swept away after having survived 233 years of lesser floods. Most of the walls and structural timbers were recovered considerably downriver. The entire structure was rebuilt in 1990-91 with some new timbers to replace those not recovered.

Ticonic Falls, a half a mile upriver, was the first

Carrying the bateaux
Courtesy, Library of Congress

major portage. The portage trail was located on the west side of the river.

18.4mi. *Following US Route 201, we turn left and cross the Kennebec at Ticonic Falls. We see that a dam has been built on the waterfall. Most of the falls on the river have had dams built on them to generate electricity. At the end of the bridge, we bear right, continuing north on 201. Immediately turn right into a small parking area.*

Point of Interest

*The portage trail around **Ticonic Falls** began below the dam next to the old C. F. Hathaway Co. parking lot, just off Water Street. The trail paralleled the river and terminated at the current site of the Two-Cent Foot Bridge. Colonel Arnold estimated the portage as sixty rods or approximately a fifth of a mile (a rod is sixteen and a half feet). Nothing remains of the trail, as roads, buildings, and fill cover it. It crossed the site of an old Native American village occupied by a subtribe of the Abenaki Nation, the Taconets. When a highway excavation was undertaken in the 1960s, many artifacts were recovered.*

Walk out onto the auto bridge to best observe the falls. Note the unusual diagonal ledge strata. The dam was built to power the huge Lockwood woolen mill complex, the red-brick buildings located just below the bridge. At its peak in the early 1900s, the mill employed more than a thousand people. The dam is still used for hydroelectric generation.

Next to the parking area is a strange-looking vehicle in a cage. This is a gasoline-driven Lombard Log Hauler. The Lombard brothers, natives of Waterville, first invented the continuous steel track, so common today on bulldozers and military tanks. The first application of the track was on these log haulers. A bigger brother of this was a monstrous (for the late 1800s) steam-powered log hauler. The only remaining example of the steam version is located at the Lumberman's Museum in Patten, Maine.

Continue north through Waterville on US Route 201.

***22.0mi.** Reach a traffic light on the main street of Fairfield.*

required to complete the mile-long portage at Norridgewock Falls. Thankfully, local farmers with oxen and sledges were available to assist the men at both Ticonic and Norridgewock Falls.

At Ticonic Falls, Arnold was grateful to be invited to dine at the nearby Crosier home. Above the falls was a fast stretch of the river called Five Mile Rips. Most of Meigs's Third Division had already floundered through this section dragging their heavy bateaux, sometimes across shallow gravel bars and sometimes pulling them through waist-deep swift-water stretches. Mr. Crosier helped Arnold avoid this difficult section of river by using his team to haul Arnold, his dugout canoe, and baggage on a sledge to a point above the islands in the river north of present-day Fairfield, where the current was more moderate.

That night, Arnold camped in the woods with Meigs and his men about a mile and a half north of the rips near what is now Shawmut Village. Morgan's First Division and Greene's Second Division were camped on the river in the vicinity of Skowhegan Falls, fifteen miles farther upriver. Enos's Fourth Division had arrived at the carry around Ticonic Falls.

On Oct. 1, the leaves on the hardwood trees were beginning to show the bright oranges, yellows, and reds of a Maine fall. Arnold broke camp early, ascending a more placid river fifteen miles to Skowhegan Falls. The valley here is broader than below Ticonic Falls, with better farmland running down to the river's shore. Arnold stopped to dine at the Weston farm, one of several that was located along this stretch of the river.

Ticonic Falls between Waterville and Winslow

Joseph Weston, Arnold's host, agreed to help the expedition over the mile-long portage around Norridgewock Falls, using his oxen team. Several days later when he arrived at the falls, he worked tirelessly in the cold rain for five days, sledging over bateaux and equipment. For his labors, he contracted what was probably pneumonia from the continual, cold wetness, and he died on Oct. 16, 1775, age forty-five, several days after arriving home. He was the first casualty of the expedition. He is buried in the old Bloomfield-Weston Cemetery, three miles south of Skowhegan off US Route 201, near the site of his home.

Arnold's party continued upriver and soon approached Skowhegan Falls, twenty-three miles above Fort Halifax. Below the falls, the river forms a large, round pool now called "The Great Eddy." Upstream from this eddy was a narrow, half-mile-long gorge containing rapids leading to the base of the falls. The men had to wade along the rocky shore of the gorge, hauling their bateaux by hand and with ropes. At the end of the gorge, a rocky island divided the river into two channels, both with high falls. The portage trail was over the island. The trail led up a steep, stony cleft where the men had to drag the craft as best they could. The bateaux were then carried an eighth of a mile farther to the upstream end of the island above the falls. The entire carry was, at Arnold's reckoning, about sixty rods.

There weren't many men portaging bateaux when Arnold's party reached the falls, as Meigs's Third Division had not yet arrived and Greene's Second Division had passed them earlier in the day. Arnold did not linger, continuing on for another five miles before darkness. From the falls, the river bears almost due west for about five miles to present-day Norridgewock before again swinging back on its northerly course. Arnold and some of his party were able to make arrangements to sleep in the relative comfort of the Widow Warren's home. This proved to be the last time he would sleep under a roof for over a month.

The next day, Arnold's party caught up with the bateaux of the Second Division, poling through the swift water of Bombazeen Rips. Several miles above the rips, they passed a large tributary, the Sandy River, which entered from the west. The river makes a graceful "S" loop at this location. A beautiful and fertile intervale formed by this loop had once been the site of a village of the Norridgewock tribe, a part of the Abenaki culture.

At one time, the Abenaki people inhabited most of

The route we are to follow continues north on 201.

Side Trip

*If you would like to see the river here up close as it was in 1775, take a break and drive to **Mill Island Park.** At the above-mentioned traffic light in Fairfield, turn right and immediately begin to cross a bridge built on two islands in the Kennebec River. As you pass a short distance onto the first island, turn left onto Island Avenue. It is easy to miss this turn, so you may have to cross the rest of the bridge and turn around. Follow Island Avenue for 0.3mi. until a park is reached. There is a large grassy area near the river, with picnic tables and a place for children to play. At the upper end of the grassy area is a loop trail along the river's edge, which will take you to the northern end of the island. The river at this point appears similar to what it was when the men of the expedition struggled past with their bateaux, poling them against the swift current. Notice how the islands funnel the river into three separate channels. After a rest, head back across the bridge to the main highway and travel north again on US Route 201.*

27.9mi. *Pass the many fine, brick buildings of the private **Goodwill-Hinckley School.** They are scattered along the left side of the highway. Glimpses of the river can be obtained on the right.*

Point of Interest

*The **L. C. Bates Museum** is located in one of these large brick buildings. It contains an extensive rock collection from all over the world, farm implements, a collection of mounted animals, several natural-history displays, an art exhibit, and a history of the Goodwill-Hinckley School. It will take an hour or more to view these exhibits. It is open during the summer. A small fee is charged. There are hiking trails right out the door. Contact:*

L. C. Bates Museum
Route 201
Hinckley, ME 04944
(207) 453-4894

29.5mi. *Turn right (an important turn) onto Route 23 and immediately cross the Kennebec on the Hinckley Bridge. A public boat landing is located on the right, just below the bridge, providing access to the river. At the far end of the bridge, turn left (north) onto the River Road, an unnumbered secondary road that follows the east bank of the river and provides several fine views. The pool behind the downriver Shawmut Dam enlarges this section of the Kennebec. You can't miss the large papermaking plant on the west side of the river, one* *of the biggest in the Northeast. The road gradually bears away from the river onto higher ground, passing several farms.*

36.4mi. *Reach US Route 2, turning left (west). After a half-mile, we are again close to the river and follow it along a beautiful shoreline with several turnouts. This stretch is about the same as it was when the expedition passed. Note the swiftness of the current that the bateaux men were obliged to navigate.*

38.1mi. *Pass* ***The Great Eddy,*** *a large circular pool formed as the river's water shoots out of a narrow canyon.*

38.6mi. *On the left is* ***Coburn Park,*** *a public park maintained by the Town of Skowhegan. It is a fine place to stop and rest. It perches high above the narrow river canyon and offers interesting views. Just beyond, we enter downtown Skowhegan.*

39.0mi. *Near the center of Skowhegan, at a point where the route becomes a multilane one-way street, turn right into a parking lot next to the Skowhegan Chamber of Commerce. Park the car and walk across the street to the river. Here we find a high footbridge providing great views of the river's canyon and falls. Looking upstream, we see that a rocky island divides the river with a hydroelectric dam built in both channels. The men of the expedition used a portage trail that climbed right up the island's steep, rocky face. They dragged their heavy bateaux up the rough trail as best they could to get past the falls. How would you haul a 400-pound bateau up that steep face?*

To continue from the parking lot, we proceed west to a traffic light, where US Route 201 turns both left and right. Turn left and follow US Route 201 and US Route 2 across the bridge leading us onto the island we viewed from the footbridge.

39.3mi. *As we reach the middle of the island, turn right onto Weston Street, which leads to a parking area adjacent to a church. Ahead is a small park on the shore of the river, aptly named Arnold Park. In the park is a boulder with a Daughters of the American Revolution bronze plaque stating that the expedition, as it portaged around Skowhegan Falls, used this island. If you walk behind the church and some industrial buildings, you can view the upper end of the island, anchoring one end of the dam. This is where the portage ended. Captain Dearborn estimated the carry as sixty rods or a fifth of a mile. The small park also provides a canoe landing, affording access to the river. Adjacent to the park is a scenic suspension footbridge leading from the island to the south shore of the river.*

what is now the northeastern United States. Until 1724, the Norridgewock Indians had an extensive community here, with cultivated lands and wooden buildings. In the late 1600s, French Jesuit priests had come down the river from Canada to convert the Indians to Christianity. Father Sebastian Rasle was their missionary priest for more than thirty years.

Boston colonial authorities and English settlers blamed Father Rasle for inciting the tribe to commit atrocities on English settlements on the lower Kennebec and the Maine coast. In 1724, a war party of colonial militia ascended the river, surrounded the village, and surprised its sleeping inhabitants. A massacre ensued in which men, women, children, and all but a few fleeing stragglers were brutally murdered by the colonial troops. Father Rasle was shot dead even though the intent had been to capture him. Native Americans never again occupied the village. Most of the few survivors packed up what belongings they could salvage and migrated to the Indian settlement of St. Francis on the St. Lawrence River, to live under the protection of the French colonial government. When the expedition passed by the site, Captain Dearborn and other officers landed and examined the remains of the village and farm fields. Only the church's foundation and some earthworks were still discernible.

The men on foot from the three rear divisions had crossed the river to its east shore at Skowhegan Falls and had camped in the open area of the old Indian village. They later recrossed the river to its west side to help in the portage around Norridgewock Falls.

Upon arriving at the base of Norridgewock Falls, Arnold found that Morgan's First Division had nearly completed the portage and was ready to embark on the next section of the Kennebec, ascending to the Great Carrying Place.

By Arnold's reckoning, Norridgewock Falls was fifty-eight miles from Fort Western. It had taken his party four days to reach it. It had taken Morgan's division eight days, including the completion of the portage. Morgan's men had averaged a slow seven miles a day to gain the ascent of the river to this point.

Before Morgan struck off upriver, he reported to Arnold that serious leakage of the bateaux had allowed water to penetrate the wooden barrels, causing spoilage of considerable amounts of flour and salted meats. This was a story Arnold would hear repeatedly for the next few days as each division reached the falls.

Chapter Eight

Norridgewock Falls to the Great Carrying Place

At Norridgewock Falls, Arnold camped for several days at the lower end of the carry in order to greet the arriving men of his army. On Oct. 3, he walked the muddy mile to the upper end to see Morgan's division off. He then returned to the bottom of the portage in time to greet Greene's Second Division, whose lead bateaux were just being pulled ashore. Because of the warning that Morgan had given him concerning the food spoilage, Arnold ordered each of the arriving companies to examine food supplies to determine their condition. A considerable amount of the flour and hard bread in the leaky pine barrels was wet, spoiled, and had to be thrown away. Casks of dried peas had leaked, swollen, and burst, making a wasteful mess in the bottom of the bateaux. Some of the dried fish, having become wet, had turned rancid, and it had to be hauled a long way from camp before being dumped. Barrels of the salted beef were opened and found to have been poorly packed. The beef had lost its brine preservative and was now good only for maggots.

How did the water get into the supposedly watertight wooden barrels, spoiling their precious contents? No evidence to answer this question is forthcoming in the journals, so we must speculate. Only eight days into their upriver journey, many of the barrels already had been opened to feed hungry men. More than a ton and a half was being consumed each day. The food was spread throughout the 220 bateaux. A quartermaster could have very little control over the handling of food supplies in a

"Oct. 2. This Day we saw an altar constructed by the Indians, and the remains of a Roman Chapel, where they paid their devotions. Their Curate, or Friar, named Francisco was killed about 40 years ago, at the time when the Provincials drove back the Indians. His remains lie buried here with a cross over them, as is customary in France, Spain, Italy and all Roman Catholic countries, when their clergy Die."

—Thayer's journal

Skowhegan to The Forks

The beautiful Upper Kennebec River Valley becomes more rural and scenic as we progress northward. The towns become smaller and farther apart. We will pass through the transition zone between the pastoral, piedmont country and the vast, wild lands of the Maine North Woods. The land changes from low, rolling hills into the much higher Appalachian Mountain chain. The mountains increasingly crowd the highway and river together in a narrowing valley.

After entering this mountain country, the expedition left the Kennebec Valley at Caratunk and struck due west into the forest over the Great Carrying Place. Even today, there are only private, gravel, wood-hauling roads penetrating this country. These roads intersect the expedition's route in several places, providing limited access. Flagstaff Lake also blocks our attempt to closely follow the route. The Long Falls Dam was constructed in 1949-1950, creating the lake that now covers twenty-two miles of the Dead River that the expedition ascended.

The Carry Ponds Side Trip in the next chapter provides a way to access this remote region between the Kennebec River and Flagstaff Lake. But first we must ascend the Upper Kennebec Valley. To start our journey north we begin at the place we ended our last section, on the river island in the middle of Skowhegan.

Set your odometer to zero again.

0.0mi. *Beginning on the island, turn left on US Route 201 northbound for a short distance. Proceed across a bridge into Skowhegan's downtown. Watch the route signs carefully. You will find yourself on a one-way street that at first heads east. After only one block, US 201 makes an acute angle left in a westerly direction. Continue on 201 for a block until you reach a traffic light. On the right is the office of the Skowhegan Chamber of Commerce. You may want to stop here to view the thirty-foot-high wooden statue of an Indian, fashioned by sculptor Bernard Langlais, at the north end of the parking lot.*

0.3mi. *At a traffic light, US Route 201 turns right. We leave 201 at this point, so* ***do not*** *turn right. Continue straight ahead across the intersection onto Elm Street. This is not a numbered highway. Follow it out of town, closely paralleling the river for the next 5.3mi.*

0.6mi. *On the left, pass the Skowhegan History House Museum on the bank of the river. This beautiful one-and-a-half-story brick cape was built in the early 1800s and has been the local historical*

society's home since 1931. It is open mid-June through mid-September, from 1 p.m. to 5 p.m. Bear left at a stop sign onto the River Road, which we will follow all the way to the town of Norridgewock.

0.9mi. *To the left, on a hill overlooking the Kennebec, is the Margaret Chase Smith Library. Senator Smith was a member of Congress from 1940 to 1973. The library contains an extensive collection of information about American political history, as well as that of Maine. It is open Monday through Friday, 10 a.m. to 4 p.m., except holidays.*

The river may be seen frequently during the next four miles. It is placid along this stretch, as it is the backwater of the Skowhegan Dam and extends upstream as far as Norridgewock village.

5.6mi. *In Norridgewock, reach the intersection with US Route 201A next to an old, concrete, arch bridge over the Kennebec, of a design no longer used. Turn right onto US 201A and proceed northbound.*

A mile from Norridgewock village across the bridge along US 2 east is the riverfront Oosoola Park, which was a campsite for Meigs's division. There is a boat-launching facility at the park as well as a historical marker identifying Meigs's campsite. Back on the main route, take US 201A northward for the next three and a half miles.

9.0mi. *Turn left onto a secondary highway, the Father Rasle Road. This is an obscure turn and easily missed, so you will have to watch your odometer carefully. This road is rough in places, even though it is paved. In the 1920s and 1930s, this was US Route 201, the main route leading north to Quebec.*

11.0mi. *Pass on the left a sweeping "S" bend in the river. You will only see the lower part of it from the road.*

11.6mi. *Reach a large cemetery to the left. This flat, fertile flood plain next to the river marks the site of the old Norridgewock indian village. The Norridgewocks were a part of the Abenaki Nation, who inhabited much of what is now the northeastern United States and parts of the Canadian Maritimes. The village was destroyed by Massachusetts colonial militia on August 23, 1724. Almost all of the inhabitants—men, women and children—were massacred. One of the objectives of the attackers was to capture Father Sebastian Rasle, a French Jesuit priest who lived with the Indians. The English colonists believed he had encouraged the Indians to attack colonial setters along the coast of Maine. He was killed instead.*

At the far end of the cemetery is the Father Rasle Monument, a prominent eighteen-foot-high white stone obelisk erected in 1833 by the Catholic bishop of Boston. In 1775, fifty-one years after the massacre, several journal writers on the expedition mentioned seeing the remains of the old village. Several

line of march twenty to thirty miles from end to end. Bateaux crews opened barrels of whatever was within their reach. Once opened, the partially full barrels were susceptible to leakage when reloaded into the boats and whenever the rains came down. Undoubtedly, they were not covered by canvas nor properly resealed once opened.

Then there was the probable rough handling. From Newburyport to Norridgewock Falls, the barrels would have had to be loaded or unloaded a minimum of nine times.

On Oct. 4, Reuben Colburn and his company of carpenters arrived and immediately went to work repairing the bateaux. They were beginning to fall apart after less than two weeks of use. Some of the soldiers were angry and voiced their opinions loudly about the poor construction of the boats. They held the builders responsible for the loss of the diminishing food supplies. Dr. Senter, the army's physician, described the bateaux as "nothing but wrecks and were stove to pieces." Colburn's men did their best to patch the hastily built craft. Repairs would prove to be only temporary in effect.

Norridgewock Falls is not a single drop, as the word "falls" implies. Rather, it is a series of violent rapids hidden by a double bend in the river. The portage path was a churned-up, muddy quagmire as a result of recent rains and many shoes. Arnold hired two teams of oxen with sledges from nearby farms to help haul bateaux and their cargo over the rocky path. These teams were kept going constantly. A steep hill along the path slowed progress of both teams and men.

Nevertheless, Greene's three companies were able to strike off upriver later that day. Meigs's four companies reached the bottom of the falls that day as well and immediately began the task of sorting food supplies and letting Colburn's carpenters repair the bateaux. The task of getting Meigs's four companies over the portage continued on Oct. 5 and 6. At midday of the sixth, the Third Division pushed off above the falls and headed upstream. Arnold, after seeing them off, again returned to the lower end of the portage just in time to greet Enos's Fourth Division. The process of repairing and transporting bateaux, checking and throwing out spoiled food, and unloading, then reloading, cargo was repeated. This process continued during Oct. 7 and 8. The men's misery was compounded on the eighth by heavy rain. Even with this impediment, the Fourth Division's three companies were able to transport most of their equipment over the portage and prepare for an early start the next day.

On Oct. 9, Arnold went upriver with McCobb's company. The other two companies of Enos's division had not yet finished transporting their equipment across the portage, but they did depart later in the day.

The river above the falls was kinder, at least for a short distance. It was sixteen miles north to the next major portage at Caratunk Falls in present-day Solon. Three miles upstream from Norridgewock Falls, the river makes a mile-long loop to the east. A portage of only thirty rods across the loop's narrow neck avoids the whole loop. At this short, relatively level portage, it was possible for ten to twelve men to line up on either side of a fully loaded bateau and carry it the short distance over the neck. Above the neck, the river remained relatively gentle to the next landmark, where Seven Mile Stream (the Carrabassett River) entered from the west. Above this junction are several large islands dividing the river. Arnold camped that night on one of the islands, along with McCobb's company. They had covered a hard, but creditable fourteen miles against a constant current to reach this point. Arnold and others commented favorably on the fine and fertile land they had passed that day. This was to be the last of such glowing observations.

On Oct. 10, Arnold's party reached Caratunk Falls, also known as Devil's Falls. These were impressive to the men of the expedition. The entire volume of the river shot through a narrow gap in the cliffs in a drop of more than fifteen feet. The portage trail began at an eddy below the falls. It followed the east shore for sixty rods to a point just above the falls and was quickly portaged. Arnold's party proceeded upstream for another twelve miles before darkness and fatigue required a halt. This would place their campsite about four miles north of the present town of Bingham.

The river north of Caratunk Falls was constantly swift, but it was becoming smaller and much shallower. This required the men continually to get out and "walk" the bateaux along the gravel riverbed. Arnold noted that the country was more mountainous. He also observed snow on the higher mountains. The valley became quite deep with high ridges on both sides. They were finally entering the Appalachians. As they passed from the coastal plain, they also encountered colder temperatures. The generally good weather that they had enjoyed on the lower river ended. Intermittent cold showers soaked and chilled the men.

The next morning, an early start enabled Arnold's party to make good headway up the shallow river. They

contingents of the army camped here.

11.7mi. *Just beyond the cemetery on the left is a boulder with a bronze plaque commemorating the site of the Norridgewock Indian village.*

11.8mi. *Pass on the left the Pines Recreation Area, a fine picnic site on the riverbank. At this point, the river flows much as it did in 1775. Try to imagine the men of the expedition poling their bateaux up this swift current. There is an old road along the river's bank leading through a grove of huge white pine, providing a fine opportunity to walk along the scenic river.*

The portage around Norridgewock Falls began three-quarters of a mile above this point on the opposite side of the river.

12.5mi. *Rejoin US Route 201A. Turn left and enter the outskirts of Madison.*

13.6mi. *At a traffic light, turn left, continuing to follow US 201A along the main street of Madison. As we approach the river, note the large paper mill on the left. Continue across the river. At the west end of the bridge, US 201A turns right following the riverbank.*

Side Trip to Norridgewock Falls

At the west end of the bridge in Anson, turn left, leaving the main highway. Go 0.2mi. to the Anson Post Office. To the right of the building, you will observe a boulder with a bronze plaque marking the route of the portage trail around Norridgewock Falls. This portage was a little over a mile long. It was necessary to avoid a long set of falls and rapids. You will notice a side street here named Arnold Lane. It closely approximates the route of the portage trail.

Following it, we will soon come to a gate often left unlocked. If it is locked, you may continue ahead on foot. Follow the gravel road for about 0.6mi. It leads down to the lower end of Norridgewock Falls, which was the lower terminus of the portage trail. Across the river is part of the large paper mill that we drove past in Madison.

Arnold camped here for seven days overseeing the four divisions of the army as they struggled on the long, muddy carry trail. The soldiers spent time trying to repair their leaking bateaux, as well as sorting and throwing away spoiled food. The upper end of the portage was just above the present dam at the Anson-Madison bridge. The trail's end now lies under the pool behind the dam. At Norridgewock Falls, the men of the expedition encountered the last habitations along the river. Above these falls was pure wilderness until they reached Sartigan (St-Georges, Quebec), 170 rugged miles north.

14.1mi. *At the west end of the Anson-Madison*

bridge, proceed north on US Route 201A. The highway closely hugs the river for the next mile. Notice the large rock piles in midstream. (Some people say these rock piles were once used to anchor crayfish traps. The indigenous crayfish living in this section of the Kennebec were so large the traps needed a firm anchor to prevent them from being dragged off. A group of crayfish captured in a trap sometimes acted like a flock of birds by darting off in the same direction at the same instant. A large number could drag traps away unless firmly chained down to these piers.)

Proceed north as the highway bears away from the river.

18.8mi. *As you cross Garland Bridge over the Carrabassett River, look left to see the spectacular, rocky falls. North Anson village is located at the north end of the bridge. Continue to follow US 201A north. Note that Route 16 diverges left toward Kingfield. On the return trip, we may use this section of Route 16 to reach Stratton.*

25.6mi. *After reaching the Kennebec, turn right onto the Emden-Solon bridge. The river at this point flows freely—similar to its condition in 1775.*

Just across the river is the ***Evergreens Campground****. This is an excellent campsite to use as a base for exploring the Upper Kennebec Valley. It is also one of the river campsites used by the men of the expedition. It is even prehistoric, as Native Americans lived here for thousands of years. Many artifacts of both expedition and Native American origin have been unearthed. On the river's west side, inscribed on rocks, are Native American petroglyphs drawn hundreds, maybe thousands of years ago.*

The campground is also the best site to launch canoes if you intend to explore the section of the river below this point (see Canoe Trip 2).

For more information about the campground, contact:

Evergreens Campground
P.O. Box 114, Route 201A
Solon, ME 04979
(207) 643-2324
www.kynd.net~evgrncp

26.7mi. *In the center of Solon village, where US 201A ends, turn left (north) onto US Route 201, the main highway in this part of Maine.*

27.4mi. *On the left, watch for a side road, the Falls Road, which leads a half-mile to Caratunk Falls (also known as Devil's Falls) in the Kennebec. In 1775, the total volume of the river made a sheer drop of fifteen feet in a rocky gorge. Today, there is a dam at the site with a footbridge over it open to the public. On the east side of the dam, you can follow the canoe path that is the exact route of the portage trail around the falls used by the expedition. The*

Upper Kennebec near where the expedition left to traverse the Great Carrying Place

soon caught up to the rear bateaux of the Third Division. At midmorning, they reached the beginning of the Great Carrying Place at the mouth of Carrying Place Stream on the river's west shore. Many soldiers were already camped here preparing for the long portage ahead. Morgan and Greene were busy starting some of their men up the steep portage trail that led out of the valley. Others were clearing areas to set their tents, building fires to dry their clothes and warm themselves, preparing meals, and organizing boats and cargo for the long carry ahead. Smoke from the wet-wood fires filled the whole area. Parts of three divisions, probably four to five hundred men, were congregated at this site. Up the river valley was a remarkable "sugar loaf"-shaped mountain (Hawk Ledges) that seemed to block the river's passage northward.

This point was where their route left the main stem of the Kennebec, 135 river miles from its mouth. It must have seemed to the men a world away from Cambridge Common. It had taken the army an entire month to reach this point. They were in an utter wilderness, dependent only upon themselves to survive.

lower end of the portage ends on a rocky ledge on the shore of a large eddy below the falls.

The bridge constructed over the dam carried the now-abandoned Somerset Railroad line northward into Bingham and then through the mountains, ending at Rockwood on Moosehead Lake. This standard-gauge line has been converted into a popular rails-to-trails path and can be followed northward to Bingham (eight miles) or southward to North Anson. The river above the dam is inundated by the pool for several miles.

We now return to the main route.

29.0mi. *On the right is a state picnic and rest area*

34.5mi. *South of the center of Bingham, we reach the junction of Route 16 (left), which we may use later on the return trip to reach Stratton or for an optional side trip to the Carry Ponds country. Continue north on US 201. If you are low on gas, Bingham is a good place to fill up. Pumps northward are scarce.*

36.1mi. *In the village of Moscow, pass on the left the Station Road, which leads a half-mile to Wyman Station, a huge hydroelectric dam built in 1936. This project transformed the Kennebec River above the dam into the present fifteen-mile-long Wyman Lake. The dam was built between two large hills that mark our entrance into the Appalachians.*

Back on US 201, the highway winds along the side of the valley, providing great views of the lake and mountains on both sides of the lake.

44.0mi. *On the lake side of the highway is a state picnic area with views south down the length of the lake. Above this point, the lake and valley begin to narrow.*

45.3mi. *Reach the Great Carrying Place turnout. Here is a boulder with a bronze plaque indicating where the expedition left the Kennebec. Look carefully directly across the lake, and you will see a small cove that marks the mouth of Carrying Place Stream. This was the beginning of the portage route. It followed the stream for less than a mile and then struck steeply uphill over the ridge that you observe. The rise in elevation to First (East) Carry Pond is about 800 feet.*

The entire carry was an incredibly hard thirteen miles. Try to imagine six or eight men struggling up this ridge, with a 400-pound bateau on their shoulders, stumbling over slippery roots and rocks. After three miles of this torture, they reached the pond, dropped their loads, turned around, and came back down the same three miles to the river, repeating the process for five or more trips to carry up all their heavy cargo.

This section of the river is still flooded by the lake

behind Wyman Dam. The small open point just south of the cove is called Arnold Landing and can be reached via the Route 16 bridge in Bingham (see the description in the next chapter, Carry Ponds Side Trip). Farther up the river valley on the west side is a high mountain (Hawk Ledges) described by several of the expedition's journal writers as a "sugarloaf" mountain that, from their perspective, seemed to block the river.

This is as far up the Kennebec Valley that the expedition went. Before you turn around and head south in order to reach Stratton, the point where we will pick up the route of the expedition, consider traveling just a few miles farther up US 201 on a side trip to see some spectacular valley country.

The Forks Side Trip

Proceed north on US 201 a short distance above this turnout, where the lake gradually ends and the river resumes its original appearance. Now you will be able to assess the nature of the Upper Kennebec much as it was in the expedition's day. We highly recommend that you continue ahead on US 201. Assuming that you will, we will continue the mileage description.

48.7mi. *On the left (west) side of the highway is a poorly marked dirt road leading fifty yards to the east shore of Wyman Lake. Watch carefully for this turn. Located here is the Caratunk boat landing and picnic area. It is only a mile north of this landing that the lake ends and becomes a river again. This landing is also the place where canoes descending the river from The Forks can be taken out (see Canoe Trip 3).*

50.7mi. *At a side road leading into Caratunk village, we cross the Appalachian Trail, which stretches from Maine's Katahdin southward more than 2,100 miles to Springer Mountain in Georgia. It is one of the longest hiking trails in the world.*

If you would like to take a short walk along a section of this famous trail, park in the small lot here. Cross the highway to its west (river) side and walk 0.3mi. along the river's edge to the point where the Appalachian Trail fords the river. The trail is marked with white blazes. This is a very pleasant and scenic walk.

Continuing north on US 201, the highway follows the shore of the swift river closely, with outstanding views.

58.0mi. *As you enter The Forks village, the highway crosses the East Branch of the Kennebec. The river's fork is several hundred yards downstream. There is a small picnic area on the right just before you cross the bridge. The East Branch above this point cuts through a narrow,*

Wyman Lake, a fifteen-mile-long impoundment

The Forks, Dead River to the left, East Branch to the right

rocky gorge that provides some of the best white-water rafting in the eastern United States. You will note the many rafting companies located in the vicinity. A day trip down the Kennebec River Gorge is a popular and exciting experience. Rafting trips are also run on stretches of the Dead River (the west branch of the Kennebec) below Long Falls Dam.

This is as far as we need to go on US 201. It would be easy to continue north to Jackman and then over the Canadian border, picking up the expedition's route in St-Georges, Quebec, on the way to Quebec City. In doing so, we would miss some of the most interesting and important parts of the route. But this would be a fast way to return from Quebec City, and you would see new and wild country.

To return to the expedition's route, turn around and head for the town of Stratton. Follow US 201 south to Bingham. There, pick up Route 16 (west) just south of the town. Be careful not to confuse it with Route 16 eastward. Follow Route 16 down the west side of the Kennebec to North Anson, where Route 16 bears west to Kingfield, then northwest through Carrabassett Valley—past the south side of the Bigelow Range—to Stratton, where we will resume the route description.

From the Forks, it is seventy-nine miles to Stratton. It will take about two hours—although, if you choose to linger, there is much to see en route, including the picturesque ski town of Kingfield with its Stanley Steamer Auto Museum, then the big ski resort of Sugarloaf USA, not to mention some of Maine's most beautiful mountains. See you in Stratton!

"We found it necessary to erect a building for our sick who had increased to a formidable number. A blockhouse was erected and christened by the name of 'Arnold's Hospital'."

—Dr. Isaac Senter

Chapter Nine

Across the Great Carrying Place

The Great Carrying Place from the Kennebec to the Dead River was by far the most difficult portage on the expedition's route. In assessing its difficulty and, more important, its effect on the army, historians have concentrated on the portage's horizontal length, neglecting to consider the huge elevation that had to be overcome. It was a very long portage, almost thirteen tortuous miles. However, both distance and elevation gain must be considered to assess the effect on the men.

The elevation at the Kennebec River at the point where the Great Carry began was 451 feet above sea level. The army had ascended to this elevation over two weeks and ninety miles of river travel. The elevation at the first of the Carry Ponds, East Carry, is 1,237 feet. Therefore, the elevation gain over the three-and-a-quarter-mile trail from the river to the pond was a phenomenal 786 feet. In addition, there was a ridge of 200 vertical feet between Middle Carry and West Carry Ponds and another of 200 feet between West Carry and the Dead River. So there was approximately 1,200 feet of climbing, slightly more than the height of the Empire State Building. And it had to be repeated by the men five to seven times to carry everything to the Dead River.

This oversight by historians is understandable since accurate topographical maps of the region were not available until the 1920s, well after the expedition's most important chroniclers had completed their writing. Nor was any estimate of this elevation given in the journals of the expedition.

The combination of the portage's length and height required an effort that took a substantial toll from the soldiers' health and strength. It would take them five or more days to complete the twelve and a half miles between the two rivers. When they reached the beginning of the portage, they were already physically worn from their efforts ascending the Kennebec, but they were still in good spirits and in reasonably good health. Subsequent events will give us a good idea of the portage's effects on the army.

Those unfamiliar with the Upper Kennebec and Dead River country might rightly ask, "Why didn't they stay with the river?" The answer is that the Kennebec's

Carry Ponds Side Trip

This is the premier side trip of our journey. It's not really a side trip, but it is listed as such because it's not on a regular auto route, and it must be reached via side and private roads. Part of it may be negotiated by car, but the heart of the experience involves a moderate hike.

It certainly wasn't a side trip for the Expedition to Quebec. When the expedition left the Kennebec River at Carrying Place Stream, it had to endure the longest and by far the most arduous portage of the journey.

To avoid an almost impassable section of the Dead River, which is the Kennebec's west branch, Native Americans used a thirteen-mile-long cross-country portage, as did all who came after them. The route took advantage of three small ponds to reach the navigable section of the Dead River to the west. This portage, because of its length and difficulty, was aptly named the Great Carrying Place. For the men of the expedition, a maximum effort was required to carry the 400- to 500-pound bateaux, tons of supplies, and their arms across these thirteen miles.

There is no public road along the route of the portage. There are several private, gravel logging roads that can be used to reach portions of the expedition's route. Much of the original portage route can be followed on foot. More than three miles between Middle and West Carry Ponds have been preserved because the Appalachian Trail has been located over portions of the old portage. In addition, the Arnold Expedition Historical Society has preserved the three-quarters-of-a-mile section of the original portage trail between East and Middle Carry Ponds.

Visiting this section of the expedition's route can be accomplished as a half-day auto trip or as a full-day trip—the latter if a nine-mile hike is included.

Please refer to the Carry Ponds map for detail of this route.

The Carry Ponds Trip: the Approach

The starting point is located at the junction of US Route 201 and Route 16 just south of the center of Bingham. There are two junctions of these highways, one north and one south of the town. Be sure to use the south junction.

Set your odometer to zero at this point.

0.0mi. *Turn west from US Route 201 onto Route 16 west and immediately cross the Kennebec*

River. At the end of the bridge, turn right (north) onto an unnumbered but paved road paralleling the river.

1.3mi. *On the left (west) is a fine spring on the roadside. It comes out of a pipe from the hillside above. This is a good place to fill your water bottles. It is excellent spring water.*

1.8mi. *At the brow of a hill on the right is a walkable side road leading a short distance to a view of the Wyman Dam, which floods the Kennebec for fifteen miles. Beyond this point, the highway follows the shore of Wyman Lake around sharp cliffs.*

2.7mi. *As the highway bears west, away from the lake, pass on the right the Moscow Recreation Area and Beach. Swimming and picnicking are available here. There is also a boat-launching ramp for access to the lake. You will not see the lake for the next six miles.*

3.6mi. *Pass on the right a foot trail leading to Houston Brook Falls. It is a fifteen-minute walk down to the refreshing falls, with cool pools for swimming below it.*

4.4mi. *In the village of Pleasant Ridge, turn right onto the Carry Ponds Road. A short distance beyond, the road becomes gravel.*

6.5mi. *Pass on the right the trail to Mill Brook Falls. It is a twenty-minute walk downhill to the falls, which are very beautiful.*

8.5mi. *On a prominent point overlooking Wyman Lake is the picturesque Honeywell Homestead.*

10.8mi. *Pass on the right a public picnic area on the Wyman Lake shore.*

12.0mi. *At a left bend in the road is an obscure tote road on the right, leading one-sixth of a mile downhill to the point where the army left the Kennebec at the beginning of the Great Carrying Place. This tote road is rough, so vehicles with low clearance should be left at the main road. The short walk will bring you to a landing on Wyman Lake. There is a small cove to the left, which is the point where Carrying Place Stream drops into the lake. Although the lake at this point covers the river by fifteen to twenty feet, this is close to the place where the expedition left the river and began the Great Carrying Place portage. The road you just walked is the approximate route of the portage trail.*

Try to visualize a hundred or so bateaux drawn up on the riverbank and men waiting their turn to start up the steep trail out of the valley. From the river, it was three and a quarter miles to East Carry Pond. Six to eight sweating, growling men carried each bateau, tripping over stumps and rocks on the freshly widened trail. It was a grueling, 786-foot climb out of the valley to the pond, a hard climb

topography changes radically above the point where the Great Carrying Place leaves the river. It snakes northerly, winding through mountains for fourteen miles of continuous swift water to The Forks, where it divides into its east and west branches. The East Branch steeply ascends northeast through the Kennebec River Gorge twenty miles to its main source, Moosehead Lake. The west branch assumes a new name, the Dead River. This branch ascends steeply to the northwest and then loops south to an upland plateau called the Dead River Valley. From the Forks to the valley above Long Falls, the river ascends more than 700 feet of almost continuous rapids and fast water, including two major falls. This rise made the river almost unnavigable.

Native Americans had used the Great Carry portage to avoid this stretch of the Dead River for hundreds, maybe thousands of years before the expedition passed this way. Natives had found three ponds that could be used to make the portage somewhat easier. These were later named the Carry Ponds.

The lead bateaux of Morgan's riflemen reached the Great Carrying Place on Oct. 6, with the remainder of the division arriving the next day. Lieutenant Church's advance scouting party had already found the obscure portage trail and was busy marking its location across to the Dead. Morgan's men immediately set to work cutting trees to widen the path. The best they could do was to hack down trees with axes, leaving low stumps to step over. The original path was only wide enough for men to pass single file carrying a light canoe. The widened path allowed the men to line along the sides of the bateaux to carry them. Thus, the new path was approximately eight to ten feet wide. The diversion of manpower for the task of path-widening caused both Morgan's division and, soon, Greene's to be slowed as they headed out of the valley up to the first body of water, now named East Carry Pond. This was a distance of three and a quarter miles.

The path began at the river, crossed a short intervale, and then climbed steeply away from the river. The first mile followed the shoulder of a deep ravine formed by Carrying Place Stream. The path then cut steeply uphill due west. The last mile to East Carry Pond was a more gradual ascent. When they reached the shore of the first pond, depositing their loads with great relief, the exhausted men had to trudge back three and a quarter miles to the river for another load. The process was then repeated. The number of trips required to portage a crew's bateau and equipment across was almost unbelievable. Dr. Senter commented it was "seven or eight" times. Each trip to the first pond was six and a half miles round-trip, times seven trips, totaling more than forty-two miles, just to the first pond. The physical effort to carry such heavy boats up out of the valley could be accomplished only by tough, determined men.

When Arnold arrived at the beginning of the carry during the morning of Oct. 11, Morgan's and Greene's divisions were strung out all along the path between the river and the second pond, which is now named Middle Carry Pond. Meigs's Third Division, which arrived about the same time as Arnold, immediately began the uphill portage over the newly cut path. Lieutenant Church was waiting to give his report to Arnold describing the discouraging details of the Great Carrying Place. On Oct. 12, Arnold joined the line of men slogging up the muddy, stump-infested path to the first pond. Bearing his own heavy load, Arnold voiced words of encouragement to each of the hard-working crews that he encountered. The men appreciated his kind words and carefully noted that he was carrying his own load.

This first long haul brought Arnold to the east shore of the first pond. The pond is pear-shaped, about one and a half miles long by a half-mile wide. The route across the pond to the next portage path was unfortunately only a short one-fifth of a mile. After crossing it, Arnold established his camp near the west shore. A dense forest of spruce and fir and a rocky shoreline surrounded all

On the last portage of the Great Carrying Place. Courtesy, Library of Congress.

even with no load. On subsequent trips, heavy wooden barrels of food, powder, lead for bullets, poles, oars, and other equipment had to be carried. Many of the men had to make five to seven round trips to get all their equipment to East Carry Pond.

Walk back to the main road. The public road ends here, but a privately owned gravel road, open to the public, continues on. It is rougher than the public road, but, with care, it is passable. Be alert for the large logging trucks that use it and have the right of way. The road parallels Carrying Place Stream to the right as it ascends out of the valley. It follows the route of the portage trail for approximately a half-mile. The trail then struck off westward, steeply uphill.

12.5mi. *Pass on the right a rough road leading downhill a short distance to the Carrying Place Stream Falls.*

12.7mi. *Pass on the left a hiking trail leading along Stony Brook one-third mile to a beautiful canyon with sheer rock cliffs through which the brook passes. It is a fifteen-minute walk to the mouth of the canyon.*

13.0mi. *Turn left onto the East Carry Pond Road. The route uphill from this point becomes rougher and steeper. If your car has low clearance, it may not be a good idea to go beyond this point. The road climbs steeply out of the river valley. Raspberries in season grow in profusion along these roads. The original portage trail lies 200 to 300 yards to the left (south), paralleling the road. The forest here has been cut many times, and the old tote road built on the portage trail is obscure and very difficult to attempt to find and follow.*

At this point, you have three choices:

1. Return to Bingham and use Route 16 to drive around to Stratton, picking up the route of the expedition there.

2. Continue up the East Carry Pond Tote Road, if you have a high-clearance vehicle, as far as the gate near East Carry Pond, where the Carry Ponds hike begins (see below).

3. Use an alternative auto route looping north of the Carry Ponds country and back to Route 16 at North New Portland, as described below.

Alternative Auto Route via the Long Falls Dam Road

At the above-described junction at 13.0 mi., the main gravel logging road you will be following continues north, then forks left, westward, and eventually joins the paved Long Falls Dam Road near Flagstaff Lake. If you choose this route, the Long Falls Dam Road can be used as an alternate route to join up with Route 16 in the town of North New Portland. From that point, Route 16 can be followed to reach Stratton, where we will resume the auto route description. While following this alternative, you cross the expedition's route only once. This crossing occurs on the Long Falls Dam Road at the junction of the West Carry Pond Tote Road. This tote or logging road was built over much of the old portage path. It is gated to cars. If you wish to walk into West Carry Pond, your hike will use this road. It is a hike of about five miles round-trip.

To explore the Carry Ponds country and follow this alternative auto route as far as Route 16, we recommend that you use the excellent DeLorme Maine Atlas & Gazetteer, obtainable at most book or sporting-goods stores in Maine. It will give you enough detail to navigate the maze of logging roads leading to the Long Falls Dam Road, thence to Route 16 in North New Portland. If time and wear and tear on your vehicle are concerns, your best bet is to return to Bingham over the route you have followed. There you can pick up Route 16. However, the alternate route is more adventurous and scenic.

Alternative to Reach East Carry Pond and the Beginning of the Hike:

13.0 mi. *At the previously described junction where the East Carry Pond Road branches left, continue steeply uphill out of the valley.*

13.8 mi. *The road forks. Take the left fork—there are no signs to help you—and proceed steeply uphill. At the brow of this hill, you will soon cross the expedition's portage route, although you will not be able to discern it because of the heavy wood-harvesting operations in this area. Beyond this point, the road becomes less steep.*

15.0mi. *Reach a locked gate blocking the road. This is as far as you can drive. Park off the road, as it is used by large logging trucks. Lock and leave your car here. It is a short walk of about a third of a mile to the east shore of East Carry Pond at the point where the portage trail reached the pond. There is a set of private camps here, so you may wish to ask permission to walk down to the shore across this private property.*

The expedition's portage trail to Middle Carry

three of the Carry Ponds. This is typical of highland ponds in this part of Maine.

The men tried their luck fishing, baiting hooks with chunks of salt pork. They immediately hit a bonanza of voracious, half-pound trout, landing them as fast as they could rebait their hooks. Some caught dozens, a welcome change from their usual diet of salt pork, salt beef, and fried flour patties. During the next several days, a steady stream of exhausted men arrived at the pond carrying bateaux, barrels, and equipment. But the men were making progress. Morgan's lead division, pushing westward, soon reached the third pond, now named West Carry Pond, and was beginning the last push to the Dead River.

An exhausted and half-starved Lieutenant Steele and two of his men dragged into camp, returning from their reconnaissance trip to the Height of Land. The bottoms of their two birch-bark canoes had been slashed by an underwater snag while descending the Dead River, causing the loss of their meager food supply and much of their equipment. Steele reported that no Indians had been seen, although a fire ring at Natanis's camp was still warm. It had been presumed that any Indians encountered here would probably be in the pay of the British. Better news yet was that the Middle Dead River, above Long Falls, was wide and deep, much easier to navigate than the Kennebec. The best news was that the ten carries to be negotiated to reach the Chain of Ponds were short and easy. Steele's party had crossed over the Height of Land as far as Chaudière Pond River (Arnold River). With this new information, Arnold immediately dispatched Church, Steele, and twenty men with axes up the Dead River to prepare a trail suitable for the main body of the army on the Height of Land.

A number of men had become sick and weak with dysentery or diarrhea. Arnold ordered a small log cabin to be built on the carry trail near the west shore of East Carry Pond. The men from Goodrich's company, who built it, dubbed it "Arnold's Hospital." The commander wrote dispatches to General Washington at Cambridge and General Schuyler in Albany. Schuyler was the officer coordinating the other attack on Canada by way of the Champlain Valley, led by General Richard Montgomery. Arnold also sent a scout, a man named Hall, and an Indian guide north to the French settlements along the lower Chaudière River to determine their sentiments toward the approaching Americans. This was a risky venture because the expedition's success was dependent upon surprising the small British garrison at Quebec. However, Arnold had to know how the French would receive his army. His orders from Washington were quite explicit: Do nothing to alienate them. They were needed as potential allies in the capture of Quebec and all of Canada.

On Oct. 14, misery came from the sky in the form of a steady, cold rain, causing the portage trail to become as muddy as thick soup. Arnold waited out the rain most of the day, finally breaking camp at about four o'clock. In a short time, his party covered the three-fourths of a mile across the portage between East Carry and Middle Carry. The trail was full of men traveling in both directions, stumbling over roots and stumps slippery from the day's rain.

Middle Carry was quite different in appearance from East Carry. Dead trees, swampy shores, and mist from the cold rain gave it a forboding atmosphere. It was much narrower, a third of a mile across. The pond's nearby inlet, Sandy Stream, formed a half-mile-long arm, which the bateaux could use to reduce the length of the next portage. Arnold and his party crossed the pond quickly and then began the longer two-and-three-eighths-mile portage over a low ridge to the third body of water, West Carry Pond.

The first part of this carry followed a small esker, thirty to forty feet high. An esker is a glacially formed gravel ridge. Then the trail descended into a 200-yard-wide swampy quagmire. The men struggled slowly through the knee-to-hip-deep muck of the bog. The rains and the bog's black, putrid waters combined to guarantee that no one would be dry that day. In the twilight of early evening, Arnold's party reached the shore of the third pond, joining several companies camping there. The men had built large fires and were trying to dry out. Their meager fare of salt pork and fried flour patties only partially satiated their hunger from the day's toil. Intermittent showers and leaky tents made for a miserable night.

The men were up before dawn building roaring fires to warm themselves and to cook their breakfasts before crossing the water. West Carry Pond (elevation 1,317 feet) is the most beautiful of the three Carry Ponds. Shaped like a large oval, it is approximately one and three-quarters of a mile long by a mile wide. The trail from Middle Carry ended on a small beach next to a long peninsula, now named Arnold Point. The morning was bright and clear. As Arnold and his men loaded their

Pond continues on the opposite shore, three hundred yards across the pond. It is maintained and marked by the Arnold Expedition Historical Society and is easily followed. The bateaux were used to cross this short arm of the pond. If you want to explore and follow more of the portage trail, read on.

The Carry Ponds Hike

Refer to the Carry Ponds map for details of this hike.

You can make this hike as short as four miles, or it can be a nine-mile, all-day jaunt through very wild country. The full nine-mile round-trip hike follows most of the expedition's portage trail between the three Carry Ponds. It is a relatively level trip. You can cover the entire portage trail between East and Middle Carry Ponds on the shorter four-mile hike. You may wish to plan the trip as open-ended, proceeding as far as time, inclination, and energy allow. The longer trip uses a part of the famous Appalachian Trail between Middle and West Carry Ponds.

We begin our hike at the locked gate near East Carry Pond, where cars are left. Hike west along the gravel logging road. It is about 0.1mi. to a fork. The right fork leads to the east shore of East Carry Pond, as previously described. Take the left fork, which swings around the south end of East Carry Pond. Many of the expedition's men who were on foot followed this route. There are a few private camps here.

After hiking slightly over a mile along this road, you will be paralleling the northeast shore of Middle Carry Pond, which is out of sight to the left. Watch carefully for the portage trail from East Carry Pond, which crosses this road from your right. It is marked by two-inch, round, orange Arnold Expedition Historical Society markers. You can follow this trail eastward for about three-quarters of a mile to its terminus on the west shore of East Carry Pond. Along this section of the trail was located the so-called "Arnold Hospital," a rough cabin thrown up to shelter the expedition's sick. The exact location has never been discovered.

Back on the main gravel road, to the left a gravel side road leads west 100 yards to the shore of Middle Carry Pond. This side road is a part of the route of the portage trail. From the shore of Middle Carry, the expedition used its bateaux to cross the pond and swing northwest up its inlet, Sandy Stream, for a half a mile to a point where the portage trail to West Carry Pond began. The road you are following will lead to that point, where we will rejoin the portage trail.

Continue hiking northwest along the gravel road

for about a mile. The Appalachian Trail will join the road from the right when you near Sandy Stream. It is marked with two-by-six-inch white blazes. From this point, we will use the AT all the way to the shore of West Carry Pond, as it uses the old portage trail between Middle and West Carry Ponds.

Just after crossing Sandy Stream, which is a small brook at this point, you will reach a fork. Turn left, following the white blazes. After 100 yards, turn sharply right, leaving the gravel road, onto the AT foot path. At this point, we rejoin the portage trail between Middle and West Carry Ponds. Follow the white blazes of the AT all the way to the pond. It is two and a third miles back to the gate where cars are parked.

If you choose to proceed to West Carry, follow the AT westward along a glacial esker for 0.2mi, then descend into a wide bog. The trail crosses the bog on a long series of log bridges. The men of the expedition did not have it so easy. They undoubtedly cussed profusely about this thigh-deep bog of cold, black muck as they carried their heavy bateaux. Several of the expedition's journal writers mention this notable bog. Beyond the bog, ascend a low ridge separating the two ponds.

At a distance of 1.8mi. from Middle Carry Pond, the trail reaches the east shore of West Carry. This is the most attractive of the three ponds. There is a pristine beach at this point. It provides an opportunity for a refreshing swim on sunny days. Arnold and a number of the expedition's companies camped at this spot.

Arnold Point juts out into the pond for several hundred yards. A mile across the pond on the west shore is a cove where the portage trail resumed westward over a gap in the ridge that is visible from here. Round Top Mountain is the low peak over the southwest end of the pond. The large, twin-peaked mountain beyond the ridge to the west is 4,108-foot Bigelow Mountain, which dominates this area. It is four miles back to your car at the gate near East Carry Pond. Allow about two hours to hike back.

The Appalachian Trail continues around the south end of West Carry Pond, ascends the north shoulder of Round Top Mountain, then descends and crosses the Long Falls Dam Road.

An alternative hike at this point would be to continue westward to the Long Falls Dam Road. This hike would have the advantage of following more of the route of the old Great Carrying Place portage trail. It would also avoid having to retrace your steps back to your car. It would have the disadvantage of the need to spot a car on the Long Falls Dam Road or have someone pick you up there—where the West Carry Pond Tote Road reaches the dam road. This would be a hike of an

craft and embarked across the pond, they observed in the distance to the west a huge, twin-peaked mountain capped with snow (Bigelow Mountain), evidence that colder weather might be on the way. The row across brought them to a cove on the west shore. It marked the beginning of the fourth and final portage of the Great Carrying Place. Some of the men who could not find places in the crowded bateaux walked along the pond's south shore rather than wait for the return of the boats.

Arnold and the men immediately began the portage westward, steeply uphill over a low ridge that separated the Carry Ponds from the Dead River Valley. The newly cut trail then led downhill into the valley. One more obstacle lay in their way. A mile-wide "savanna," now locally called a spruce bog, had to be crossed before they reached the end of the portage. The crossing of this open, treeless area was deceptive. Although it gave the appearance of easy going since there were few trees, these bogs hide a quagmire of black mud under a thin, grassy surface. The men sank up to their hips as they struggled along with heavy loads. Some men's boots, weakened by weeks of wetness, literally fell apart or were sucked from their feet. The bateaux were dragged and slid across the ooze. Buried wooden snags and roots constantly tripped the men. They often fell headlong into the black muck accompanied by laughter and derision from their companions. There was a treed "island" of slightly higher, dry land in the middle of the bog. It offered temporary relief from the mud.

The portage trail ended at Bog Brook, a deep, narrow tributary of the Dead River. The men were elated to finally reach navigable water again. As soon as all their cargo reached the brook, and the mud was washed off, they launched their bateaux and poled or rowed down it for about a mile until the placid and welcome Dead River appeared. The hardships of the Great Carry were thankfully over. Could there be anything worse ahead?

additional four miles from this point.

To do this, follow the Appalachian Trail for 1.3mi. around the south end of the pond to a point where the AT turns west and leaves the pond. At the point where the trail turns to leave the pond, leave the AT and continue along the shore of the pond, soon picking up a camp road that parallels the west shore about half a mile to a prominent cove, where the portage route resumes.

The old gravel West Carry Pond Tote Road is then followed for two miles westward uphill and over the ridge, then down to the Long Falls Dam Road, where the tote road ends. This junction is approximately a mile north of the Appalachian Trail's crossing of the Long Falls Dam Road.

The next twenty-plus miles of the expedition's route, up the Dead River, are now under the waters of nearby Flagstaff Lake. To pick up the expedition's route, we must drive south around the Bigelow Range and then north to the town of Stratton.

Before the flooding of the valley, the Dead River was a quiet, meandering watercourse paralleling the Bigelow Range. At what is now the town of Stratton, the river divided into two branches. The expedition followed the North Branch into the Boundary Mountains. The former town of Flagstaff and two smaller communities also lie under the lake. The village was built near the site of the cabin of the Indian Natanis on a point along the Dead River. The expedition's men, as local tradition has it, erected a flagpole at that site, but there is no written record of this event in the expedition journals. So let's move onward to Stratton to resume the route of the expedition.

The west end of Flagstaff Lake with dry-kye along the shore

"We were awakened by the freshet which came rushing in on us like a torrent . . . We had a small hill to retreat to. . . We passed the night in no very agreeable situation . . . "
—Benedict Arnold

"Last night, our clothes being wet, were frozen a pane of glass thick, which proved very disagreeable, being obliged to lie in them."
—Thayer's journal

Chapter Ten

Ascending the Dead River to the Chain of Ponds

The Middle Dead River stretched upstream from Long Falls twenty miles to the valley's west end, where the Dead divided into two main branches, the North and the South. Across this upland valley, it meandered toward every point of the compass. The gentle and dark waters of this middle stretch of the river had led travelers to dub it the Dead. Today, we cannot see this section of the river as the men of the expedition saw it in 1775. It was inundated in 1950 when the Long Falls Dam was built to form Flagstaff Lake as a reservoir for the downriver hydroelectric dams of the Kennebec. However, the rest of the river's North Branch above the present village of Eustis is very much as is was when the expedition passed.

Mountains surround the valley, the largest being the fourteen-mile-long Bigelow Range, isolating the Dead River Valley from the Atlantic coastal plain. Bigelow's massive, bare 4,000-foot peaks were the highest encountered by the expedition. As they passed up the river, several of the journal writers observed the snow on top.

The North Branch is the larger of the two, and it was the route the expedition followed into the maze of mountains that divide Canada from Maine. It becomes much smaller as it weaves northwest through this wild country. By the time it reaches its source near the Canadian border, the beautiful Chain of Ponds, it is normally little more than a shallow mountain stream.

These ponds are shaped like the rattles on the tail of a snake. Native Americans called the Kennebec, with its many twists and turns and rattle-shaped ponds at its end, "Manitou Kennebec" or "The Snake." This small, shallow river with its series of picturesque falls was, for the men of the expedition, about to become a dangerous, raging torrent that almost ended the mission in death and destruction.

Of course, when the army exited the terrible hardships of the Great Carrying Place and rowed along the calm and pleasant Middle Dead, they could not have suspected the disasters soon to befall them. But as the men began the ascent of the Dead River, they had been weakened in several ways. First, carrying heavy bateaux and many tons of cargo on their backs over the Great

Stratton to Lake Megantic

We resume following the route of the expedition in the small town of Stratton located at the junctions of Routes 16 and 27. Stratton and its satellite village of Eustis are the last communities before crossing the border into Canada via Route 27. Gas up the car here, as gasoline is substantially more expensive in Canada. Also, the couple of banks in Stratton are good places to exchange some of your U.S. dollars into Canadian. The exchange rate fluctuates from day to day. During the winter of 2002-2003, it was approximately $1.47 Canadian for one American dollar.

There are few restaurants or overnight accommodations north of Stratton-Eustis until you reach Woburn or Lake Megantic (Lac-Mégantic) in Quebec Province. So this may be a good place to stay overnight, as you will need a full day to explore the next section to Lac-Mégantic. The country north of Stratton, all the way to the border and beyond, is the wildest that you will encounter during your entire journey.

Bigelow Mountain Range from the northwest

In the Stratton region, there are many hiking opportunities. The Appalachian Trail crosses Route 27 four miles south of town. This crossing provides access to either Crocker Mountain to the south or the ***Bigelow Mountain Range*** *to the north. Both are four-thousand-footers. Another possibility is the easier Bigelow Range Trail, which begins in Stratton and leads three miles along the west end of the Bigelow Range to Cranberry Peak and beyond. The entire fourteen-mile Bigelow Range is protected from development. It lies within the state-owned Bigelow Preserve, established in 1976 by a referendum vote of the state's citizens to prevent the range from becoming a giant ski resort. You can obtain maps of these trails locally or consult the Guide to the Appalachian Trail in Maine for details.*

Bigelow Mountain is named after Major (later

Colonel) Timothy Bigelow, an officer in Greene's Second Division. Local tradition has it that he climbed or attempted to climb the mountain from the Dead River in order to see Quebec City. There is no verification of this event in any of the expedition's many journals. As one of the key officers in the army, he was likely aware that the mountain lay more than 150 miles from Quebec City and the St. Lawrence River, well beyond a possible sighting. Considering that the men of the army were already running seriously short of provisions, he would probably have been busy hurrying his men forward rather than climbing mountains. Major Bigelow was a native of Worcester, Massachusetts, and played a prominent role in many Revolutionary War battles.

We begin this section heading northward at the junction of Routes 27 and 16 in the center of Stratton. Route 27 leads us all the way to the Canadian border at Coburn Gore.

Set your odometer to zero at this junction.

0.0mi. *Bear right onto Route 27 northbound. On the right is a notable hostel called the* ***Widow's Walk****. This is a fine bed and breakfast in which to stay while in the Stratton area. For more information, call or write to:*

Widow's Walk
P.O. Box 150
Stratton, ME 04982
(207) 246-6901

On the opposite side of the street is the ***Dead River Area Historical Society*** *building. In front is a replica of a bateau with roughly the same dimensions as those used on the expedition. Inside are a number of local-history exhibits of interest to followers of the expedition's route. There is also a collection of pictures, articles, and histories of the flooding of the valley and the inundation of Flagstaff village in 1949-50. The building is open during the summer.*

0.9mi. *Cross the bridge over the South Branch of the Dead River. At this point the river is still flooded by the flowage of Flagstaff Lake. There are fine views of the west end of the Bigelow Range, including nearby Cranberry Peak, East Nubble, and the Horns.*

3.6mi. *As we pass through a forest of red pine, to the left (west) is a road leading two miles to* ***Eustis Ridge****, with outstanding views of the entire Bigelow Range and the Dead River Valley. There is a small picnic area at the viewpoint.*

3.7mi. *On the right is a turnout with several historic plaques relating to the expedition. There are good views here of narrowing Flagstaff Lake and Bigelow. A short distance north of this point, the lake ends and the North Branch resumes its normal*

Carry had required an extreme physical effort. The toll on them was made worse by a marginal diet, which did not renew them. Second, the size of the army had shrunk. In a letter to Washington written at East Carry Pond, Arnold estimated that he had "950 effectives." If accurate, this meant a reduction of approximately 150 men from the 1,100 that had left Fort Western. After only three weeks, many sick or injured men had been sent back downriver. Many had contracted severe cases of dysentery, a sure sign of bad food, bad water, or poor sanitation, all of which were not uncommon in armies of the day. The need to construct a log " hospital" near East Carry Pond was further evidence that men were succumbing to this and other afflictions. A few men had melted into the woods after concluding that soldiering through wilderness country with lousy food, enormous daily hardships, and low pay was not the glamorous adventure they had envisioned.

The diminishing food supply had become a serious problem and was obvious to all. The bulk of their forty-five-day supply had been consumed or lost to spoilage. There would be no more food other than what they carried until they reached the French settlements on the Chaudière, unknown days ahead. The men tried to supplement their food by fishing, with some success, but the toil from sunup to sundown of rowing, poling, hauling, and carrying bateaux and equipment did not allow much time for it. As for hunting, the noise and odors of a thousand active men drove potential game well away. Their last two oxen, which had been driven along with the army, were butchered and quickly consumed by Meigs's division at the end of the Great Carry. Arnold's awareness of the rapidly diminishing food supplies forced him to establish a daily food ration of three-quarters of a pound of flour and an equal amount of salted pork for each man, not enough to sustain hard-working men. Because the army's units were strung out over twenty miles of river and often out of communication with each other, Arnold was unable to ensure equitable distribution of the remaining food. Also, the remaining food was unevenly dispersed throughout the expedition's thirteen companies.

At this time, unknown to Arnold and the lead divisions, there were serious morale problems developing in Enos's rear Fourth Division. Arnold had managed only brief contacts with this unit since leaving Fort Western. He also had not enough time to assess the leadership qualities of Lieutenant Colonel Enos, as events will show.

The Fourth Division seemed to be constantly falling behind the others. It might have been expected that, with a cleared path at each portage, these men would have moved faster and caught up with the three other divisions. But there were serious mutterings and wild rumors among the Fourth Division about the dangers, hardships, and possible death that lay ahead. Wise officers would have dealt harshly with such morale killers. Seeing a stream of sick and injured men heading the other way did not help morale. Conditions within the army were changing fast and not for the better.

Arnold's party left the Great Carrying Place and paddled down narrow but deep Bog Brook on the morning of Oct. 16. Meigs's Third Division launched their bateaux at the same time. A small detachment from Meigs's division was detailed by Arnold to return over the last carry to improve the quagmire in the "savanna" for the Fourth Division. After less than a mile, Arnold reached the Dead River. After turning upstream to the west, the river's meandering made the distance traveled two or three times the distance a crow would fly. The men in the bateaux grumbled, as they seemed to be making no progress when measured against the snow-capped, twin Bigelow peaks to the south. In fact, they made good progress that day. As they rowed farther west, the river gradually straightened. It was eight miles from the mouth of Bog Brook to the first carry on the Middle Dead River at Hurricane Falls. This was a short, forty-yard portage around an eight-foot drop over rapids. All the falls on the Dead consisted of several sharp rapids over ledges, rather than a single cataract. Surprisingly, Arnold found Morgan's First Division camped at the falls, with Greene's Second Division ahead of them. Greene's Division had gone ahead at the end of the Great Carry. The path-clearing activities assigned to Morgan and his division had slowed them down.

Arnold's party pushed on another five miles to a prominent point on the river. Here in a small clearing was the bark cabin of the Indian Natanis, strategically placed to view the river in both directions. Local tradition has it that the men erected a flagpole here, although none of the expedition's journal writers mentions it. Many years later, this site became the village of Flagstaff. The village and the point now lie under the waters of Flagstaff Lake.

Arnold continued upriver for another three or four miles. Just as dusk fell, he caught up with Greene's Second Division camped on the south shore. Arnold's

river course.

Located here is the entrance to the beautiful ***Cathedral Pines Campground,*** *located in a grove of huge red pine. This is an excellent campground to use as a base while exploring the area. There are accommodations for both recreational vehicles and tent camping. It has a swimming area in the adjacent lake. There is a public boat launch that is the launch point of Canoe Trip 4. For more information, call or write to:*

Cathedral Pines Campground
P.O. Box 146
Eustis, ME 04936-0146
(207) 246-3491

4.0 mi. *Pass the* ***Flagstaff Memorial Chapel*** *to the left. Much of the chapel was moved here from the town of Flagstaff in 1949, just before the lake flooded the Dead River Valley. The graves in the nearby cemetery were also moved to this location.*

5.6mi. *Turn right onto a side road leading into Eustis Village. We will rejoin Route 27 on the north side of the village. On this side road, after a short distance, pass a Maine Forest Service station on the right.*

5.8mi. *Turn right onto the Mill Road and follow it for fifty yards to its end. Park here. Directly ahead is Eustis Dam, a small hydro station built on a falls portaged by the expedition. The pool behind the dam covers Black Cat Rapids, which also was portaged. Somewhere between this point and the Cathedral Pines Campground to the south is the place where Enos's Fourth Division decided to abandon the*

The Dead River near Eustis

expedition. There is a portage trail for canoes around the dam. It approximates the trail used by the expedition's men. Drive back to the main street and turn right.

6.2mi. *Turn right (north), rejoining Route 27.*

7.9mi. *Park your car at an unmarked turnout on the right. There is no sign to identify this site, so*

Ledge Falls

watch your odometer reading. A short trail leads down to ***Lower Ledge Falls****, another of the many portages the men made on the North Branch. The portage trail was on this side of the river. The river was at a flood stage when the men passed this point. A Caribbean hurricane dumped heavy rain on the valley for several days. Try to imagine the drenched and cold men struggling with their bateaux against the river's heavy current. Arnold estimated that the river rose nine feet in one night.*

9.2mi*. Pass a small pond on the right. The river flows just beyond the pond, around its east side.*

10.7mi*. Cross Alder Stream, a large tributary of the North Branch. Some of the expedition's men moving on foot had to detour far upstream to ford it.*

11.0mi. *To the right can be seen a short stretch of the North Branch. Note how small the river has become.*

12.0mi. *As the main highway makes a left-hand curve, to the right is an obscure turnout that was part of an old roadbed. Watch your odometer carefully to identify this hard-to-find location. Park cars here and walk a narrow gravel road downhill about fifty yards to the North Branch. Here we see* ***Shadagee Falls****, where seven of the expedition's bateaux were overturned and wrecked, losing their cargo of food and supplies. This was the day after the hurricane roared through, and the river was raging. The disheartened men camped here, appropriately naming it Camp Disaster.*

15.4mi. *Pass, on the right,* ***Sarampus Falls*** *Picnic Area. The falls are a small drop over a ledge in the river. The portage trail was on the left, or road side, of the falls.*

15.9mi. *Cross the North Branch of the Dead River. This will be your last view of it before we reach its source, the Chain of Ponds.*

17.9mi*. At the brow of a hill on the left is an obscure, narrow gravel road. Check your odometer mileage to help you identify it. You will have to watch sharply for this road. It leads 200 yards to the*

party had managed to cover a good seventeen miles that day. It would be the last such good day on the Dead River.

The next morning Greene and his officers conferred with Arnold about a very serious problem. His officers had discovered that the men were exceedingly short of food rations, certainly not enough in their estimate to reach the French settlements. How this shortage had occurred mystified them. It was suggested that, when Greene's Division passed through Morgan's lead troops on the Great Carrying Place, some barrels of food had been siphoned off and placed in Morgan's bateaux instead of Greene's. This could not be proven, but what to do?

It was widely assumed that Enos's Fourth Division had enough reserve food to support the three front divisions. Therefore, Arnold ordered Major Bigelow and about eighty men in twelve bateaux back down river to meet Enos's men and bring up the reserve food. The rest of Greene's three companies stayed put for the next five days, awaiting the food to be brought up.

To keep the men busy, Arnold ordered them to start preparing paper cartridges. This was accomplished by putting a lead ball and a standard charge of powder in a small piece of paper, rolling it into a cylindrical shape, and twisting it at the ends so that it would stay together. When used, a soldier would rip the paper open with his teeth, hold the lead ball in his mouth, pour the powder down the barrel, cram the paper in to form a patch, and then push the lead ball down the barrel using a ramrod.

Five days later, Major Bigelow's detachment returned with long faces and a meager two barrels of flour. This was alarming news. It meant that there was no food reserve. Greene's Division would be forced to try to stretch out what little food they had left until the French settlements were reached. Arnold had already gone ahead, so he was unaware of the implications of this startling news until several days later.

On Oct. 17, while Major Bigelow and his detachment headed back downstream to obtain food supplies, Morgan's three companies worked upriver past Greene's camp to regain the lead. Because of the missing food, there must have been some hard looks from Greene's men as Morgan's men passed. The following day, Meigs's Third Division passed Greene's camp, which was approximately five miles east of present-day Stratton. Ominously, it began to rain, quite steady and hard.

On Oct. 19, Arnold had left Greene and continued

westward along the still-placid Dead River. His party proceeded about four miles farther west to a short portage around a waterfall later called Arnold Falls. Just beyond these falls was the fork of the Dead River. The South Branch continued west, farther up the valley. Some of Meigs's soldiers had mistakenly followed this branch. Men were sent to catch up with them and inform them of their error. The North Branch winds into the wild hills now known as the Boundary Mountains. This branch, reduced by the water volume from its southern sister, becomes a shallow, twenty-yard-wide stream, usually hardly worthy of the label of river. But the recent rains were transforming this narrow branch into something far from shallow and dead.

The Hurricane

Over the next few days, the expedition's luck was dealt an almost mortal blow by the weather. On Oct. 19, no one thought much of the persistent light but steady showers. The men had experienced these conditions many times before. Most storms in this area come from the northwest or west. Unusually, though, this storm blew in from the southwest.

Arnold's party camped at the falls just below the fork in the river. This site is currently under Flagstaff Lake. All during the night, the rain continued to pick up and was accompanied by increasing winds. Many of the men did not have tents and had to crawl under an overturned bateau for shelter. Some just huddled around smoking campfires with blankets wrapped over their heads.

On Oct. 20, the two lead divisions were able to progress only about five miles up the North Branch to a point near what is now the village of Eustis. In the cold, gray morning, the showers shifted into a downpour, driven by increasingly strong winds. Meigs's drenched men came up to Arnold Falls and began the unpleasant task of carrying their bateaux and rain-soaked equipment over the thankfully short portage. The river had already risen, by Arnold's estimate, about three feet, making progress upstream much more difficult. Meigs told Arnold that he intended to continue on just a short distance and quit early to give the soggy men a chance to build fires and try to dry out. The rain did not abate at all during the afternoon. It rained even harder during the night. The wind picked up, tearing wildly at the tents and causing them to leak badly. Keeping dry was next to impossible.

North Branch of the Dead River's confluence with Alder Stream

outlet dam of the Chain of Ponds. The dam is only six feet high, so the ponds' environment closely resembles what it was when the expedition passed. This is the take-out or put-in point for canoeing the length of the ponds (see Canoe Trip 5). Cars with high clearances can drive to the dam, but most people will choose to park on the main highway and walk in. The views of the rocky cliffs hemming in the narrow ponds are spectacular.

18.5mi. *On Route 27, we reach a high point with good views of the Chain of Ponds stretching to the northwest. The region here was and is quite wild. In fact, no road was constructed along these ponds as late as 1904. The high granite ridges blocked penetration of this area for many years. Except for periodic timber-harvesting operations, the country remains close to the wilderness conditions that existed in 1775. The State of Maine has acquired considerable acreage along the shores of the ponds to preserve them for future generations.*

21.8mi. *On the left, turn onto a gravel road leading to the* ***Natanis Point Campground,*** *which is open to the public. Stop at the entrance to seek permission to view the very attractive point. This is an excellent place to camp if you are tenting or have an RV. Canoes may be rented here. It's also a launch or take-out site for Canoe Trip 5. For more information, call or write to:*

Natanis Point Campground
HC 73, Box 270
Eustis, ME 04936
(207) 297-2694
www.natanis@tdstelme.net

The road leading out to Natanis Point passes between Round Pond to the right (northwest) and Natanis Pond to the left (southeast). The view south on a clear day is breathtaking. The large mountain you will see through the mountain gap southward is Bigelow. It is approximately thirty air miles away.

Natanis Point is historic and prehistoric. Native Americans used it for thousands of years in their passages between the St. Lawrence River and Chaudière Valley to the north and the Kennebec River and Atlantic Ocean to the south. The point is at the south end of the long portage and series of small ponds that the expedition used to pass over the Height of Land into the Chaudière watershed and Canada. Travelers descending or ascending the route would camp at this excellent site where the bugs were manageable and one could see who was coming from either direction.

Some of the men of the expedition camped here before beginning the arduous eight-mile portage over the Height of Land. On the point is the grave of an Indian woman Natanis who was murdered here in 1863. This is obviously not the expedition's Natanis.

The portage trail is located at the west end of the point and follows the southwest shore of Round Pond. This trail is not well marked or maintained, and timber harvesting has obliterated its middle portion. The water route that some of the expedition, including Arnold's party, used is via Horseshoe Stream and four small ponds, ending at Arnold

The author at the international boundary at Coburn Gore

Pond. The entrance to the stream is located on the northwest side of Round Pond.

24.4mi. *Back on Route 27, continue northwest. Cross Hawthorn Brook, which some men of the expedition mistook as the stream leading to Arnold Pond.*

27.4mi. *Pass Arnold Pond on the left. A private sporting club owns the shore of the pond on the highway side. Access is difficult. Note the mountain with the sharp cliffs to the east.*

28.4mi. *Reach the United States - Canada*

When Arnold awoke on Oct. 21, he decided that he had to continue despite the incessant rain. His small party left the fork of the Dead River, battling into the swollen waters of the North Branch. It was now difficult to ascend against the powerful current. Arnold passed Meigs's division and struggled about six miles to a short rapid, later named Black Cat Rapids, just north of the present village of Eustis. This rapid required a short carry. A half a mile farther brought them to another falls requiring a portage. They continued on against the swollen river about three miles to Ledge Falls.

Arnold found Morgan's division camped here in a poor location. He decided to continue a little farther to a better campsite. He made camp after dark in the unrelenting heavy rain driven by high winds. He and his men did not get dried out and into their blankets until after 11 o'clock because of the difficulty of getting fires started in the downpour. The two days of steady rain had saturated every piece of potential firewood. Adding to the misery was the sieve-like canvas of the tents, which had lost most of its ability to shed water. Attempts to sleep and rest were fitful at best. The loud reports of falling trees and limbs sounded like gunshots in the surrounding woods.

The men were awakened about 4 a.m. by the roar of the river, which had risen an unbelievable nine feet during the night! They rushed to grab their boats and baggage, frantically hauling them up a small hill behind their camp. They spent the rest of this night miserably huddled in small groups and without warming fires. Dawn exposed the seriousness of their plight, The rain continued, adding even more water to the flooded river before them. The water overflowed the river's banks and made lakes of any low land. The storm's high winds had downed trees throughout the adjacent woods. Whole trees, roots and all, were being swept down the river. Attempts to navigate boats were a constant game of dodging the floating trees hurtling past them. Small, trickling tributaries had become dangerous torrents, making it almost impossible for the soldiers on foot to cross without detouring far upstream away from the main river.

This was no ordinary fall rainstorm. They had been hit by a late-season hurricane that had cut a path inland from the coast. The four divisions were strung out more than twenty miles along the river, and they were for the most part unable to support each other. Enos's Fourth Division was far down the Dead River near the first carry at Hurricane Falls (named, later, after this storm). Greene was still camped four miles below the fork of the Dead, awaiting food to be brought up. Meigs's division was near present-day Eustis, and Morgan was at Ledge Falls just below Arnold's encampment.

All along the route, the Dead River was at flood stage. What were they to do? Quebec lay far to the north, and the nearest American settlements were weeks to the south. They were running out of food. To the discouraged men, the sight of the almost impassable river and its surrounding flooded land made Quebec seem an unattainable dream. They were wet, tired, and extremely hungry.

Working against the flood on Dead River
Courtesy, Library of Congress

Despite this terrible discouragement, they picked themselves up and continued to forge ahead. The men loaded their bateaux and set off upstream against the floodwaters of the not-so-Dead River. There was the constant danger of being swept away and drowned. The current was so powerful and the river so deep that paddling or poling upstream was almost impossible. The men resorted to grabbing onto trees or bushes to pull the boats ahead. In some places, the bateaux were maneuvered between partially submerged trees in the flooded adjacent woods.

The men on foot had to leave the river in some places as much as a quarter of a mile to avoid the flooded land. They often became lost, not being able to distinguish swollen tributaries from the main river. Constant wading in cold water further sapped their strength. Some of the foot soldiers mistakenly followed Alder Stream, a large tributary of the North Branch. Men had to be sent several miles to catch them and bring them back. Despite these dreadful and dangerous obstacles, the army slogged forward.

boundary at the small village of Coburn Gore. Most of the Maine wilderness is divided into six-mile by six-mile squares called Unorganized Townships. Irregularly shaped slices are sometimes left over. These are called "gores." At this point, everybody must check through Canadian Customs. Usually, a valid driver's license is sufficient documentation to enter Canada if you are a U.S. citizen. Noncitizens will require a passport.

Proceed "Nord" (north) into the province of Quebec. The route number changes to Provincial Route 161. The road ahead passes through a gap in the mountains, which was the route of the Height of Land portage over to the Arnold River in present-day Woburn. This highway approximately follows the route of the now-obliterated portage trail. The border is the divide between the Atlantic and St. Lawrence watersheds. Beyond this gap, the highway abruptly breaks out of the Appalachian Mountain Chain.

30.9mi. *As the forest gives way to the first of Quebec's fields and farms, we reach the Arnold River, at this point a rocky mountain stream. Downstream a short distance from the bridge is the site of the so-called "Beautiful Meadow" that the journal writers describe so glowingly. It was the first open area they had encountered since passing through the lower Kennebec Valley, which to them must have seemed a world away. In 1974, the author saw six-foot-diameter elm stumps here marking the meadow's location. But lumber mills now occupy this site on both sides of the river, and the stumps have been bulldozed into the past.*

Part of the expedition followed the Arnold River north to Lake Megantic, nine perilous miles away. Only a few bateaux were brought across the Height of Land, so most men walked along the river's banks.

31.4mi. *In the center of the town of Woburn, pass on the right the Arnold Motor Inn.*

33.7mi. *Route 161 turns more easterly to swing around the Lake Megantic swamps at the south end of the lake. We soon recross the Arnold River. There is a place to launch canoes just below the bridge. It is possible to canoe through the swamp all the way to the lake.*

The swamps almost destroyed the expedition. A few men did die here. The swamps were thigh- and waist-deep. It was late October when the soldiers struggled through to reach the lake. The water was quite cold, and ice was forming along the stream's edges. To complicate matters, they became lost among several false rivers or "sloughs" within the swamp.

The road ahead bears easterly in the general direction taken by another large contingent of the expedition's men who were on foot. Becoming lost, they went easterly around Spider Lake, found to the east of this road, where more swamps were encountered. The nearly 400 men following this route were saved and guided back to Lake Megantic by an Indian who seemed to materialize out of the wilderness. Some chroniclers believe he was Natanis.

The highway cuts north between Rush and Spider Lakes, which are out of sight from this road.

***38.4mi.** Cross the Spider River, the connector stream between that lake and Rush Lake, which flows into Lake Megantic. The highway soon reaches the east shore of Lake Megantic, which is fourteen miles long. A point of land near here is where the men emerging out of the swamps regrouped. On the point, there was an Indian hut that Arnold used. A campground and private camps now occupy the site. Ahead, the highway parallels the lake northward.*

***47.8mi.** Near the center of the City of Lac-Mégantic, we reach a traffic light at the junction of Routes 161 and 204. Route 204 will be our route over the next section. The main street turns left and immediately crosses the outlet of the lake, which is the beginning of the Chaudière River.*

***Lac-Mégantic** is a small but picturesque city (population 15,000) at the north end of the lake. It has a number of restaurants and overnight establishments. There is a fine park behind the main street with good views of the huge lake. A large dock here once was the landing for steamers plying the lake. During the summer, tour boats depart for trips up the lake. On the main street on the left is the Hôtel de Ville, which means City Hall. On the main floor are displays and a wall plaque celebrating the expedition. A visit to the dam at the outlet of the lake is also of interest.*

Two miles west of the city center on Route 161, on the south side of the highway, is the town's Information Center. Here are two interpretive panels and a replica of a bateau commemorating the expedition's passage.

(The Travel Guide will continue on page 77 at Lac-Mégantic.)

On the morning of Oct. 22, Arnold and his party reorganized the equipment they had so hastily saved from the flood during the night and then spent the day trying to get their blankets and clothes dried out. The rain had lightened to intermittent showers, and the gale had died to a breeze. Morgan's company struggled past Arnold's camp, trying to make some progress. Downriver, Greene's Second Division, after waiting five days for food to be brought to them, decided to move on.

On Oct. 23, Meigs's division passed Arnold's camp. The colonel and his party packed up and joined the upriver struggle. The river's flow had diminished somewhat, but it was still at flood stage and still dangerous. With extreme effort, the two lead divisions worked their way upstream to the next frothing obstacle at Shadagee Falls. Just below the falls, a line of bateaux was working by a narrow point in the river. The lead bateau lost control and swung broadside, hitting and overturning the next in line. In rapid succession, like tumbling dominoes, seven bateaux overturned and were swept downstream. Men fought for their lives as they were carried down the rapids. Miraculously, they were able to grab onto trees and bushes along the flooded shoreline and pull themselves to safety. Fires were immediately started to warm the chilled and water-soaked men. All their precious provisions and equipment were lost, as were the seven bateaux, bashed into floating boards. The crews downstream eyed with misgivings the wreckage as it swept past them. The downstream crews snagged some clothes, barrels, and equipment, but all the guns, powder, and balls were gone.

It being late in the day and with many men needing to dry out and recover from their close call, camp was made at Shadagee Falls. The soldiers accurately dubbed this site Camp Disaster. That evening, Arnold called a council of war with the officers of Morgan's and Meigs's divisions. Greene's and Enos's divisions were farther down the river and out of contact. The serious predicament in which the army now found itself was the only item on the agenda. After much discussion around the campfire, a series of actions was decided upon. Since their food was almost gone, all speed was needed to reach the French settlements where more could be procured. The council decided to send back the sick and injured who might slow them down. After the officers combed the ranks, twenty-six men from the two divisions were found to be too sick or weak to continue. The following morning, they were loaded into several bateaux and sent on their way home with a meager supply of rations.

Captain Hanchet and fifty men were ordered as a "flying column" to proceed ahead at all speed to the French settlements on the Chaudière to procure food and transport it back to the starving men. Arnold, who had positioned himself throughout the expedition to aid and oversee the entire army, decided that he also needed to shoot ahead to reach the settlements and expedite the shipment of food back.

On Oct. 24, the army moved slowly up the flooded river. They portaged over the eighth and ninth carries on the Dead, around what is now Sarampus Falls. Arnold's party camped about a mile above these falls, near the present Highway 27 bridge over the North Branch. The following morning, the horrors of the Dead River were gratefully left behind. Arnold and his party finally reached the first of the Chain of Ponds. The lead division was not far behind.

Unknown to Arnold and the men in the lead divisions, a grave drama was unfolding at the rear of the expedition that was to have crucial effects on its fate.

Chain of Ponds

"To add to our discouragement, we received inelegance that Col. Enos had turned back taking large stores of provisions."
—Abner Stocking

[After the 7-6 vote was taken to proceed] ". . . on which they [Lieutenant Colonel Enos and his five officers] held a council of war amongst themselves, of which were the Capts. McCobb, Williams and Scott, and unanimously declair'd that they would return, and not rush into such imminent danger . . . Col. Enos advanced, with tears in his Eyes, wishing me and mine success and took, as he then suppos/d and absolutely thought, his last farewell of me . . . "
—Captain Simeon Thayer

Chapter Eleven

Retreat of the Fourth Division

While Arnold and his advance party fought head-winds and snow squalls on the Chain of Ponds, an event was unfolding far down the Dead River that would vitally affect the expedition. The Fourth Division, led by Lieutenant Colonel Roger Enos, had slowly progressed a short distance up the North Branch to a campsite south of the present village of Eustis. Greene's division was five miles ahead near Ledge Falls. Morgan's and Meigs's divisions were farther upriver, nearing the Chain of Ponds. Enos's and Greene's divisions, like the others, were still battling against the swollen river, although it was beginning to recede. The rains had finally stopped as well.

Enos's three companies, under Captains Scott, Mc-Cobb, and Williams, totaling about 250 men, constituted somewhat more than a quarter of the army. With Enos was also a remnant of Captain Colburn's company of carpenters and shipwrights, although the bulk of them had returned home after repairing bateaux at Norridgewock Falls. Also with them were a number of sick and weakened men from the lead divisions, ready to start downstream back to Fort Western. The division had fallen behind by three days since leaving Fort Western. The hurricane had hit them while on the Middle Dead River in the vicinity of Hurricane Falls.

Their inability to keep up with the rest of the army had troubled Arnold. He had sent messages back several times urging Enos and his division forward "at all haste," but these messages had little effect. From the time the expedition had left Fort Western, Arnold had made personal contact with Enos only once, briefly, at Norridgewock Falls. Closer supervision by Arnold might have prevented the unfortunate events that were to unfold, but he had thought he was needed more urgently, as commander, at or near the head of the line of march. Lack of communication with the rest of the army may have created within the ranks of the Fourth Division a feeling of not being a vital part of the expedition. A pivotal issue within the army was the amount of food

Flagstaff Lake and the Bigelow Range

the Fourth Division carried. It was widely assumed by the officers and men of the rest of the army that the division had a reserve of food and supplies that the other divisions could draw upon. This became a crucial matter when the lead divisions began running out of food. Greene's division waited for five days for this food reserve to be brought up from the Fourth Division. It was a shock when Major Bigelow and his contingent returned to Greene's men, in the midst of the hurricane, with only two barrels of flour. At that time, there was no way for Greene to communicate this vital information to Arnold and the two lead divisions, who were many miles ahead. Enos had claimed that his men had no reserve and were short of food themselves.

As a result of the council of war held at Camp Disaster on Oct. 23, Arnold sent orders to Enos to send his sick back to Fort Western along with the twenty-six men from the first two divisions that were being returned. Arnold also ordered that the remaining able men from Greene's and Enos's divisions be sent forward with "fifteen days' provisions," enough to sustain them until they reached the French settlements. This order would prove to be the key point that decided the Fourth Division's fate.

On Oct. 25, Greene's division was camped near Ledge Falls trying to dry out from the hurricane. Enos and his officers came forward to their camp to discuss the plight of their situation with Greene and his officers and to decide what to do in light of Arnold's orders. Observing the large group of sick men heading home from the forward divisions had added to their discouragement.

Enos and his three captains claimed to Greene that they had no food left to provide anyone with the fifteen days' food supply specified in Arnold's orders. They also claimed to have barely enough left to get their own men back down the river to Fort Western. Their men were in no condition to go farther, they said. Enos and his officers, arguing at some length, implored Greene and his officers to return with them.

Because the commander, Arnold, was not available to settle the issue, the entire group of officers decided to take a vote on whether both divisions were to continue or retreat. The five officers with Enos cast votes to return. Greene and his four officers voted to continue. Enos then cast the tiebreaker, voting to continue. It was thus a six-to-five vote for both divisions to press on. Enos and his officers then briefly conferred by themselves and announced that they were refusing to abide by this vote, as their minds had already been made up to retreat. Enos was distraught, claiming that, even though he had voted to proceed, as leader of the division he must accompany his men back. This point ignored the fact that he was the division's commander. The meeting soon broke up with very ill feelings between the two groups of officers.

As a pacifier to Greene's men, Enos had agreed to give them as much food as he could spare. Captain Thayer was sent downriver with a Mister Odgen in a bateau to collect these supplies and bring them back. When Thayer arrived at Enos's camp, he was contritely told that there was no food to spare for Greene's men. Thayer vehemently cajoled, swore, and implored Enos and his three impassive captains to give him any amount of food, as they had promised. Captain Williams finally caved in, returned to his men, and was able to "find" two barrels of flour. After quickly loading the two barrels into his bateau, Thayer tersely bid Enos farewell. Enos said that he was afraid that he would never see him again. Thayer commented in his journal that Enos had tears in his eyes when he said this farewell. Thayer and Ogden felt extreme bitterness and anger toward these men who, in their judgment, were deserting them. With heavy hearts, they returned to their upstream camp with the two meager barrels of flour.

Enos's division began its retreat downstream the next day, Oct. 26. Many of the sick from the lead divisions accompanied them. It took a mere ten days to reach Fort Western. The downstream current sped them along very fast. They procured additional rations at the fort to get them back to Cambridge. They had to go by land through Brunswick, Falmouth (Portland), Portsmouth, and Newburyport. They were considerably impeded by storms and knee-deep snow most of the way below Fort Western. The main body of the three companies arrived in Cambridge on Nov. 23, four weeks after turning back on the Dead River. By comparison, Arnold and the rest of the army had reached the walls of Quebec on Nov. 14.

The effect of the loss of Enos's three companies on

the outcome of the attack on Quebec can only be speculative. These additional two-hundred-plus guns definitely would have helped. In their six weeks before Quebec, Arnold and General Montgomery lacked sufficient men to conduct an effective siege. They also had other serious manpower and morale problems. Some of the men and officers whose enlistments were expiring threatened to go home.

After the arrival of Enos's tattered troops in Cambridge, a displeased General Washington ordered a court of inquiry of Lieutenant Colonel Enos on the subject of his decision to retreat with no orders to do so. The only men to testify were Enos's three company captains, Scott, Williams, and McCobb. They strongly supported "Enos's decision." Other officers who might have disputed their statements were fighting and dying at Quebec. With no information to challenge the statements made by Enos and his officers, it was a short inquiry. Enos was cleared of any wrongdoing and returned to service. However, for the rest of his life, doubt and suspicion about his retreat followed him.

The Fourth Division's retreat was probably a case of a weak commander whose style of leadership was consensus. This type of leadership was not uncommon in colonial militia companies. Officers were often elected by popular vote and remained commander only as long as they remained popular. In this case, General Washington had appointed Enos. But instead of asserting the normal military line of authority, he continued to practice leadership by committee. Although he was convinced his division should proceed, as evidenced by his vote on the Dead River, his officers overruled his decision. The three company captains, Scott, Williams, and McCobb, called the shots. They simply ignored their indecisive commander. The actions by the three captains revealed that Enos had little respect from, or real authority over, his officers.

The bigger question was how much food did the Fourth Division actually have? Enos and his company captains concluded that, since they could not comply with Arnold's orders requiring that men going forward be provided with fifteen days of food supplies, that they had no choice but to turn back. Whether they did or did not have enough food will never be known. There is no record or statement that would help determine this fact. It is reasonable to assume that they could have scraped enough food together to send forward some able men. The decision to turn back took place on Oct. 25. At that point, they were one day behind Greene's division and four days behind Arnold at the head of the column. The lead companies received new food supplies on the Chaudière on Nov. 2. At most, the Fourth Division was ten days from the French settlements and replenishment of their food supplies. It took them an equal time, ten days, to reach Fort Western. Greene's division, which was only five miles ahead of Enos, reached the French settlements on Nov. 3 and 4, only eight days after the decision to retreat was made.

The frightening four-day rains of the hurricane probably broke the Fourth Division's will. The decision to turn back was made the day after it ended. The river ahead was still at flood stage. The negative experiences of driving wind, uprooted trees, constant rains, and the isolation in an utter wilderness would be enough to unnerve many people. Strong leadership would have overcome the psychological effect of such terrible conditions. It was not found in the Fourth Division.

"The day was very cold and the ground covered with pretty deep snow... our progress much impeded . . . Some of us frequently slipping into bogs."
—Simon Fobes

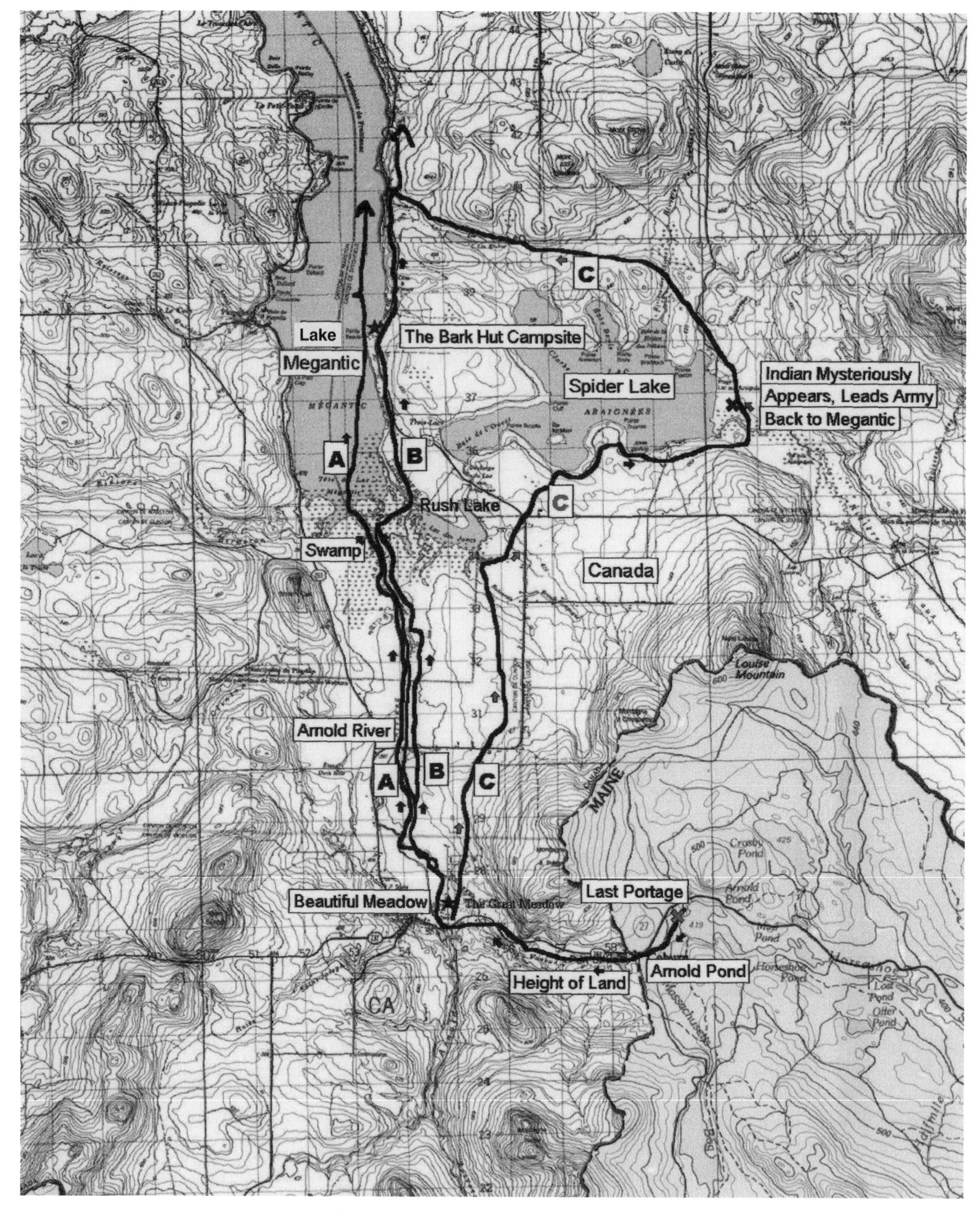

Map of Lake Megantic and the Height of Land Border Country

Showing the routes of the three separate contingents as they left the Beautiful Meadow on the Arnold River. Courtesy of NG Maps.

A. Route of Arnold's party, Hanchet's and Morgan's companies following the Arnold River to the lake.

B. Dearborn's and Goodrich's companies followed the river on foot and were trapped in the swamp.

C. The six remaining companies, including all of Greene's division, and some of Meigs's and Morgan's divisions, totalling about 350 men, followed this route and became lost near Rush Lake. They were rescued by an Indian who mysteriously appeared and led them back to Lake Megantic.

Chapter Twelve

Over the Height of Land

On a snowy, windy day, Arnold and his party emerged from the Dead River onto the Chain of Ponds. There they fought through huge whitecaps whipped up by a freshening northwest wind. The Chain of Ponds is hemmed in on both sides by high mountain peaks with big shoulders coming down to the ponds and forming cliffs on the ponds' shores. Heavy wind-driven flurries swirled down through this natural funnel, pelting snow and whipping freezing water into the faces of the men in the boats. Several times they had to go ashore to bail out the bateaux from leaks below and waves above.

Morgan's and Meigs's divisions were only a few miles behind Arnold, fighting the last stretch of the swollen North Branch to reach the ponds. Arnold was now ahead of all four of his divisions. It was his intent to hurry to the French settlements to expedite the shuttling of food back to his starving army. Ahead of him were Lieutenants Steele and Church and their trail-clearing party. They were working on the eight-mile carry trail over the Height of Land. And several hours ahead of Arnold's party were Captain Hanchet and his fifty men. They had been dispatched the previous day from Camp Disaster to obtain food at the French settlements.

The Chain of Ponds is a series of five interconnected ponds about five miles in length. After plowing through wind and waves for most of the day, Arnold's party finally reached the last of the chain, Round Pond. They then had difficulty finding the route that Church and Steele had marked and cleared. The snow and gathering darkness did not help, hiding the pond's inlet, which they assumed was the correct route. Finally, the inlet, Horseshoe Stream, was discovered, and in the twilight they proceeded about a mile and a half up its winding course. As the stream became narrower, trees and brush had to be cut to allow the boats to proceed. Arnold and his men were confused. If this was the correct route, why had not Church and Steele cleared the way? As darkness came upon them, they called it a day and made camp in the thick woods along the stream.

In the morning, Arnold's party continued up Horseshoe Stream. As the stream grew shallower, the men gave up poling and paddling and climbed out into the cold water, resorting to pulling and pushing their craft along the shallow stream over rocks and gravel. After two cold miles of slogging, the portage trail was found paralleling the stream near Lost Pond. Church and Steele's party had cut a trail directly from Round Pond to Lost Pond, bypassing the shallow, winding stream. In the darkness and snow, Arnold had missed the beginning of the portage trail near what is now Natanis Point on the Chain of Ponds.

After quickly crossing the very small Lost Pond, they found another portage of about three-fourths of a mile that took them to Horseshoe Pond. A similar quick crossing of this small pond brought them to another short carry to the even smaller Mud Pond. Beyond this was another brief portage to reach the final body of water of this maze, now named Arnold Pond. This is the western source of the mighty Kennebec River. A one-mile paddle across the pond brought them to a three-mile portage through a gap in the mountains—over the Height of Land—and into Canada. Fresh-cut trees and bushes were evidence that the advance party had been hard at work clearing the trail. Even though it was four o'clock in the afternoon, Arnold's party pushed ahead for another two miles over the portage. Bogs, rocky ravines, and a thick, spruce-fir forest impeded their passage through this mountain gap. But, unlike the Great Carrying Place, this carry had only a relatively moderate elevation gain to overcome. Finding their way with torches through the darkness, near midnight, Arnold's crew stumbled into a camp of twenty men from Church and Steele's party. Their warm campfires were most welcome.

The next day, Oct. 27, Arnold and his group, with good information about the route ahead, rapidly completed the remaining mile downhill to what is now known as the Arnold River in present-day Woburn, Quebec Province. The Height of Land marks the dividing ridge between waters flowing south into the Atlantic Ocean and north to the St. Lawrence River. The Arnold River was the first stream encountered on the expedition's route that flowed northward.

Near the end of the carry, Arnold and his party were amazed to enter an open meadow, which in the journals was called the "Beautiful Meadow." It was almost park-like in appearance. Large elms and tall grass made easy passage, a welcome relief from the dense forests and rocky country they had just passed through. At the meadow, Arnold caught up with Captain Hanchet and his detachment. They had been delayed by confusion about the route across the Height of Land and what lay ahead, since Church and Steele's trail ended at the river. There had been no scouting of the route beyond this point. This oversight would cause near-fatal hardship to the men over the next several days.

The Arnold River was a small, rocky stream flowing out of the nearby mountains northward to the huge Lake Megantic (*lac Mégantic* in French), eight miles distant. As soon as the portaged bateaux arrived, Arnold's party packed their baggage and headed downstream with the current. Captain Hanchet and his men crashed through the woods on foot along the river's shore. The river soon received a number of tributaries, increasing water volume enough to speed Arnold and his group along. After four quick miles, the river became deeper, slower, and began to meander as it entered a huge swamp. This swamp is at the south end of Lake Megantic, and it is several miles wide.

In the late afternoon, Arnold's party broke out of the swamp onto the fourteen-mile-long lake. A row about two miles along the east shore brought them to a prominent point, where they found a bark hut, obviously built by Indians who frequented the area. Hanchet's contingent had followed the course of the river into the swamp. Having no boats, they had waded knee-to-waist-deep in the freezing water for miles to reach the lake, where they found themselves trapped in the swamp as night approached. Luckily, as they neared the lake, they spied Arnold's campfires on the lakeshore and literally shouted for their lives. It was now dark and there was no high ground near them. They had no idea how to extricate themselves. Building a fire in the swamp was impossible. A night in that cold swamp water would have meant certain death for many of them. So they shouted with all the strength they had left.

Arnold and his men, upon hearing the shouting, immediately sent his three bateaux across the lake to rescue the stranded soldiers. It took several trips to save all of Hanchet's fifty men. The campfires were kept blazing most of the night to warm and dry the exhausted men as they were brought in. It had been a very close call for them.

The bulk of the army was strung out all along the route from the Chain of Ponds to the end of the Height of Land portage at the Beautiful Meadow. In view of Hanchet's near disaster, Arnold realized that the entire army, almost out of food and near exhaustion, was in danger of being trapped in the swamp. The army had to be warned not to descend along the river.

In the morning, he dispatched one of his bateaux with a messenger back up the river. The messenger carried two orders. First, the soldiers were to abandon their bateaux and proceed on foot. The army had to move faster since so little food was left. They had to reach the French on the Chaudière as quickly as possible—or perish. Second, he directed the men not to follow the Arnold River down to the lake. Rather, they should swing farther east to avoid the swamp-trap. This dispatch was sent on the morning of Oct. 27. After writing this and other dispatches, Arnold and twelve men in four bateaux and a birch-bark canoe struck off along the east shore of Lake Megantic and proceeded twelve miles to its north end. There they found its outlet, the beginning of the Chaudière River.

While Arnold rushed north toward the French settlements, the men of the main body of the army were about to experience the greatest crisis of the expedition. Each of the three remaining divisions made good time across the five miles up the length of the Chain of Ponds. Having lost many bateaux, many men had been forced to walk along the shore. They had to struggle along the ponds' rocky, precarious edges by climbing over snow-covered ledges and outcrops. Even with these obstacles, they still made relatively good progress, no longer having to contend with the flooded river.

As each detachment reached the northwest end of the Chain of Ponds at Round Pond, they followed the portage trail cleared by Church and Steele's party. The three divisions became strung out all along the eight-mile carry to the Beautiful Meadow. Morgan's rifle company was the first to reach the portage over the Height of

Land. He decided to carry his remaining seven bateaux across. Even his tough men were in a weakened state, stumbling and frequently falling as they carried the bateaux. They paid a dear price, sapping much of their remaining strength by carrying the heavy, battered boats over the rugged mountain gap.

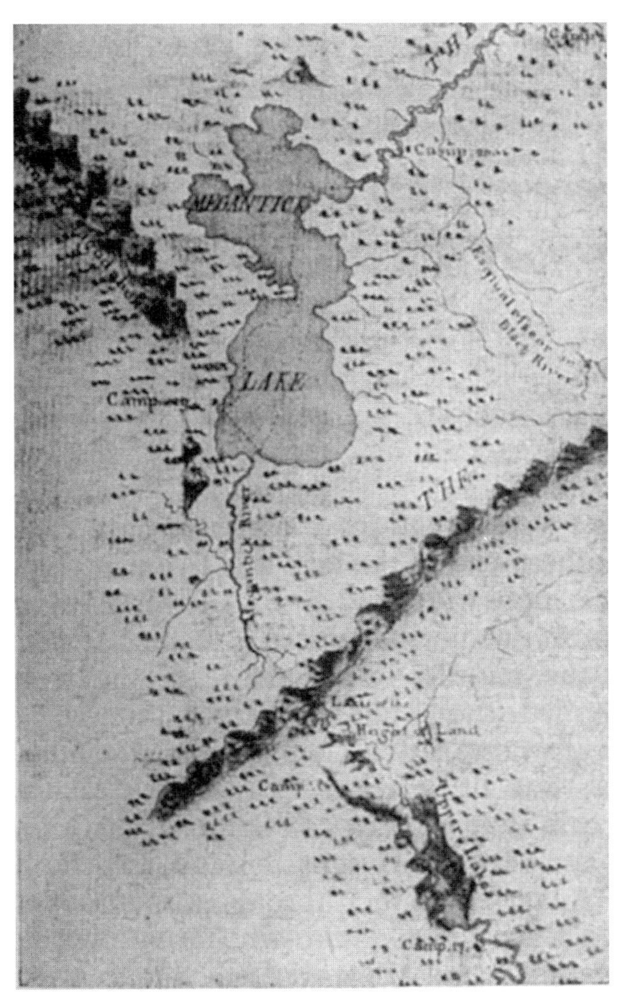

A portion of Montresor's map
Note the absence of Rush and Spider Lakes and of the huge swamp

They had just arrived at the end of the carry at the Beautiful Meadow when they encountered Arnold's messenger coming up the Arnold River. His message to leave the bateaux and proceed on foot came too late for them. The courier then walked back over the portage trail, meeting company commanders in turn and delivering Arnold's order to abandon their bateaux. Some companies decided to carry over just one bateau in order to carry their sick and their remaining equipment.

The total number of bateaux carried over the Height of Land by the army is unknown, but it would probably be twenty or fewer. Approximately 200 of the bateaux, ninety percent of those that had left Colburn's shipyard a month earlier, had been destroyed, abandoned, or had gone back with Enos's retreating division.

After Arnold's message was received, bateaux, oars, paddles, and poles were discarded all along the route back to the Chain of Ponds. With great relief, the men gathered up the remaining food, powder, guns, and equipment, and continued much more rapidly over the portage trail toward the Beautiful Meadow. This order substantially lightened their loads, eliminating the need for multiple trips over the same portage trail. In their weakened condition, it was a godsend.

Meigs's division reached the Beautiful Meadow during the morning of Oct. 28. Greene's now-lightened division, the last to cross the Height of Land, arrived by mid-afternoon. This was the first time the bulk of the three remaining divisions had been together since they left Fort Western. It was here that Greene's men angrily gave the discouraging news that Enos's division had abandoned them. It does not require much imagination to picture the men's anger and oaths directed at Enos and his men.

The rendezvous at the Beautiful Meadow was, of necessity, brief. The supply of food was now perilously short, and the men were in a weakened condition from their daily hard toil and the havoc caused by the hurricane. They were still days away from possible relief at the first French villages down the Chaudière. The company commanders decided to divide the remaining flour and salt pork equally. Although there is some disagreement by the journal writers on the exact amounts, the best estimate by several of the journalists was five pints of flour and a few ounces of salt pork allocated to each man. This larder was supposed to last for six days, the time estimated to reach the settlements. Some men were so starved they devoured a large portion of their rations on the spot before their officers could restrain them. The army was now consuming the last of its meager food supplies.

Since Arnold had ordered the men to leave their bateaux on the other side of the Height of

Land, the army had been transformed from primarily a water-borne force to an army on foot.

The next several days were by far the worst that the army would experience during its journey. Death from starvation threatened all the men. And, at the Beautiful Meadow, the command organization began to unravel. The expedition's commander, Benedict Arnold, was racing for the settlements to procure desperately needed food. Now each company more or less acted independently and chose its own route and speed. At this point, the distinction among the three remaining divisions largely ended. Morgan's company chose to descend the Arnold River to the lake because it had its seven bateaux to enable it to do so. The other two rifle companies theoretically under Morgan's command proceeded on foot with the main body. Dearborn's and Goodrich's companies chose the river route on foot. Their departure from the Beautiful Meadow almost immediately after reaching it indicates that they may not have received Arnold's orders not to follow the river into the swamp. The other six companies spent the night at the Beautiful Meadow, then as a body struck off into the trail-less woods on higher ground to the northeast, heeding Arnold's warning to avoid the swamps. This company-level organization and decision-making would continue until Arnold halted and gathered the straggling army together far down the Chaudière at Ste-Marie. As conditions along the route worsened and the army was further weakened, its plight approached each man for himself. As starvation and exhaustion reached the crisis stage, men simply tried to survive.

There was no lingering at the Beautiful Meadow. To linger was to die! Goodrich's and Dearborn's companies left during the afternoon of Oct. 28 after receiving their pitifully small portions of the remaining food. They struck off following the river. There was no trail for them to use, so they bushwhacked through the woods, going down the east side of the small river with no knowledge of the swamp ahead. All they knew was that the river led north to Lake Megantic, where they could then pick up the Chaudière.

Arnold had ordered advance parties to mark and clear portage paths along the Kennebec and Dead Rivers and over the Height of Land as far as the Beautiful Meadow. Because of the press of time and the condition of his army, he had not ordered any further trail marking or clearing beyond that point. This oversight of not having a trail scouted and marked to the lake proved almost fatal to the army.

Arnold and his company commanders were using copies of the only map of the route available, drawn by the British engineer Montresor fourteen years earlier. Montresor had descended the Arnold River from the meadow late in the afternoon and early evening, missing some important features around the south end of Lake Megantic. Arnold had also missed some of these features, although he had recognized the dangers of the huge swamp along the lake's south shore. They were both ignorant of the existence of a small pond in the swamp, now named Rush Lake, and a much larger lake just to the eastward, Spider Lake. Further complicating the water route was the discovery that the swamp contained many dead-end branches of the Arnold River called logans, plus an unfordable connector waterway from Rush Lake. The topography of Spider Lake was, as its name implies, distinguished by a number of arms radiating in every direction from the lake's main body. Into this watery labyrinth entered the unsuspecting army.

The first to encounter this maze was Hanchet's detachment, which was saved by Arnold's party. The next company to wade into the trap of the swamp was Goodrich's, soon after it left the Beautiful Meadow on the afternoon of Oct. 28, followed several hours later by Dearborn's.

As the crow flies, it is only eight miles from the Beautiful Meadow to the south edge of Lake Megantic. The soldiers covered the first few miles in good time, as the river ran through relatively level, dry ground. When they drew near the lake, continuing to follow the river, they entered a continuous marshy area. They waded across a branch of the river in waist-deep, cold water. Ice was forming along the edges. Beyond, they entered the main swamp. They continued to wade in the chilling water, which became deeper as they approached the lake. Finding no solid ground, they swung east, attempting to reach high land in that direction. As darkness came, they reached an unmapped, deep channel that was unfordable. They were now lost with night coming on—and caught in the trap.

Not knowing what to do, Captain Goodrich left his men and tried to scout a crossing up the unknown stream. Near dark, he was overjoyed to spy Captain Dearborn and one of his men in a birch-bark canoe that Dearborn had found farther up the river. Dearborn's company also was separated from its commander and lost somewhere in the swamp. In the darkness, Goodrich and Dearborn paddled slowly about, not finding any way out.

Meanwhile, Goodrich's exhausted and frozen men found a small hummock and climbed out of the water. With some effort and skill, they finally coaxed a fire out of the wet wood. The fire that night was, for many, the difference between life and a frozen death. The hummock, just barely out of the water, was so small that the men lay like spokes of a wheel with their feet to the fire and their heads almost touching the surrounding swamp water. Most of their food was stored on their one bateau, which was lost somewhere in the maze, so they had little food that night. A few tried to cut up and boil leather apparel or shot pouches and chew on them to gain some sorry sustenance. Some men died that night.

Several men had already died of drowning or sickness after leaving Fort Western. The deaths of men over the next few days until the expedition emerged from the wilderness was never documented nor quantified by company commanders. But, according to journal writers, men did die over the next few days as conditions worsened. Goodrich lost at least one man this night.

Goodrich and Dearborn, knowing that their men were suffering terribly, continued to paddle their canoe around in the dark, seeking a way out of the swamp. As they neared the lake, they joyously spied a campfire on the east shore at the site of Arnold's former camp. He had left two men there to provide a rallying point as the men reached the lake. They paddled across the lake and joined the soldiers camped there, spending a troubled night worrying about the fate of their men.

In the gray of morning, Goodrich and Dearborn recrossed the lake and reentered the swamp. They found Goodrich's men still on the hummock next to the impassible river. Dearborn's men, who had spent a similar horrible night in the swamp, heard the shouting and joined them. All now were confronted with the problem of trying to cross the deep channel. They finally agreed that the only way was to try to ferry all the men across with the single, small, birch-bark canoe. This was no easy task for such a frail craft. Luckily, the one bateau belonging to Smith's company came around a bend. The rest of Smith's men were somewhere up the river. The addition of this larger craft greatly speeded the process of shuttling the two companies to the other side of the channel.

But the swamp wasn't done with them. Only sixty rods beyond this channel was a second, wider channel coming from the uncharted Rush Lake. The boats were portaged over and a second ferry was conducted for the now nearly spent and frustrated men who desperately sought to be rid of this swamp. Finally, in the late morning, the two companies dragged themselves onto higher ground on the east shore of the lake. They were all very wet and dangerously chilled. They immediately marched along the shore to the bark hut campsite on the point. Here they rested with a roaring fire and ate what little food they had. Their lost bateau carrying their food and supplies had finally rejoined them.

Morgan's company, riding with relative ease in their seven bateaux, also emerged from the swamp and joined them. They had descended the river from the Beautiful Meadow that morning. Time could not be wasted. As soon as each company reorganized itself, it marched north along the east shore of the lake. Morgan's men in their bateaux paralleled the companies that were on foot. All converged on the lake's outlet, the Chaudière, at the north end.

But what had happened to the other six companies? On Oct. 28 at the Beautiful Meadow rendezvous, some time had been required to divide the remaining skimpy supplies of food. After the departure of the two companies down the Arnold River, the remaining troops decided to encamp, it being late in the afternoon. Arnold's message had arrived, imploring them to stick to the high ground in order to avoid the dangers of the swamp. They spread out around the meadow, building warming campfires in the bitter cold.

They discussed the good news contained in Arnold's message that he would send back food in about three days. They mistakenly assumed this meant food would reach them in three days. Some nearly starved men, upon hearing this, began to devour much of their entire remaining rations of flour and salt pork.

On the morning of Oct. 29, they broke camp early. Morgan's company climbed into their bateaux and began their descent of the Arnold River. The remaining companies prepared to march. These included Captain Hendricks' company, all of Greene's three companies, under Captains Thayer, Topham, and Hubbard, and parts of several other companies, all totaling about 350 men. The senior officers leading this contingent were Lieutenant Colonel Greene and Major Meigs. The guide Arnold had sent them was leading the way through country that was completely new to him. This column, bushwhacking through the dense woods, swung north. They soon encountered the edge of the swamp and swung farther east around the south shore of Rush Lake. This confused the guide and the officers, as Rush Lake was not shown on their maps.

The guide was now lost. He led the column eastward to somewhat higher ground. The men soon reached the connector stream between Rush and Spider Lakes. At this point, they were only two miles or less away from the campsite on the east shore of Lake Megantic where the rest of the army was resting after emerging from the swamp. The fact that the guide and the officers did not turn north indicates that they were thoroughly lost. Instead, they led the entire column eastward, skirting the south shore of Spider Lake, which also was not on their maps. The guide finally admitted he was lost and had led the column astray.

By now all the men knew they were lost and in serious trouble. Around the south and east sides of three-mile-long Spider Lake are a number of arms, making it difficult to follow the lake's shoreline. To make matters worse, swamps lined the southeast corner of the lake. The men had to pass through them in order to follow the lake's shoreline. They trudged on through this terrible country, not knowing where they were going. They finally gave up when it was near dark. They were wet, cold, and as dispirited as would be any men who were lost. During the evening, the officers discussed what route to follow at morning's light. They knew they could be going directly away from Lake Megantic—which, in actuality, they were. The next day would be decisive.

They started early, at dawn. There was little food to prepare, and most men had to move to get warm. Every man knew that if he could not march with the column, he would have to be left behind, and death would be certain. Soon they slogged through more swamps, up to their knees in muck and ice-coated water. At the southeast end of Spider Lake, a large stream, now called the Spider River, was encountered. It was deep, and ice had formed on both shores. There was no way around it, so the men reluctantly peeled off their clothes and waded with their guns, powder, and equipment held over their heads.

A short distance beyond this stream, the lead officers miraculously encountered a lone Indian who spoke English. He told them that he knew the country and would be willing to guide them back to Lake Megantic. In Kenneth Roberts' novel *Arundel*, the Indian is identified as Natanis. But, in fact, there is no record of this Indian's name. The men were near the end of their strength and thoroughly lost. They needed little convincing to accept his offer. He led them around the east end of the lake onto higher ground and then northwest, back toward Lake Megantic. The exhausted companies lost all semblance of a military organization. They were strung out for miles, the stronger ahead, the weak dropping farther and farther behind.

Toward the end of the day, Oct. 30, the men were overjoyed to see Lake Megantic through the trees. They soon encountered a wide and recently used trail leading north. All being exhausted and weak, the bulk of the troops stopped and made camp to allow the stragglers to catch up. At this point they had intersected the route of the rest of the army. From where they were, it was approximately six miles to the north end of the lake and the beginning of the Chaudière.

The army had barely survived the terrible swamps of Lake Megantic. Before them lay a descent down an unknown river into a foreign land. But, at least, it was toward food and survival.

Chapter Thirteen

On to the St. Lawrence

Lake Megantic lies on a plateau about 1,100 feet above sea level just north of the present American-Canadian border. The lake is approximately ninety air miles from the St. Lawrence River, which is at sea level. The Chaudière River, which is the lake's outlet, flows north and empties into the St. Lawrence only six miles above Quebec City. The greatest portion of the river's descent in elevation to the St. Lawrence, more than 600 feet, is in the first fifty miles. This upper section descends so fast that it is almost continuous rapids, with a couple of big falls thrown in for good measure. It passes through a deeply cut valley that even today has no roads, houses, or other signs of civilization for much of its way.

In 1775, the Upper Chaudière was a wild, uninhabited river valley from its source to Sartigan, the present city of St-Georges. There were at that time several small farming communities situated along the river northward to the St. Lawrence and Quebec. The French word *chaudière* means "boiler," describing a feature near the river's mouth: A major waterfall cascades into a circular gorge.

As each contingent of the army reached the outlet of Lake Megantic, the men quickly began their pell-mell descent along the wild river. They were out of food and near the end of any remaining strength. Their clothes were in tatters, and more than a few were without shoes or hats. And the Canadian winter had arrived, compounding their misery.

On the morning of Oct. 28, Colonel Arnold with his lead party left the bark hut on the southeast shore of Lake Megantic. He had four bateaux and one canoe, carrying thirteen soldiers and his aide, Captain Oswald. Arnold reached the unmistakable outlet of the lake during the late morning. As soon as the slower bateaux caught up, they lashed their baggage and started down the rapids, which commence almost immediately upon entering the river.

They had no guide and no knowledge of the dangers ahead. Normally, the descent of an unknown river would be undertaken with careful scouting to avoid upsetting their boats. But this was no time to be cautious. Arnold and his party were driven by the knowledge that their comrades behind them were starving and dying. They had to reach the French settlements and send back food

Travel Guide 8

Lac-Mégantic to Quebec City

This is the last leg of our journey following the American army's footsteps from Cambridge to Quebec. The section is a beautiful trip down the Chaudière River Valley with its mixture of old and new, of quaint villages and modern towns, of farm fields and forest, a mixture that changes every few kilometers.

Far down the Chaudière near the town of Ste-Marie, the route of the expedition leaves the river valley and cuts directly to the St. Lawrence River near Lévis, opposite Quebec City. From Lac-Mégantic

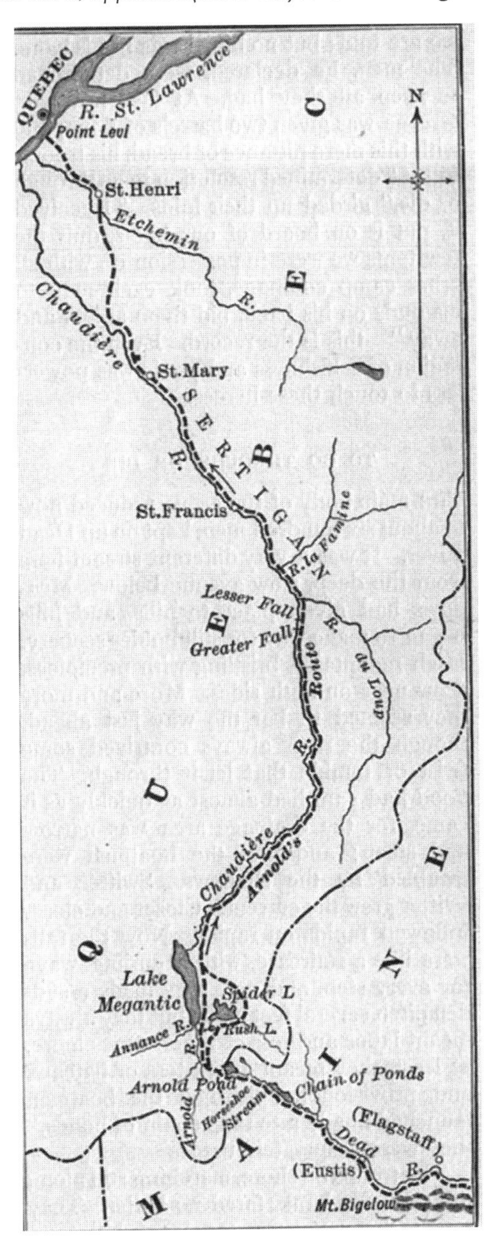

Map of expedition's route from Dead River to Quebec
Courtesy, Arnold Expedition Historical Society

to Quebec it is only 113 miles. (Don't forget that Canada uses the metric system, so all signs and maps will be in kilometers. The rough conversion factor is one kilometer equals 0.6 mile.)

As you plan how to traverse this section you will need to make a decision about how you will approach Quebec. There are two ways. One is to use the Pont Pierre LaPorte (Pierre LaPorte Bridge) on the expressway, Route 73, which crosses the huge river about five miles upstream from the city. The other is to drive into Lévis, opposite Quebec, and use the ferry. The ferry transports both passengers and cars and departs every thirty to forty-five minutes.

The ferry choice has three big advantages. It is much more scenic, it more closely approximates the expedition's route, and it is much more fun. It also provides the opportunity of choosing overnight accommodations in Lévis, which are less expensive than in Quebec City. You can then use the ferry on a daily basis to reach the city. The ferry terminal in Quebec is right in the Lower Town. Most of the sites you will wish to visit in both the Lower and Upper Towns are within a reasonable walking distance or can be reached by public transportation. Parking

Arnold's expedition descending the Chaudière in an unrealistically large bateau. Courtesy, Library of Congress.

with great haste. Their speed could be the difference between life and death for their men. So down the rapid river they flew.

Arnold estimated the continuous rapid current carried them along at an amazing eight to ten miles per hour, even while frantically dodging rocks. They barely saw the shore that flew by. This success was too good to be true. About fifteen miles down the river, they hit several fast, rocky sets of rapids. In quick succession, two of the four bateaux were smashed into kindling. Their crews were carried through the rapids, struggling for their lives, for hundreds of yards before they managed to catch and cling precariously to rocks. These men lost all their guns, equipment, and whatever food remained. The other two bateaux swamped but were able to be maneuvered to shore along with the fragile birch-bark canoe. These were used to rescue the men on the rocks. When Morgan's men hit this same rapid two days later, they were not so lucky.

Arnold's party immediately built fires to warm the chilled and exhausted soldiers rescued from the river. Some of their equipment was salvaged, and they loaded it into the two remaining bateaux. As soon as the men were sufficiently recovered, they turned back to the river, but with much more caution than before. Some men had to proceed on foot, as there was not enough room for everyone in the three remaining craft. This swamping might have been a blessing in disguise. A short distance below was a hidden waterfall that would have drowned them all. They camped here as darkness fell—wet, tired, hungry, and discouraged.

The following day, the advance party continued downriver. Arnold estimated that they covered more than forty miles because of the swift current. The men on foot were unable to keep up and were separated from the boat crews. During the day, the bark canoe hit a rock, sprang an unrepairable leak, and was abandoned.

On Oct. 30, Arnold's party in its two remaining bateaux reached the roaring Grand Falls of the Chaudière. There they met two Penobscot Indians who helped them portage the half-mile around the falls. The Indians conveyed the good news that it was only a short distance to the first settlement. Only one last, small falls and portage had to be negotiated. Below these falls, the Chaudière's main tributary, the Rivière des Loups, entered from the east. Four miles farther downriver joyously brought them to the first farmhouses of Sartigan (also spelled Sertigan in the journals). The exhausted men dragged their two remaining bateaux ashore and rested while curious farm families came down to meet them.

Arnold lost no time in organizing a relief party to head back upriver with food for his men. The relief party departed the next morning, commanded by the ever-reliable Lieutenant Church, who had accompanied Arnold down the river. It consisted of horses to help transport the sick, cattle to be slaughtered for meat when they reached the men, flour, mutton, and such other food as could be procured in a small, poor farming community. To the starving men, some of whom had not eaten in days, this would be the best meal of their lives.

The rest of the army was scattered along the river from Lake Megantic. Three of the four companies that descended the Arnold River through the swamp reached the lake on Oct. 30, the same day Arnold reached Sartigan. After resting at the bark-hut campsite, they set off along the east shore, with Dearborn's company in the lead. Morgan's company in his seven bateaux made quicker time by rowing down the lake. The remaining six companies, which had gotten lost near Spider Lake, did not reach Lake Megantic until the next day, Oct. 31. All converged on the lake's outlet, the beginning of their long downriver journey.

The army's march down the Upper Chaudière was a march into hell. Morgan's company, upon reaching the outlet, immediately began the descent using their bateaux that they had so laboriously hauled over the Height of Land. Like Arnold, his men had no idea what lay ahead. In the same rapid in which Arnold's party had lost his two bateaux, they met a similar disaster. In short order, all seven bateaux were overturned and smashed on the rocks. Much of their remaining food, ammunition, precious rifles, and other vital supplies were lost. Worse, one of their comrades drowned. The survivors dragged themselves ashore and lit fires to keep from freezing to death. This event marked the end of the expedition's flotilla of bateaux. Morgan's men could go no farther that day.

The following day, the other lead companies caught up with Morgan's. They shared what little they had with the unfortunates. Then they all continued on foot, following the river northward.

The next day the river destroyed the single food-carrying bateaux possessed by each of the other companies. The river below these rapids must have looked like a bateau graveyard. The rapids simply could not be navigated by such clumsy craft crewed by

within Quebec is at a premium during the summer months. The route description of this section assumes that most people will choose the Lévis-Quebec City ferry option.

Here is a point about timing your travels: If you leave Lac-Mégantic during the late morning or early afternoon, a good choice is to stay overnight in the St-Georges area, which has a wide variety of accommodations and good restaurants. Plan at least a full day to explore the many interesting sights and venues in the Chaudière Valley. The valley's mixture of modern and older French culture features many family farms that still flourish. Some are succumbing to the same economic and social forces that have so diminished the number of family farms in New England and in much of the rest of the United States. However, the Chaudière Valley is still pastoral and very beautiful. So go slow and resist the temptation to speed onward to Quebec.

As you descend the valley, the main highway, Route 173, tends to bypass most towns. We suggest turning onto the old main streets and fully view the hearts of these wonderful communities. These turn-offs into the villages are not always well marked, so you will have to watch closely as you approach each town's outskirts. It will be impossible not to note and admire the fine architecture of the churches that dominate each village.

The men of the expedition followed the east bank of the Chaudière from its beginning at the outlet of Lake Megantic as far as the village of Scott, just north of Ste-Marie. At this point, almost all the 650-

Chaudière River at St-Gédéon

675 men left were on foot. They were near starvation and reduced to boiling and eating their leather musket-ball pouches. Only a few tents remained. Most soldiers had to sleep out in the open or in makeshift brush shelters. Their clothes were in tatters. Some men were shoeless or hatless and few had gloves. It was more a disorderly and desperate trek for survival than a military march. However, at Ste-Marie they pulled themselves together into an

Grand Falls of the Chaudière near Jersey Mills, Quebec

army once more, although the local citizenry must have wondered if this tattered rabble had any chance against the powerful British.

There were no roads or paths along the river's banks from Lake Megantic to Sartigan (St-Georges). The army had to bushwhack through the thick woods bordering the river as best it could. After reaching Sartigan, the army followed a rough, rutted road that connected each of the valley's scattered settlements.

Lac-Mégantic to St-Georges, 49 miles (78 km)

We start the last leg of our march to Quebec at the junction of Routes 161 and 204 next to the dam and bridge over the Chaudière River in the city of Lac-Mégantic. Turn onto Route 204 nord (north). This is a main highway all the way to St-Georges. We will not see the river for another twenty miles until we near the village of St- Ludger. The road swings east, away from the river on higher, more level land. After leaving Lac-Mégantic behind, pass through the hamlets of Frontenac and Audet. The country here is wooded with some scattered, older farms.

As we begin to descend and return to the river valley, the Chaudière will be seen to the left (west). The river at this point seems more like a small, rocky upland stream than the raging river described by the men of the expedition. It will soon pick up tributaries to swell its size. A short distance downstream, at the small settlement of St-Ludger, we rejoin the expedition's route.

Route 204 now closely follows the pathway used by the expedition's men. From St-Ludger, it is 8.7mi. to the village of St-Gédéon, then another 8.7 mi. to St-Martin. The road follows the river closely. Note how rocky its bed is. This is why the few remaining bateaux were swamped and destroyed along this section. The country along this stretch is pastoral, and the farms extend to the river's edge.

weakened men. From this point, the army became entirely a land operation, as it had been when the men marched so proudly out of Cambridge.

The six remaining companies, which had been almost destroyed around Spider Lake, reached the outlet and began their descent the next day. They had no bateaux to lose. They carried what little supplies they had on their backs.

The entire army in its descent down the Upper Chaudière lost any semblance of an organized military force. The weary groups of haggard scarecrows struggled to keep alive, each barely able to take another step. Goodrich's men were so ravenous that they were able to persuade Captain Dearborn into giving them his dog. They wasted little time killing and cooking the poor pet. Dearborn, in tears, did not partake when offered a share.

Dearborn's company was now in the lead. Several miles above the Grand Falls, his men were overjoyed to meet the relief party led by Lieutenant Church. One of the cattle was quickly killed, butchered, cooked, and consumed on the spot. The men had not had fresh meat in over a month. The officers admonished the men to eat slowly so as to not become sick. This took place on Nov. 2. After refreshing themselves and resting, they cut off large chunks of meat and continued down the river toward the settlements ten miles away.

Church and his relief party continued to work slowly upstream for several days, meeting each successive group of desperate men. The scenario of starving men devouring freshly slaughtered cattle was repeated at each encounter. Finally, Church reached the tail end of the column of stragglers. He sent men farther up the trail to see if there were any more left alive. They found only the now-frozen dead. The following summer, a soldier named Forbes who escaped from the British noted at least two bleached-bone corpses beside the trail as he worked his way back home. There were more that he did not find.

From Lake Megantic, it took most soldiers four days to reach Sartigan and escape from the wilderness. Most had survived, but many needed time to rest and recover their strength. Their commander, Colonel Arnold, did not let them rest long. Quebec City was only sixty miles away and awaited their attention.

Arnold spent one night at Sartigan at a private home near the Rivière la Famine in present-day St-Georges. He assigned some of Hanchet's men, who had arrived among the first, the task of dispensing procured supplies to each company in turn when it dragged into Sartigan. Arnold himself moved about eight miles downriver to the equally small settlement of Gilbert, where he collected more supplies for the army. There he met with a group of seventy Indians who lived in the vicinity. They were decked out in full war paint and beautifully costumed. Here he met Natanis, whom he had thought to be a British spy, and who, some thought, had guided the lost army out of the swamps of Spider Lake. Arnold, seeking fresh allies, implored the Indians to join the expedition against the British, for whom they had little love. About fifty agreed. This was a welcome addition to the army, as they had no scouts who knew the area. Arnold persuaded some of the Indians to perform the important task of screening the army from ambush.

He also assigned them the task of descending to the St. Lawrence to try to collect enough boats and canoes to ferry the army across the river. Arnold had gained intelligence that the British in Quebec now knew of the American army's approach. They were burning or destroying anything that could float for some distance up and down the river's south shore in an attempt to prevent the colonial army from crossing the St. Lawrence. This was extremely bad news. It meant that the army had lost the critical element of surprise.

Arnold and his party marched down the river valley, stopping at each village to set up supply depots for the following army. The villages were located about ten miles apart. He reached the large village of Ste-Marie on Nov. 5, and he worked feverishly to gather food and other supplies, including critical gunpowder, to replace all that had been lost. The bulk of the army arrived at Ste-Marie the following day. Fortified by fresh food, they had been able to march rapidly down the valley using a rough road connecting the villages. Ste-Marie was large enough to house the men under roofs and provide warm fireplaces for the first time since they had left Newburyport so long ago. This was a godsend. The Canadian winter had arrived. Snowy and quite cold weather were with them constantly.

Arnold established his headquarters at the Taschereau Manor, the largest and finest home in the village. He sent Major Meigs and other officers around the area to purchase boats and canoes to carry an estimated seventy-five sick men down the Chaudière to the St. Lawrence. The boats later would be used to cross the river. Stragglers coming down the river continued to collect in the village. Arnold worked diligently with his

Approximately seven miles beyond St-Martin, watch for a high bridge over a ravine. Look to your left and catch a glimpse of the massive Grand Falls of the Chaudière. There is no good parking here, so you will have to park on the road's shoulder as best you can. If you wish to obtain a closer look, you will find a rough path that passes under the bridge and goes down the ravine to the river's edge. There are private homes along this stretch of road. They make it harder to view the huge falls. Please respect the privacy of these homes. You can view the lower portion of the falls from the bridge.

The two remaining boats in Arnold's advance party were almost lost here, but the sound of the falls warned them, and they pulled out and portaged around.

Three miles from the falls, we reach Route 173, the main highway between the U.S. border and Quebec City. We will follow this most of the way to Lévis. Turn left onto this road nord toward St-Georges.

If you are planning to stay overnight in the St-Georges area, we recommend the Auberge (Inn) Benedict Arnold. It is located about 1.5mi. south (turn right) on the east side of Route 173. In 1975 during the 200th anniversary reenactment of the expedition, one of the bateaux used was donated to the proprietor of the inn and is now on display. It is a full-service motel and offers excellent cuisine.

Auberge Benedict Arnold
18255 Boulevard Lacroix
St-Georges, Beauce
G5Y 5B8 Canada
1-800-463-5057
www.aubergeamold.qc.ca

Back on Route 173, the outskirts of St-Georges are soon reached. It is a city of nearly 25,000 people and has the usual fast-food stops and malls. There is a helpful tourist information center in the large mall on the right (east) side of Route 173. There are many good accommodations and restaurants in St-Georges. The old main street and center of town is located downhill near the river about a half mile away from Route 173.

St-Georges to Ste-Marie, 33 miles (53 km)

Continuing on Route 173, the highway rejoins the river. Note how broad the valley has become and observe the interesting land-settlement patterns. The farms extend from the high ridges all the way down to the river's edge.

Seven and a half miles north of the center of St-Georges, watch for a narrowing of the valley. On the river side of the road, stop at a signed, public turnout. Walk down a short trail to a narrow, rocky

Taschereau Manor, Ste-Marie, Quebec

falls named Chute du Diable (Devil's Falls). There is a fine picnic area here as well as delightful views of the falls and river.

From this point it is 1.8mi. to Beauceville, then ten miles farther brings us to St-Joseph-de-Beauce. The main highway bypasses the latter town's center.

Here Route 73, the valley's expressway, diverges right, and leads north to the Pierre LaPorte Bridge, the fast way to reach Quebec City. We recommend this route for the return trip, as it is faster and bypasses the valley towns. It swings well away from the river, leaving the route of the expedition.

The continuing description assumes the choice will be to proceed on the much more scenic Route 173. Be careful to distinguish between Route 73, the expressway, and Route 173, the older valley road.

From St-Joseph to the next town, Vallée-Junction, it is 5.0mi., then 8.0mi. farther to Ste-Marie. The latter was an important town to the men of the expedition. Arnold selected it as the best place to regroup, rest, and reorganize his ragged troops before making the final push to the St. Lawrence.

Today it is a truly beautiful town on the banks of the Chaudière. It has lovely homes, fine churches, and pleasant parks. We recommend a little exploration here.

As you approach the town, watch for a side road to the left, which is the old main road that hugs the river. Turn here, as it is much more scenic than continuing on Route 173, which bypasses most of the town. The Taschereau Manor, Arnold's headquarters while in Ste-Marie, is located on the main street just north of the center of town on the east (right) side of the road next to Saint Anne's Chapel. The manor has a large, white-pillared front entrance. It is used as a museum and is open to the public during the summer.

commanders to reorganize the companies into effective fighting units. Most of the men began to slowly regain their strength, but not all. Captain Dearborn, who had been sick the entire distance down the Chaudière, had to take to bed in a private house and was unable to rejoin the army for almost a month. Others were still seriously sick and weak.

The inhabitants of the valley had welcomed the men of the expedition and had been most helpful in meeting the men's needs. Arnold, heeding Washington's orders, had impressed upon his officers the need to take no action that would alienate the native French. Arnold was also careful to use hard currency to pay somewhat premium prices for the food and supplies he was able to buy. The local people themselves hated the conquering British in Quebec, and they welcomed anyone who might weaken the British hold on their country. Even the local Catholic clergy gave support to the ragged army.

Arnold, ever impatient, felt the army sufficiently reorganized by the afternoon of Nov. 6 to assemble the ten companies and march them north on the river road in a single long column. The number of soldiers that left Ste-Marie was, the author estimates, about 550 men. More than a hundred recuperated somewhere along the valley in private homes.

Five miles north of Ste-Marie, at the site of the present village of Scott, the column left the river road and turned northeast onto the road cross-country to Point Lévis, a town on the south side of the St. Lawrence immediately opposite Quebec City. The farm fields and houses ended, and the men once more entered forested country. The terrain from the Chaudière Valley to the St. Lawrence is a flat coastal plain, a welcome change for the men from the ups and downs of the valley they had just left. The Justinien Road they were following was not much better than a muddy, rutted path covered with knee-deep, fresh snow.

The men marched until almost midnight to reach the village of St-Henri on the Etchemin River. It was cold that night, and the village was too small to accommodate the army. They slept as best they could under the stars. The men built roaring campfires in an attempt to keep warm in the bitter cold. They had covered a rough twenty miles from Ste-Marie. St-Henri was ten miles from the St. Lawrence, well within the reach of the British troops in Quebec. The army had shifted from the challenge of surviving a wilderness to that of surviving a war with its nearby enemy.

The current main road to Lévis bears northeast away from the Etchemin River. Arnold did not go that way. To end up in Lévis would place them opposite the battlements and cannons of Quebec. Crossing the river there was unthinkable. He directed the army to follow the Etchemin River north, using the parallel Pavement Road. In those days, muddy roads were sometimes paved with "corduroy"—small logs, usually cedar, laid perpendicular to the line of travel to prevent wagons from becoming mired in the mud.

Arnold now proceeded warily, as his intelligence of the whereabouts and activities of the British forces was sketchy and unreliable. He sent a scouting force of twenty men north along the Etchemin River. The army edged forward that afternoon, Nov. 7, and that evening in two short marches of three miles each. It stopped to await the return of the scouting party. On the morning of Nov. 8, the army received word that the south shore of the St. Lawrence was clear of British forces, so it marched toward the river.

The men soon reached the main road paralleling the St. Lawrence River's south shore. The river over eons had cut a deep valley with 150-foot-high palisades on both sides. The region was thickly settled with large farms. Patrols were sent in both directions along the main road, but the bulk of the army followed the Mill Road down to the St. Lawrence. No opposition was found, so camps were established close to the shore of the river near Caldwell's Mill and near the mouth of the Etchemin River.

Quebec lay only three miles downriver on the opposite shore. Although the British had tried to confiscate or destroy all boats on the south shore, because of Arnold's foresight other boats and canoes were being gathered along the Lower Chaudière and brought down to the St. Lawrence. They were held in a cove three miles upriver from Caldwell's Mill.

The river was still unfrozen, and the British had two warships at Quebec at that time: the *Lizard*, a small, twenty-six-gun frigate, and the *Hunter*, a smaller sloop-of-war. In an obvious attempt to prevent the Americans from crossing, these were positioned near where the army had reached the river at the mouth of the Etchemin. On the night of Nov. 8, a small patrol boat from the *Hunter* slipped into the cove near Caldwell's Mill. An officer landed, but Arnold's alert sentries captured him. The boat was hailed and fired upon but managed to escape. The captured officer proved to be the younger brother of

Ste-Marie to Lévis, 27 miles (45 km)

After leaving the Taschereau Manor, continue along the highway next to the Chaudière. This road parallels Route 173 and rejoins it in Scott, 4.0mi. downriver. This road is the route the expedition followed. At the village of Scott, the highway leaves the Chaudière for the last time.

After rejoining Route 173 (do not confuse this with the expressway Route 73, which crosses the highway here), Route 173 soon emerges onto a plain that extends to the St. Lawrence, approximately twenty miles away. The troops at this point followed

The review of Arnold's detachment near Point Lévis
Courtesy, Library of Congress

a rutted wagon road, only somewhat better than the raw wilderness from which they had just emerged. During this part of their journey, the men marched in ankle-to knee-deep snow. The road goes through the farming communities of St-Isidore and St-Henri. The fine farms along this route are pleasing and a remembrance of how things used to be in New England.

At the village of St-Henri, the expedition turned to the north, following an old road along the Etchemin River to its mouth, where it empties into the St. Lawrence three miles above Lévis. The crossing of the river took place near that point.

As you leave the center of St. Henri, where Route 173 forks right, turn left onto a side road named Chemin des Isles. This parallels the Etchemin River closely. The expedition followed this road.

After 5.0mi., the road will gradually bear away

from the river, pass a refinery, and eventually reach a major highway, Route 132. If you turn left onto this road, you can go a short distance downhill to the St. Lawrence at the town of St-Romauld. We venture in this direction only as far as the bridge over the Etchemin River. Near this point once stood Caldwell's Mill, which was the headquarters for the army while Arnold waited for the right conditions to cross the river. The mill is long gone, with no mark. Unfortunately, there is no public access to where the Etchemin meets the St. Lawrence. Wolfe's Cove is on the north shore of the St. Lawrence directly across from this point.

This is as far in this direction as we need go. It is time to head for Lévis and Quebec, leaving the expedition's route. We will see where the army landed on the opposite shore of the river when we visit Quebec.

Turn around and follow Route 132 northeast. After 4.0mi., it will bring you into the commercial center of Lévis. Route 132 is one of Lévis's main streets. Restaurants, motels, malls, and other commercial establishments line the highway. Lévis has a population of about 40,000.

At the center of the commercial district is the intersection of Routes 132 and 173. If you are planning to stay overnight in Lévis and day-visit Quebec via the ferry, numerous motels in this area may be the best bet.

At the junction, continue straight ahead on Route 132 for a short distance. Keep in the left lane, and at the second traffic light turn left onto the Côte du Passage, an important turn. This is the main thoroughfare through Lévis, leading down to the river and ferry. Follow this through the old commercial part of Lévis approximately a mile and gradually begin a descent with the river in sight.

As you begin winding steeply down the high cliffs of the river's palisade, watch carefully for a road to the left when you see a park high on a cliff ahead. Turn left and proceed uphill. Immediately, turn right near the brow of the hill. This will lead to the Terrasse de Lévis on Rue William-Tremblay. Here is an outstanding overlook of the river and Quebec City on its high promontory directly across the St. Lawrence. King George VI dedicated the terrace in 1939. The Laurentian Mountains to the north of the city can be seen in the distance. Your camera should get a fine workout here. Some of the men of the expedition must have used this place to spy on the city's fortifications and shipping.

After leaving the Terrasse, return to the Cote du Passage and descend the steep cliffs to the river. A short distance brings you to the ferry terminal. There is plenty of parking near the terminal. A round-trip ticket on the ferry is an economical $5 Canadian per

the captain of the *Hunter*. When the ship's boat reached the *Hunter*, the captain, learning of the loss of his brother, must have been livid, as the ship's guns fired on the area around the mill. No one was hurt, but the first shots of the war in this part of Canada had been fired.

During the next several days, stragglers from the rear came overland from Ste-Marie to join the troops around Caldwell's Mill. Arnold and his officers worked feverishly to collect provisions and additional boats. They were seriously short of gunpowder. The army was mustered and paraded every day to reestablish its edge. They were a sorry-looking lot. Many wore clothes in tatters. Many were without shoes, warm clothes, or hats. Some had fashioned crude animal hides into moccasins to protect their feet. The hatless used cloth kerchiefs to protect their head and ears. Some had no firearms, their muskets lying on the bottom of a river or bog somewhere on the route they had traveled. But they were hard, lean, and ready to fight. They had proven their courage and determination by surviving the severest of wilderness gauntlets. Still, the French population must have wondered who these strange scarecrows were and if they would have any chance at all against the powerful and polished British army.

Arnold ordered an army-wide inventory of usable gunpowder and shot. He was surprised to learn that the men had only an average of five rounds each. This obviously was not nearly enough to successfully attack a flock of birds, let alone a fortified city.

Patrols were sent out along the river to guard against any surprise sorties from the city. Arnold wrote reports to both Washington and Montgomery informing them of the condition of his army and the disposition of the enemy. Arnold learned that General Montgomery had just captured an undefended Montreal much farther up the St. Lawrence. Meanwhile, the men busily prepared for the river crossing. They constructed scaling ladders and grapples in anticipation of storming the city's walls. However, a strong wind whipped up whitecaps, making a crossing in small boats out of the question at that time.

During the afternoon of Nov. 13, five days after reaching the river, Colonel Arnold called a council of war with his company commanders at his headquarters near Caldwell's Mill. The decision was made to cross that night. The boats hidden at the mouth of the Chaudière three miles upriver were sent for. The commanders went off to their respective companies to prepare the men. This would be a dangerous crossing. The river was over a half-mile wide at this point, with powerful currents, and there were the two British warships at station. The ships had small guard boats patrolling between them. The small size and number of the American boats would require them to run the gauntlet several times to get everybody across.

The loading of the boats and canoes began in the darkness around nine o'clock. Luckily, it was a moonless night. No lights were used to guide the flotilla of small boats. Arnold went over with the first load, passing near one of the British warships. He aimed his men for Wolfe's Cove on the north shore, the same landing spot that had been used during the British landing in 1759. That landing had led to the decisive battle on the Plains of Abraham that resulted in the British conquest of Quebec and the end of French rule in Canada. Arnold intended to use the same route from the river up to the plains as that taken by the British General Wolfe.

His men greased their oarlocks and remain absolutely quiet in order to ease by the anchored British ships and patrol boats. The fleet of small boats became scattered in the dark, so they did not all land at the same spot. After dropping off the first load, the boats returned across the dark river for another. Meanwhile, the officers worked rapidly to collect the scattered men on the north shore into a fighting unit. Amazingly, the second and third trips were again made without detection.

The boat carrying Lieutenant Church and a few others was swamped, the men losing some of their fire-arms. When they reached the north shore, they built a fire in an abandoned house to warm themselves. Enough light escaped from the house to attract the attention of a passing British patrol barge. As the barge approached, the overanxious colonials hailed it and ordered it ashore. The British instead turned and rowed for their lives. The men on shore fired on them. The resulting cries indicated that some balls had found their mark, but the barge escaped downriver to Quebec to spread the alarm.

It was now four o'clock and the cover of darkness nearly gone. The moon rose, making any further crossings that night too dangerous. The three trips completed had transported about five hundred men, a good night's work. Arnold called off any further ferrying, assembled his troops, and marched them up the steep slope to reach the Plains of Abraham, just as had General Wolfe and his redcoats sixteen years earlier. The expedition had reached its long-sought goal, the almost mythical city of Quebec. Now to take it!

person (as of 2002). You can take your car across, if you wish. The parking in Quebec's narrow streets is brutal, and you don't really need a car. Most of the city's key sites are compactly situated in the historic Lower and Upper Towns. And almost all of the city's features are better seen on foot.

After two months of one of the toughest military expeditions in history, the ragged army had reached its objective. And you have reached yours as well!

"This day with much exertion we got forward to Hell Gate Falls [Grand Falls of the Chaudière], which are of astonishing heigh and exhibit an awful appearance."
—Abner Stocking

". . . taking up some raw-hides, that lay for several Days in the bottom of their boats, intended for to make them shoes or moccasins of in case of necessity , which they did not then look into so much as they did their own preservation, and chopping them to pieces, singeing first the hair, afterwards boiling them and living on the juice or liquid that they soak'd from it for a considerable time."
—Capt. Thayer's journal

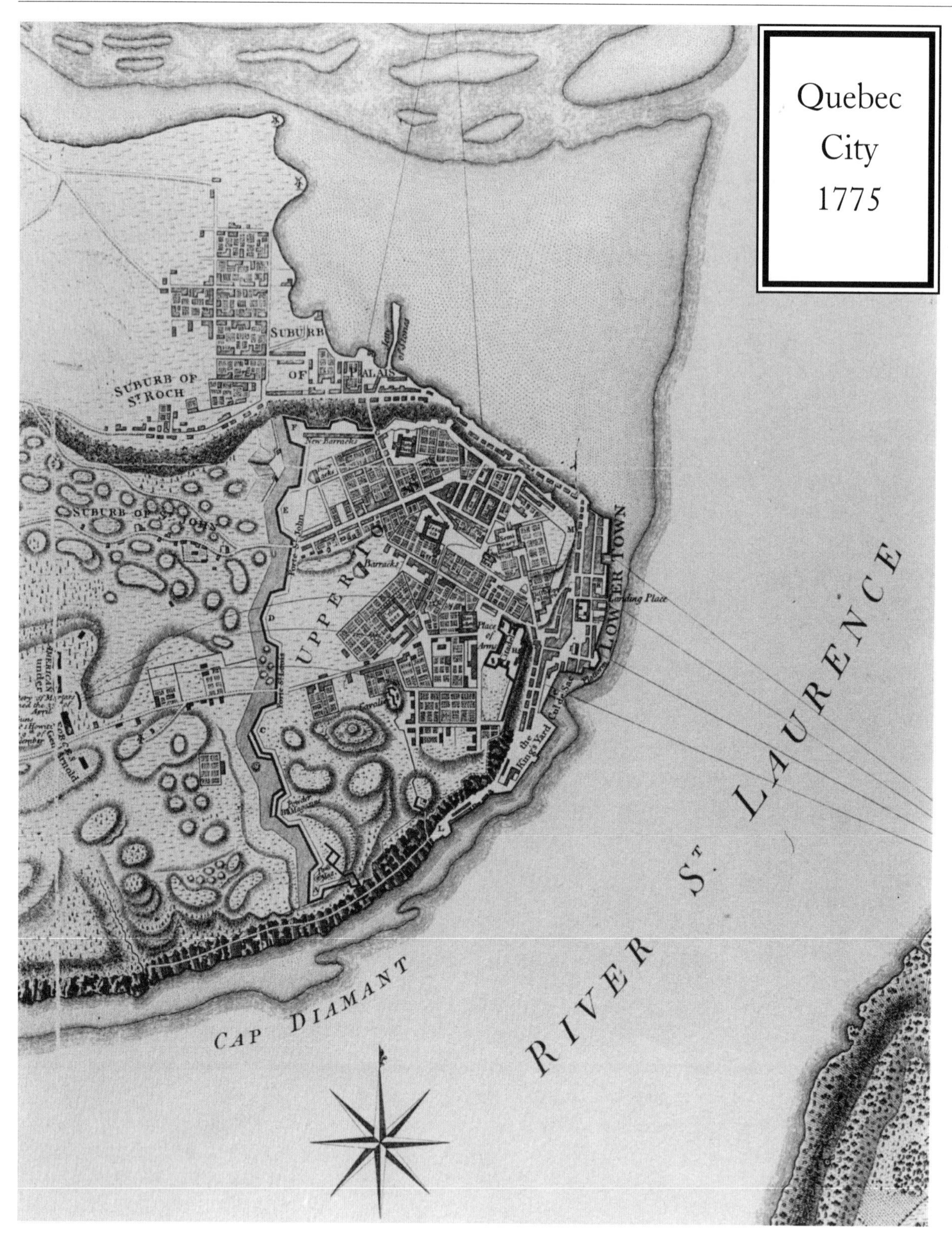

A. Bastion of Cap Daimant
B. Bastion of La Glaciere
C. Bastion of St. Louis
D. Bastion of St. Ursula
E. Bastion of St. John
F. Bastion of La Potasse
G. Porte De Palais, Col. Arnold was wounded near this point
H. Governor's House
I. Lower Town Church
K. Nuns of the Congregation
L. The place where General Montgomery began his attack
M. Le Sant du Matelot, at the second barrier

Old map and key courtesy of La Société historique de Québec.

Chapter Fourteen

Before Fortress Quebec

On the morning of Nov. 14, the Expedition to Quebec, having made three perilous trips across the half-mile-wide St. Lawrence, began to make war. Colonel Arnold organized his more than 400 soldiers and marched from Wolfe's Cove up the steep, rough road to the Plains of Abraham. The men covered the half-mile in quick order, arriving on the plains about daybreak and then spread out, occupying several farm buildings. To the east lay open, snow-covered fields all the way to the stone and earth walls of the fortified city. The officers studied the formidable fortress, noting with disappointment that the two western gates were closed. Sentries could be seen moving along the top of the walls. Church spires and other tall buildings in the Upper Town could be seen beyond the walls. Undoubtedly, heavy cannons were aimed their way from the walls' embrasures.

The army moved forward over the rolling farm fields to within half a mile of the fortress. These snow-covered fields gave little cover from cannon fire. To the right were the sheer cliffs of Cap Diamant, dropping two hundred feet to the river. To the left were woods and farms on a slope of a hill that crested and overlooked the St. Charles River Valley to the north. At the foot of this hill and near the St. Charles River was the small suburb of St-Roch, just outside the walls.

Quebec City was perched on a high, rocky point forming a triangle with the St. Lawrence and St. Charles Rivers on two sides. The third, westerly side was the land upon which the American army now stood. Samuel de Champlain had chosen New France's capital very well. Below the cliffs at river level was a narrow strip of land wrapped around the point. Located upon this strip was the city's seaport, known as the Lower Town. The Lower Town was outside the protective walls of the fortified Upper Town, but it also had batteries with large-caliber cannons that faced toward the river. Barricades were under construction on both sides of the Lower Town. Quebec was the most heavily fortified city in North America, but it was still vulnerable because it had a relatively small garrison at that time.

Quebec had been under siege five times before. In 1759, a huge army of more than 9,000 of the best troops the British could muster had been sent westward into the

Quebec City

Quebec is a wonderful place to end our journey retracing the footsteps of the 1775 Expedition to Quebec. The city oozes history at every step. So much of American history is closely related to events that occurred here. Founded in the early 1600s by Samuel de Champlain, Quebec was the capital and gateway for all of Canada until supplanted in the late 1800s by Montreal and Ottawa. Much of the exploration of North America began here. The long, brutal French and Indian Wars, which so influenced colonial history, ended here in a decisive battle on the Plains of Abraham in 1759. The resulting peace treaty signed in 1763 ceded all of Canada to the victorious British, ending a century of French rule. However, the French language and culture have been proudly retained over many generations and are very much in evidence during a visit to the city.

Quebec City remains the center of French culture in North America. Today, it is a modern city of 600,000 mostly French-speaking citizens (more than 90 percent) who treasure their past but build for the future. The city's citizens have been able to showcase its rich history and culture better than any other in North America.

Quebec City from Lévis

The city's center is perched on the precipitous 200-foot-high cliffs of Cap Diamant, which overlooks the St. Lawrence River. These cliffs divided the original, old city into the Upper Town and the Lower Town, the latter located at the base of the cliffs at the river's edge. An extensive fortified wall, with six main gates, encloses the Upper Town. The castle-like Château Frontenac, the city's premier hotel and meeting place, dominates the Upper Town. A massive fort called the Citadel was constructed adjacent to the Upper Town during the 1830s to further strengthen the city's fortifications.

The Lower Town was and is the city's seaport

and commercial district. It was historically the entry point for goods and people traveling into Canada's interior as well as the chief export point for the country. It has been masterfully restored to much of its former self, with its cobblestone streets and seventeenth-century stone buildings preserving the original French architecture. There are many fine specialty shops with a wide variety of goods from all over the world located here. A long staircase, the Escalier du Casse-cou ("Break Your Neck Stairway"), and the Côte de la Montagne, a winding street, connect the Upper and Lower Towns. Also available between the two towns is the unique and popular cable-car lift, called the Funiculaire.

The Plains of Abraham are adjacent to the Upper Town and are now a combined national monument and beautiful urban park named the National Battlefields Park. It is perched between the cliffs of Cap Diamant and the Provincial Parliament buildings to the north. Several museums and numerous historical sites are located on or near the plains. The park's breathtaking location along the cliffs overlooking the river and the obvious care taken to preserve the grounds combine to make the Plains of Abraham one of the world's finest urban parks.

Surrounding the historic Upper and Lower Towns is a much larger modern city stretching along the St. Lawrence and inland for miles. The city has the usual four-lane throughways, malls, commercial districts, a modern international airport, and residential areas that are part of any modern city.

We suggest that you plan to spend a minimum of three days to begin savoring what the city offers. Before you arrive, it would be wise to contact the city tourist bureau for more detailed and up-to-date information to plan your visit. Contact:

Greater Quebec Area Tourism and Convention Bureau
835, Avenue Wilfrid-Laurier,
Quebec, Canada GIR 2L3
(418) 649-2608
www.quebecregion.com
Email: bit@cuq.qc.ca

There is so much to see that you will have to pick and choose from a wide variety of possible itineraries. The cost of hotel accommodations and restaurants varies greatly with the season, similar to any modern city. Because of the favorable exchange rate for Americans, however, Quebec seems a bargain. American dollars are readily accepted everywhere, but the best exchange rates are obtained in Quebec banks or money exchanges. There is an international money exchange at the information bureau just across the square from the Château

mouth of the St. Lawrence, transported by a powerful fleet of heavy warships. After this army landed on the Isle of Orleans, just downriver from the city, a siege commenced. The highly experienced and competent General Montcalm commanded the French troops in the city. General James Wolfe commanded the British army. Admiral Sir John McKenzie commanded the British fleet. After months of intensive siege, during which several bloody battles were fought east of the city and during which the British fleet bombarded Quebec with more than 40,000 cannon balls and nearly 10,000 rockets, French possession of the city remained solid. There seemed to be a stalemate.

The decisive element was the absolute British control of the sea approaches and the river. In a daring and dangerous night maneuver, British transports clandestinely sailed up the river under the powerful cannons of the city, undetected, to a point west of Quebec near what became known as Wolfe's Cove. General Wolfe moved 4,000 troops up a narrow ravine onto the Plains of Abraham. General Montcalm immediately realized that the city was now surrounded. He decided to risk all in a frontal assault on the plains, rank to rank. In a little over an hour, the proud French army was defeated. The remains of the French army retreated behind the city walls. Both commanders had been wounded, and both soon died. Knowing that it was just a matter of time before heavy cannons and mortars would be mounted on the plains and the city demolished, the French surrendered. Four years later, all of Canada was ceded to England. Canada had become a part of the British Empire mainly because of the fall of Quebec.

Washington, Arnold, and the other planners of the American invasion of Canada had hoped the American invasion could exploit the French Catholic population's latent hatred of the British, igniting an expansion of the colonial rebellion. If this occurred, it would be a serious blow to the British. However, the French reception of the small, ragged American army in the Chaudière Valley had been friendly, but cool. Only a few of the inhabitants joined the American cause. Maybe they were not convinced that such a small, scruffy force could beat the most powerful military power in the world. French support outside and inside the walls of Quebec never materialized to a degree that would influence the invasion's outcome.

On the Plains of Abraham, Arnold's small army cautiously approached the city's walls. They were detected, and cannons roared. The men ducked behind the rolling hills, and the cannon balls plowed harmlessly into the snowy ground. The army could not return fire because the British were well beyond musket range, even out of range of Morgan's long-reaching rifles. The men gave three cheers to taunt the British and moved back out of cannon range. Arnold was in a quandary. His small force of close to 500 men was not large enough to mount an immediate attack on a city as well fortified as Quebec. The gates were closed and the walls manned.

Governor Guy Carleton, an able military leader, commanded all the British forces in Canada. He had been in Montreal, then only a small frontier town, directing military operations against the American force under General Montgomery, who was advancing through the Champlain Valley. Upon learning of Arnold's approach down the Chaudière, Carleton gathered up all troops that could be crammed into several small ships available and sailed hurriedly down the St. Lawrence to his bastion in Quebec. He had arrived at Quebec with his troops only three days before the expedition crossed the river. Carleton had been overjoyed when a contingent of 150 soldiers from Newfoundland had come upriver to reinforce Quebec. He energetically pressed any reluctant city dwellers, sometimes at the point of a bayonet, to help defend the city. Those who would not help or were under suspicion of being American sympathizers were sent to the Isle of Orleans or outside the city walls.

Arnold had no cannon or mortars to lay an active military siege to the city. Nor did the Americans control the river and sea approaches to it, as had the British navy when Wolfe had taken Quebec. The Americans had no navy at all. Worst, Arnold's small army, which was really no more than a single regiment, had a minuscule five rounds for each musket, a small fraction of what was needed to properly arm his men. The best that could be done was to threaten and harass its occupants. They were barely able to cut off food, other supplies, and communications coming into the city—hardly an effective siege.

During the next several days, the army probed around the walls, occasionally drawing cannon and musket fire from the defenders. Arnold established temporary headquarters in the small village of Sillery, near Wolfe's Cove. The rest of the men still on the south shore of the river were gradually ferried over. As soon as they were able, the men who were recovering in the Chaudière

Governor (later Sir) Guy Carleton
Courtesy, Musée du Québec

Frontenac. Gasoline, sold in Canada by the liter, is expensive. On certain items, there are both provincial and federal sales taxes. French is the predominant language, but most inhabitants who deal with the public are bilingual, so you should have little trouble communicating.

Relevant Venues to Visit

The American attack on Quebec in 1775-76 left few indelible marks upon the city. The Americans were able to muster only a few light mortars and cannons for their bombardment, causing minimal damage to buildings. In comparison, during the siege of 1759 the British navy, with more than forty ships, lobbed an estimated 40,000 canon balls and nearly 10,000 rockets into the city, mainly into the Lower Town! As one might imagine, this bombardment caused great damage and loss of life.

The armies on both sides during the 1775 American siege were also considerably smaller, involving an estimated 1,200 men on the American side and about 1,500 within the city. Consequently, the historically minded visitor will hear and see much more of the capture of Quebec in 1759 than of the American attack sixteen years later. There are only three small bronze plaques that mark the sites of the final battle for the city on the night of December 31, 1775.

Below are listed six recommended venues that will provide the best understanding of what the American army was up against when it arrived at the city's gates on November 14, 1775. We recommend that you balance these with the many other marvelous places to visit in and around the city. A steady diet of history can become tedious, though, even for the most fanatical history buffs. If you have children in tow, careful planning will have to be considered to avoid the "Do we have to go there!" downer.

Aspen Point (Point-aux-Trembles), where Montgomery joined Arnold. Courtesy, Library of Congress.

1. The wall walk

Quebec's survival for more than two centuries depended upon its massive walls and fortifications. Most of these walls are still intact, although much of the outer walls, the fortifications, and the six gates have been rebuilt and strengthened since 1775. The St. Louis and St. Jean Gates are much different in appearance from those that blocked the American army.

We suggest that you select this walk first. It will provide an overview of the city. This walk is approximately three miles in a loop around the outer walls and fortifications enclosing the Upper Town. Although we could begin the walk at any point, the most convenient place to begin and end is at the

Valley came to rejoin their companies, although Captain Dearborn and others were still very sick and recuperating in private homes. Arnold had left Captain Hanchet and sixty men on the Lévis side of the river to guard against possible British sorties in that area. Temporary quarters for the soldiers were found in private homes nearby and in a nunnery in St-Roch, north of the city.

It snowed off and on almost every day, and the temperature became colder as the Canadian winter descended in earnest. The poor condition of the men's clothes and equipment hindered their ability to conduct military operations in the worsening winter weather. The river had not yet frozen, but it was icing out farther from the shore each day. After five days, it became obvious that an immediate attack was not possible. There was a need to consolidate and better organize operations against the city from a safe place, free from fear of enemy sorties. Arnold moved his headquarters and some of his men upriver to a small village at Point-aux-Trembles, eight leagues (a league is three statute miles) from the city. This was done on Nov. 19. Arnold continued to direct harassing activities while collecting much needed supplies, especially powder and lead.

Meanwhile, in Montreal, General Montgomery gathered forces and supplies to march and join the siege. The British were active as well, reinforcing the city's fortifications and sending out for help. The *Hunter* sloop-of-war and three smaller ships worked upriver near Point-aux-Trembles to harass the Americans and to try to deny them the use of the river. The Americans, having no cannon at all, could only swear and grit their teeth while the ships sailed by, untouchable.

On Dec. 1, General Montgomery arrived at Point-aux-Trembles to the joy of Arnold's troops. He had brought much-needed winter clothing, shoes, food, powder, and even light artillery to be used against the city. Small ships brought most of these supplies. He also brought about 300 much-needed New York troops to reinforce the army. General Montgomery, as senior officer, assumed command, and with Arnold's help he set to the task of capturing Quebec.

With some light canons and mortars, they could now lay at least a limited siege against the city. A mortar battery was constructed at St-Roch and immediately began to lob balls into the city. A second battery of cannons was constructed on the plains to cover the two west-facing St. Louis and St. John (Jean) Gates. As these were small-caliber cannons, the effect was not as great as was hoped. The British fired back, also with little effect, as the American mortars had been placed behind a small hill, keeping them out of sight of the city's defenders. Much of the firing was done at night to further mask positions and make return fire more difficult.

Morgan's men with their long-distance rifles were sent to St-Roch as snipers to shoot any head that appeared above the walls. They set up shop in several buildings near the Palace Gate. Every day they were able to cause considerable harm to the wall's defenders. To counter this, several cannons were brought to bear on the buildings from which Morgan's men were positioned, and the cannon balls started to batter the walls to pieces. Morgan's men had to make a retreat out of range of the cannon fire.

In the meantime, Montgomery and Arnold devised a plan of attack within the capability of the limited men and arms at their disposal. During December, the American army grew to about 1,200 men, as more troops came downriver from Montreal. Governor Carleton had about 1,500 men under arms inside the walls. Military strategy of the day held that to successfully assault a fortified city, a five-to-one ratio was required, including a heavy advantage of artillery. A frontal assault was ruled out. So Montgomery decided to try a surprise attack at night into the less heavily defended Lower Town. A two-pronged attack on both sides of the Lower Town was planned to cut off Quebec's access to the river and reinforcements by sea. If successful, it would increase the chances of persuading the city's defenders to surrender, it was believed. The army prepared for the attack, although the details were kept secret from the soldiers. On Dec. 28, an attack was almost put in motion, but Montgomery called it back at the last moment because the weather cleared, eliminating the cover the men needed to mask their attack. However, the men remained on alert, as they knew that more bad weather was on the way.

prominent statue of Samuel de Champlain next to the Château Frontenac.

La Société historique de Québec, 72, Côte de la Montagne, (418) 692-0556, has published an excellent brochure, entitled American Invasion, 1775-1776, that describes a self-guided walking tour. The tour within the brochure includes a loop through the Lower Town that is not the route described here. The sites suggested in the Lower Town are only the two bronze plaques marking the locations of the First and Second Barricades. We recommend that you obtain this brochure to help you identify other possible sites around the city that you may wish to visit. The society's office is conveniently located halfway up the street that leads from the Lower to the Upper Town.

If a self-guided tour is not your preference, there are guided tours (for a fee, of course) that originate at the tourist information office, previously mentioned, which is located across the square from the Château in the Upper Town. It is well marked, and you can't miss it. To help you navigate through the narrow, sometimes confusing streets, obtain a

View of the Lower Town and the St. Lawrence River

street map of the Upper Town at this tourist office before you begin.

Beginning our walk at the Champlain statue next to the Château Frontenac, go southwest along the Dufferin Terrace. Take advantage of the magnificent views out over the St. Lawrence below. As you walk along the terrace, to the left of the Château you will see a small park, the Jardin des Gouverneurs. Here is located a large obelisk dedicated to the two commanding generals, James Wolfe and the Marquis de Montcalm, who both died in the British-French battle on the Plains of Abraham in 1759.

Cross the park to its west side and pick up the Avenue Sainte-Geneviève westward. Bear right onto the Avenue Saint-Denis for a block. When you reach Rue Saint-Louis (St. Louis Street), turn left toward the Porte Saint-Louis (St. Louis Gate) to reach the beginning of the walled fortifications.

Before you begin to follow these walls, take a turn left onto the Côte de la Citadelle for about a hundred yards. Here is a memorial plaque marking the point where General Montgomery and his two key officers were buried a few days after the attack. In 1818, his remains were exhumed and reburied adjacent to St. Paul's Cathedral in New York.

Return to the Porte Saint-Louis. From this point, pick your own way along the walls northward. There are several stairways that lead to the top of the walls where redoubts are located, bristling with large-caliber eighteenth-century cannons. The stone fortifications here are quite remarkable. The Plains of Abraham are seen off to the west. A mile or so west along the edge of the plains is the point where the men of the expedition first emerged from the river valley on November 14, 1775. Pass the Porte Kent on Dauphine Street as you continue along the massive walls. In a short distance, reach the important Porte Saint-Jean.

Just outside the walls is a small park, the Place d'Youville. During the attack of December 31, 1775, Capt. James Livingston led a diversionary attack on this gate from the shelter of several houses outside the walls. The attack was short-lived and did not fool the garrison into thinking the main attack would be here, as was intended.

From the Porte Saint-Jean proceed along the wall to the Parc-de-l'Artillerie located in the Redoute Dauphine. This is a major stop along our walk. See the separate section below describing this key place.

After leaving the Parc-de-l'Artillerie, work your way north along Carleton and de l'Arsenal Streets, which will bring you out onto a broad intersection at the top of a steep hill. Here was located the Porte du Palais (Palace Gate). All signs of it have long been demolished. It is now a major entrance to the city. This gate played an important role during the battle. When Governor Carleton realized the main attack was focused on the Lower Town, he shrewdly ordered a large body of soldiers to sally down the hill to attack the rear of the American troops. At the bottom, they encountered the late-arriving Captain Henry Dearborn's company and captured the entire lot. Not only did this deprive the Americans of these badly needed reinforcements, it put a British force at the Americans' rear and cut off their route of withdrawal.

From the site of the Palace Gate, continue along the top of the walls following des Ramparts Street. Occasionally, look down into the streets of the Lower Town directly below. Arnold's troops, then being led by Captain Daniel Morgan, were exposed to deadly fire from all along this part of the walls. Watch for a side lane coming in on the right, Hamel Street. Directly below this point in the Lower Town was the

The attack at midnight in a snowstorm
Courtesy, Library of Congress

Place Royale and Notre-Dame-des-Victoires church, Lower Town, Quebec, where Arnold's and Montgomery's forces were to meet

The Attack on Quebec and Its Aftermath

On the afternoon of Dec. 31, 1775, General Montgomery and his officers decided to attack. It was snowing hard outside, just the kind of cover they would need to conceal their soldiers' approach to the Lower Town, where the main attack would take place. Montgomery would lead his New York troops along the St. Lawrence below the cliffs of Cap Diamant. Here, the men would follow the narrow strip of land between the river and the towering cliffs to reach the southwest side of the Lower Town. This contingent would have about 400 men.

Arnold and his 600 men would pass through the suburb of St-Roch, dangerously close to the walls of the fortress, to attack the north side of the Lower Town. A third, smaller group under Captain Livingston was to make a feint at the west side of the wall at or near the St. John Gate, even trying to set fire to the gate in order to draw the defenders away from the two main points of attack.

It was a sound plan, but it had a weakness. The three contingents would be out of communication with each other. Coordination and timing of the initial attack was crucial to success. Since events of a battle require adaptation and change, especially one conducted in the dark and in the confusion of a snowstorm, coordination was crucial. In this case, it was difficult if not impossible. This inability to communicate proved to be the decisive issue of the battle. There were other weaknesses, as we shall see.

At 4 p.m., orders for the attack were issued to each company. Morgan's rifle company would lead Arnold's column, as usual. Dearborn's company was to be second, though, unfortunately, it was billeted some distance away on the other side of the St. Charles River, and it would be late arriving for the battle. Arnold ordered that each of his men wear sprigs of hemlock in their hats to distinguish them from the enemy.

Near midnight, Arnold's force worked silently through the suburb of St-Roch under cover of the heavy snowstorm. Close by but invisible in the darkness and heavy, blowing snow were the cliffs and walls of the Upper Town. To their left were the mud flats of the St.

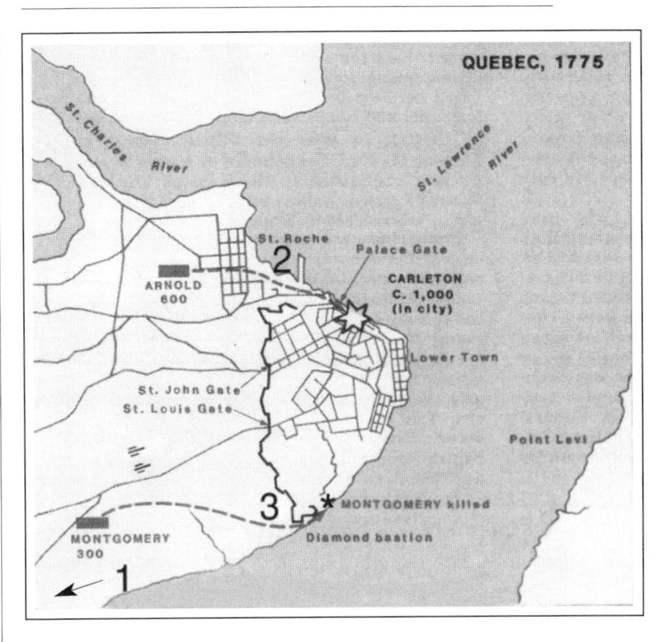

1. To Wolfe's Cove, where the expedition landed on Nov. 13.
2. The suburb of St. Roch, through which Arnold's column of approximately 500 men passed on their attack of the Lower Town. The large star indicates the location of the First Barricade.
3. The route of General Montgomery's attack with 300 New York troops eastward along the base of the cliffs of Cap Daimant into the Lower Town. He and two of his chief aides were killed instantly by a cannon blast of grape shot.

Courtesy, *Encyclopedia of the American Revolution*

site of the First Barricade, which the men of the expedition attacked and successfully captured. All along the walls at this point are batteries of cannons to protect the city.

Beyond this point, des Ramparts Street and the walls swing more southerly. Watch for another side street coming in from the right, named de l'Université. Directly below this point in the Lower Town was the location of the Second Barricade, where Morgan and the soldiers were stopped. Unable to overcome this barrier, receiving fire from the walls above, and with British troops closing in from the rear, Morgan and almost 400 American soldiers surrendered in the morning as the cover of darkness faded.

Continue along the wall as the St. Lawrence comes into sight. The cannons facing the river here are huge. Cross a small park, the Parc Montmorency, to the last gate, the Porte Prescott, which passes over Côte de la Montagne, the main street leading up from the Lower Town. Cross the top of the gate and reach a steep staircase. This leads a short distance up to the plaza next to the Champlain Statue, thus completing the loop and the walk. You have accomplished one of the most historic walks in North America.

2. Parc-de-l'Artillerie (Artillery Park)
2, rue d'Auteuil
C.P. 2474, Terminus Postal
Quebec, Canada G1K 7R3
(418) 648-4205
www.parcscanada.risq.qc.ca/artillerie/

This park is located next to the Saint Jean Gate on Rue St-Jean. It is the old military barracks and armory for both the French and later the British military forces stationed in Quebec. It consists of four buildings containing great historical artifacts, cannons, mortars, and every type of arms manufactured and stored here during almost three centuries of use. After the American attack on Quebec, many of the prisoners were locked up within the lower floor of the main barracks building. As you tour the facility, sit down in some of these sparse, stone dungeons and you may hear the low voices of the American captives plotting to escape. Some did! It is well worth the visit. It is open daily during the summer and for limited hours in the spring and fall. An admission is charged. A visit can often be combined with the wall walk.

3. La Citadelle (The Citadel)
Côte de la Citadelle
C.P. 6020, Succursale Haute-Ville
Quebec, Canada G1R 4V7
(418) 694-2815
www.qbc.clic.net/-citadel

The Citadel is a massive fort built between the Upper Town and the Plains of Abraham battlefield. In 1775, this almost impregnable fortress was not yet built. It was constructed in the 1830s, strengthening the city's defenses to perceived threats from an expansionist United States. At that time, there also was strife between the British and the French separatists agitating to throw off the British yoke and establish their own French nation.

The fort is only partially visible from the outside. It has many underground passages leading to hidden batteries all along Cap Diamant, even under the present Dufferin Terrace. What you can view represents the final evolution in fort-building design in the nineteenth century. The star-shaped bastions with internal moats on all sides made the fort virtually unassailable by the military technology of that period.

The one public access is through the narrow Dalhousie Gate, which is reached from the Côte de la Citadelle, a short distance from the Porte Saint-Louis. Since 1920, the Citadel has been home to the famous Canadian Royal 22nd Regiment. As it is an active military establishment, the fort is only visited by guided tours. The "changing of the guard" occurs daily at 10 a.m., weather permitting. There is also a

Charles River, which were also invisible in the darkness. The men moved as silently as possible in the deep snow, passing darkened houses. The falling snow and the darkness made the men unsure of where they were. To show a light would destroy the element of surprise. The pickets on the walls above would have detected them and given the alarm.

The way ahead between the cliff and the river began to narrow like a funnel. Arnold's men passed by the first houses of the Lower Town and slowly worked their way down a narrow street. The troops had mounted a six-pound brass cannon on a sled, but hauling this heavy piece in the new snow proved difficult and slowed the advance. The rest of the column could not wait for the gun and continued ahead. The snow came down so hard that many of the men wrapped the flintlock firing mechanisms in cloth in an attempt to keep their powder dry.

Without being detected, the silent men passed the road leading steeply uphill to the Palace Gate. A short distance beyond, they approached the first barrier, a makeshift wall thrown across the street from house to house. They were finally challenged in the dark and snow. In response, the lead men opened fire toward the dark wall. The defenders fired two cannons that were mounted through ports in the wall. Morgan's company, closely followed by the rest, pressed forward. The defending fire increased. The roar of cannon and rattle of muskets from the barrier ahead joined intense spits of flame from the musket-armed pickets manning the walls of the Upper Town.

Colonel Arnold, in the lead, was soon knocked to the snowy ground by a musket ball that went through his upper leg, shattering the bone. Several men picked him up. With pained voice, he urged his men forward toward the barrier. The two men supporting him then carried their wounded commander to the rear. This was a great blow, as his inspiring leadership was lost to the attackers.

Morgan's men were able to work their way around to the rear of the barrier. Several well-placed volleys into the rear of the crowded British defenders forced them to surrender. The rest of the Americans poured over the first barrier and pressed forward along the narrow street, which was lined with two- or three-story houses. Only the few soldiers in the front ranks could shoot, but the enemy could concentrate a devastating fire into the advancing, close-packed Americans. In the darkness, several side streets confused the Americans about the route to be taken. Fire from the defenders in front of them was supplemented with sporadic musket fire from dark windows in the houses lining the street and from the walls above. Church bells in the Upper Town began ringing the alarm, adding to the din.

Several hundred yards farther along the main street, the attackers encountered a second, more formidable barrier. More cannons fired into the approaching attackers, mowing down the lead ranks with grape shot. Men all along the column were dropping from the increasing gunfire from the walls of the Upper Town. Several key company captains were wounded or killed. As the advance bogged down before the continuous fire, many Americans tried to use houses as protection. Morgan, the lead officer after Arnold had been reluctantly carried off, could not find any way around the barrier. The defensive fire steadily increased as defenders from all parts of the city rushed to stop the Americans. Where was Montgomery's force that was supposed to attack the British rear from the other direction?

General Montgomery had led his troops in darkness along the shore of the St. Lawrence under the cliffs of Cap Diamant. Darkness and heavy snow slowed their advance, as had happened with Arnold's men. Montgomery's force quickly cut through two unguarded wooden barriers. About a half a mile from the Lower

retreat at 7 p.m., Tuesday-Thursday-Saturday-Sunday, weather permitting, during July and August. Guided tours are available in both English and French. Allow at least two hours for the tour. Check the website for current schedules.

4. Parc des champs-de-bataille (Battlefields National Park)

The park is a part of the Plains of Abraham, west of the Upper Town and the Citadel. The plains are the site of the decisive battle in 1759 between the French and British. The area is now a 250-acre park along the edge of Cap Diamant, with magnificent views overlooking the St. Lawrence, 200 feet below. Allow half a day or more just to begin to sample the park.

The best place to start is the reception center, which is called the Discovery Pavilion. It will give you an excellent overview of the park and how to get around. It is located several hundred yards northwest of the entrance to the Citadel and not far from the Porte St.-Louis. It is open daily during the summer season from 8:30 a.m. to 7:30 p.m.

The Discovery Pavilion
835, avenue Wilfrid-Laurier
Quebec, Canada
(418) 648-4071
www.ccbn-nbc.gc.ca

Withstanding the attack of Arnold's men at the second barrier. Courtesy, Library of Congress.

On the night of Nov. 13-14, 1775, two months after leaving Cambridge, Arnold was able to sneak more than 400 soldiers in small boats and canoes across the half-mile-wide river between two anchored British warships. In the early morning, the expedition's men climbed steeply onto the Plains of Abraham, repeating the feat accomplished by General Wolfe and his 4,000 troops.

The first shots of the American attack were fired here. However, the gates of the city were closed, and the walls were manned. The men moved about the plains that day, just out of cannon range, then retired to the west, upriver, to await the arrival of General Montgomery and reinforcements.

In addition to touring the plains on your own, there are guided tour buses originating at the pavilion. Also available at the pavilion are audio-tour headphones.

Part of a dungeon in which the expedition's men were imprisoned in the winter of 1776 at the Redoute Dauphine

4. The Battlefields Park Interpretation Center and the Musée du Québec

This wonderful facility is really two in one, both located farther west in the park. It consists of the Battlefields Park Interpretation Center and the connected, much larger Musée (Museum) du Québec. Both are well worth visiting. The interpretation center has been converted from the old Quebec jail. It emphasizes the history of the city and the various battles that have taken place in and around it over several centuries. It has a fine audio guide through the many exhibits. For information, call (418) 648-4071.

The connected Musée du Québec is a large national museum consisting of three buildings. Its main building has twelve galleries displaying both modern and historic works of art. It has more than 18,000 art objects and paintings. It is an extraordinarily fine museum. For more information, contact:

Town, his troops came upon a group of houses and a fortified barrier looming in the darkness ahead. The general turned to his men and exhorted them to charge the barrier. The defenders heard the charge, touched off one of the cannons, and then ran in fear back toward the Lower Town. This left the fortification undefended, but terrible damage had been done with that one lucky cannon blast.

Montgomery and his two chief officers lay dead in the snow, chopped down by the grape shot from the cannon. Captain Campbell, next in command, was unaware that the barrier had been left undefended. He stood stunned by the horrible sight of his general lying dead in the snow. The door to the Lower Town was wide open, and they could have walked in, virtually unopposed, but Campbell only felt the horror of seeing his commander dead. Not knowing what to do, confused about where he was, and most likely overwhelmed by the responsibility suddenly thrust upon him, Campbell called for a retreat. It was revealing that he did not even take time to order the removal of the body of the general and the other officers, leaving them in the snow for the British to recover the next day. Captain Campbell heard no objection from the remaining officers or men. The loss of the general had shocked them all. The entire column headed rapidly back the way it had come, leaving Arnold's attack to whatever fate might befall it.

Because this half of the attack had been abandoned, the city's defenders soon realized that the main thrust was by Arnold's column, which was stalled in the narrow streets of the Lower Town. Many British defenders rushed to the second barrier and concentrated their fire at the soldiers led by Morgan. Musket fire became so intense that it was sure death to climb a scaling ladder and stick one's head above the twelve-foot-high barrier.

Another serious matter had been overlooked in planning the attack and now sealed the outcome of the battle. The Palace Gate, having been easily passed early in the attack, was now in the column's rear. No force had been detailed to watch the gate with orders to prevent a sortie from it. That is exactly what happened. In the gray of the approaching dawn, British troops sallied forth, rushing down the steep road to the Lower Town. This placed them in the rear of Arnold's men.

Captain Dearborn's company had arrived at the battle late. It had become lost among the side streets below the Palace Gate. His men soon became engaged with the British troops advancing down from the gate. Dearborn himself was at that moment separated from most of his scattered men. He managed to collect some of them into a nearby darkened house and tried to fire back, but the powder charges on their muskets had become wet and would not fire. After several minutes of receiving intense fire, balls whining through the windows, with the frustration of not being able to fire back, Dearborn told his men to try to escape any way they could. He and a few remaining men cried for quarter and surrendered. The British defenders placed Dearborn and his men under guard and marched them off to prison.

The British defenders then worked their way along the streets into the rear of the American column. The Americans left alive were now trapped between the two barriers, both occupied by the British. They had lost Arnold and several company commanders. The officers still alive were unsure what to do. Increasingly intense fire came down on them from windows in the surrounding buildings, and fire was now coming at them from the rear as well. Morgan's attempts to probe along the length of the barrier from the cliffs to the river's edge had found no weak point to go over or around. Morgan and the officers still standing could not find a way to get their men out from under the stabs of light that marked death from all sides. The attack had stalled, and they were surrounded.

The men began to speak of surrender. Morgan was still defiant, but the full light of morning revealed how exposed and untenable their situation was. He and the other officers could devise no plan to extricate themselves from the deadly balls that crumpled man after man into the red-stained snow. The soldiers began to cry to their officers for quarter. By mid-morning, the firing tapered off as the British troops moved into the mass of men, disarming them at gunpoint. The British marched the dejected Americans off into captivity. The attack ended in a most disastrous defeat. Those not captured lay wounded or dead in the snow. Some bodies were not discovered until spring.

This was New Years' Day, 1776, a day of death, dejection, and defeat for the American army. General Richard Montgomery and two of his chief aides lay dead in the snow. Colonel Benedict Arnold lay in a nunnery hospital in great pain from a ball in his leg. He had much company that day as other wounded men were carried in. The nearly 400 captured soldiers of Arnold's command were herded into cellars and prison rooms in the Upper Town. The remaining men of the American army

Musée du Québec
Parc des champs-de-bataille
Quebec, Canada G1R 5H3
(418) 643-2150
www.mdq.org

6. The Musée du Fort

Located on the southeast side of the small park next to the Château Frontenac, the Place d'Armes, this museum has an interesting half-hour program that uses a diorama to provide a quick but comprehensive overview of the city's rich military history. It includes a sound and light show with a 400-square-foot model of the city as it was in the eighteenth century. All six of the sieges of Quebec are portrayed with graphic and visual details.

Included as one of the six sieges is the American attack of 1775. It depicts where Arnold was wounded and where General Montgomery died, both in the Lower Town. This show will be most useful to help to visualize how the attack was conducted and why it failed. Shows occur every half-hour and alternate in French and English. A fee is charged.

Musée du Fort
10, rue Sainte-Anne
Quebec, Canada G1R 4S7
(418) 692-1759

There are four other noteworthy sites related to the expedition. Because of the city's change during two centuries, these sites bear little resemblance to what the expedition's men encountered in 1775.

The Redoute Dauphine near the St. John Gate

*1. The **First Barricade** in the Lower Town. Arnold was wounded near here. A bronze plaque marks the site. It is on the corner of Côte de la Canoterie and Rue St-Thomas. This is the point where Captain Daniel Morgan assumed command after Arnold was carried from the field.*

*2. The **Second Barricade** is also in the Lower*

Town. Here the attack stalled and faltered in the narrow, snow-covered streets and roughly 400 men of the expedition were captured. A bronze plaque marks this location at the corner of Rue de la Barricade and Rue Sault-au-Mâtelot.

3. The site where General Richard Montgomery and two of his aides died during their aborted attack is in the small village of ***Près-de-Ville*** *along the edge of the St. Lawrence. A bronze plaque is affixed to the cliff on the Boulevard Champlain, approximately a half-mile west of the ferry terminal.*

4. ***Wolfe's Cove*** *is the point where the expedition's men landed after crossing the river on the night of Nov. 13-14. Today, many commercial establishments crowd around the cove. Drive about two miles west of the ferry terminal along the St. Lawrence River on the Boulevard Champlain. Following this route, you will also pass the site where General Montgomery was killed. At a traffic light where the Côte Gilmour turns right, a left turn will bring you down to a public boat-launching site where you may view the cove and obtain some idea of the perils of the river crossing. The Côte Gilmour leads uphill to the Plains of Abraham and is the route followed by both Wolfe's force and, later, the expedition. A plaque commemorating Wolfe's feat is located near the intersection.*

We hope you have enjoyed and have been enriched by your long journey from Cambridge to Quebec. If you have faithfully followed their footsteps, then, we hope, you have created a life-long link between yourself and the brave men of the expedition who passed this way not so long ago.

(End of the Travel Guide)

Château Frontenac, Quebec

returned to their now considerably thinned billets, mourning the loss of so many of their comrades. They did not know if they had been captured, wounded, or killed. It would be several depressing days before they would find out.

The dreadful casualty list would show that, in Arnold's command, officers dead included Lieutenant Humphrey, Captain Hendricks, and Lieutenant Cooper. Key officers that had been captured included Captains Morgan, Thayer, Topham, Dearborn, Ward, Hanchet, and Goodrich. Of the ten company commanders who descended the Chaudière, eight were either captured or killed; only Captains Smith and Hubbard had escaped. Of the higher command, General Montgomery and Captains Cheeseman and McPherson had been killed; Colonel Arnold and Captain Ogden were wounded. Lieutenant Colonel Greene, Major Meigs, Major Bigelow, and Captain Duncan were captured. The loss of so many key officers made reorganization of the remaining troops into an effective fighting force extremely difficult.

Apparently, Governor Carleton didn't know how weak and leaderless the Americans were at this time. If he had, he would probably have convinced them to surrender or driven them off completely. Approximately two-thirds of the expedition's men that had completed the march to Quebec were killed, wounded, or captured. The totals were 35 killed, 33 wounded, and 372 captured. The total for the New York contingent was thirteen killed, one wounded, and none captured.

However, the remnants of the American army did reorganize themselves. In the next few days of recovery, the army learned that many of their comrades were safe, but in captivity. Montgomery's body had been recovered by the British, given a decent burial with full military honors, and interred in the city. Arnold was beginning his recovery in the hospital in St-Foy while writing reports to General Washington and others about the terrible outcome of the attack. He implored Washington to send more troops and supplies for a spring campaign against the city. He estimated it would take six thousand troops to successfully capture Quebec. Now the senior officer on site, but in pain and bedridden, he was hardly in a position to effectively command the army. He received the discouraging news that some of the American troops and officers were heading up the St. Lawrence River, on their way to the colonies and home. They claimed that their enlistment had expired.

Over the next several winter months, Arnold gradually regained his strength as his leg wound healed. He requested of Washington that a more experienced senior officer be sent to Quebec to assume command.

Military operations on either side were limited because of the icy Canadian winter and shortages of men and supplies. The waterways all the way back to Albany were frozen solid, making movement of supplies and men difficult at best. Occasional harassing fire from the American cannons on the Plains of Abraham was conducted with little effect. The mortar battery in St-Roch had been captured several days after the attack, through negligence by the officer in command, who had left them improperly guarded.

It was a dismal winter of frozen stalemate. The nearly 400 American captives in the city were treated harshly, with minimal food, as they languished in cold, bleak, stone rooms. The officers received somewhat better treatment.

In April, American General David Wooster, who had managed to antagonize most of his command in Montreal because of his fondness for flip, a rum-based drink popular in colonial times, arrived and assumed command. Arnold was reassigned to the command of the small American force in and around Montreal. In late April, when the ice in the St. Lawrence broke up, a full regiment of crack British troops arrived from Halifax along with several powerful British warships. Several days later, this new regiment spearheaded a sortie-in-force from the city's gates and captured the American fortifications and batteries on the Plains of Abraham. General Wooster and the remaining American forces hastily gathered what they could and retreated up the St. Lawrence.

The expedition to, and siege of, Quebec were now at an ignominious end. Never again would Quebec be subjected to a siege or attack by foreign forces.

Views of Lower Town, Quebec

THIS TABLET
MARKS THE HEADQUARTERS OF
COLONEL BENEDICT ARNOLD
SEPT. 21 — 23, 1775
WHEN HE WAS THE GUEST OF
MAJOR REUBEN COLBURN
DURING THE TRANSFER OF HIS ARMY OF
1100 MEN AND SUPPLIES FROM
THE TRANSPORTS TO THE 220 BATTEAUX
BUILT BY MAJOR COLBURN
FOR THE EXPEDITION TO QUEBEC
TO COMMEMORATE THIS EVENT THIS TABLET
IS PLACED BY
SAMUEL GRANT CHAPTER
DAUGHTERS OF THE AMERICAN REVOLUTION
1913

History Epilogue

An adjective such as "ill-fated" is often used by writers and historians to characterize the 1775 Expedition to Quebec. Such a word accepts that the expedition was a failure, specifically because the city was not captured. This view is retrospectively reinforced by the fact that Benedict Arnold, its leader, later became an infamous traitor, joining the very enemy he had fought against so valiantly. If one considers only that the city was not captured and the army was badly defeated, with the loss of many men, it would be reasonable, of course, to conclude that the expedition was a failure.

However, if one views the results of the expedition as a single battle in the American army's northern campaign, with a wide-angle rather than a telescopic lens, a much different view emerges. The story of the expedition is really two stories in one. The first is the saga of the journey itself, describing the gauntlet of incredible hardships the men of the expedition had to endure and overcome. The second is the military campaign to capture Quebec and bring Canada into the Revolution.

Historian Justin Smith, in his great *Arnold's March from Cambridge to Quebec,* recognized this dichotomy by writing only of the first part, the march itself, ending his narrative at the crossing of the St. Lawrence River. There is little doubt that the Expedition to Quebec was an extraordinary story of great human courage and perseverance. The men of the expedition overcame hardships that surpass the American army's extreme experience at Valley Forge. The second story, the defeat of the American army at Quebec, tends to dim the brilliance of the first, the expedition's march through the wilderness.

And, to illuminate the issue of "the failure" at Quebec, we must also consider the events there in the context of the entire northern campaign of the American army. It began, of course, with the initial invasion by General Montgomery's and Arnold's small, relatively inexperienced forces in the fall of 1775. It ended two eventful years later in October of 1777 at a place called Saratoga. Let us see if we can fit the events at Quebec into this larger picture.

Quebec was simply the beginning battle of a long series of ignominious and deadly defeats suffered by the northern American army during the first two years of the rebellion. After Quebec came Trois Rivières and the Cedars, the rout of the American army at Soral, the defeat of Arnold's tiny fleet at Valcour Island on Lake Champlain in October of 1776, another rout at Fort Ticonderoga, and another at Hubbardton during the summer of 1777. All these defeats were a prelude to Saratoga in October of that year.

For Arnold's small force to succeed in capturing Quebec, it would have required rapid movement of his troops and a surprise attack upon an unprepared city, which was the original plan. Because of unanticipated difficulties encountered on the march and the inexperience of the fledgling army, they achieved neither rapidity nor surprise.

The late start in the season, the hasty construction of the bateaux, the river conditions that caused the boats to leak badly and fall apart, the loss of so much food and most of their military supplies, the inexperience of the men in handling the bateaux, and the generally poor intelligence regarding the route—all these factors contributed to the loss of the critical element of surprise. And the expedition had just plain old-fashioned bad luck! The horrendous hurricane that struck them on the Dead River could not have been anticipated. Hurricanes in inland mountain country, so far from the coast, are extremely rare.

Washington and Arnold were counting on his force walking into a lightly defended, open-gated city, similar to what Arnold and Ethan Allen encountered when they captured Fort Ticonderoga in April of 1775. The Quebec expedition carried no artillery or siege equipment because no such strategy was intended.

When the army arrived before Quebec on Nov. 14, the able British leader Guy Carleton and his reinforcing contingent had just descended the St. Lawrence from Montreal. Arnold estimated that if the expedition had arrived at Quebec just ten days earlier, it would have walked through the gates and the city would have been theirs. History would have then treated these soldiers much differently, most likely proclaiming them to be great heroes of the Revolution.

Let us assume that Arnold and Montgomery had taken Quebec. They would have spent a more pleasant winter within the walls as masters of the city. But what might have happened when the ice broke up in the St Lawrence River in the spring?

During the winter of 1775, while the remnants of the defeated American army were languishing outside Quebec's walls, the British lords and generals were devising a master plan to wipe out the audacious rebels and restore the colonies to British rule. The plan was to send forth two great armies, one to New York, which would capture that city and advance northward up the Hudson River. A second army was to be sent to Quebec and advance up the St. Lawrence, south down the Champlain Valley, and on to Albany, where it would meet with the other army advancing north, thus cutting the colonies in half. With this plan accomplished, the British reasoned that they could then deal with the remnants, including the most hotheaded rebels, who were perceived to be in New England where the rebellion began. This plan was adopted and put into motion in the spring of 1776.

Captain Dearborn and Major Meigs, who had been captured during the attack on the Lower Town, were paroled in May of 1776. They were on board a British frigate sailing down the St. Lawrence on their way to Halifax, Nova Scotia, and then on to home. While on deck, they were amazed to see the spectacle of a great fleet of forty-three ships, which carried 9,000 British troops under the command of General John Burgoyne, heading in the opposite direction toward Quebec.

What if Arnold and the army had arrived earlier to find an undefended Quebec and walked through its open gates as had been intended? That victory might have led to a great defeat. When spring arrived and the river became clear of ice, the 9,000 British troops aboard their forty-three warships and transports would have simply sailed upriver past Quebec, as Wolfe and his army had done sixteen years earlier. After landing their troops and cutting the Americans' supply line and only route of retreat, all the British would have had to do was wait.

Inside the city walls, the 1,200 American soldiers would have faced hostile or unsupportive inhabitants. Outside, they would have faced the well-equipped redcoats and a powerful navy controlling the sea and river. They would have been hundreds of miles from their base of supply at Albany. There would have been no help for them.

Following this scenario, Quebec would have been a trap instead of a fortress for the Americans. General Montgomery, Colonel Arnold, and their 1,200 men would have eventually been forced to surrender to the vastly superior British forces, dealing the rebel cause a terrible blow. If, when the fleet arrived, they would have elected wisely to retreat (the most likely course of action) up the St. Lawrence River, then the military significance of capturing and holding Quebec for six months would have been negated.

To speculate about scenarios and outcomes beyond this point has too many variables to seriously consider. The only probable outcome is that, because of events unknown to Montgomery, Arnold, Washington, or any of the American leaders, Quebec, if it had been captured in November of 1775, could not have been held beyond the arrival of Burgoyne's army in May of 1776.

In 1775 the Americans had to build an army from scratch. The most critical of many shortages in the early phases of the war was experience, both in its leadership and in its ranks. British General Burgoyne was not far from the truth when he disdainfully labeled the Americans as a "rabble in arms," which was to become the title of Kenneth Roberts's famous novel about the northern campaign. Burgoyne would rue this arrogance when he lost his army and his sword at Saratoga. Washington and some other officers privately voiced similar sediments about their army. The early, rawboned victories at Concord and especially at Bunker Hill were more a case of British stupidity than colonial excellence.

This lack of experience was evident throughout the entire northern campaign leading up to Saratoga. The inexperience was equally evident in the outcomes of battles and campaigns fought by Washington's army in New York and New Jersey during the first two years of the war—one loss after another, except for Trenton.

In a sense, the Expedition to Quebec was part of a process of the American army learning how to form and operate an army and fight a war. It is often true in military history, as it is in our lives, that we learn best from our mistakes. This was very true of events at Quebec and in their aftermath.

The northern campaign was a long series of deadly defeats and humiliating retreats, all leading to one place and one momentous battle, Saratoga.

The importance of Saratoga is sometimes minimized as a northern sideshow to the campaigns of Washington's army. However, by the fall of 1777 the ragged Americans had suffered two years of defeats. Granted that the rebels had inflicted heavy losses on the British at Bunker Hill and had forced them out of Boston, but those episodes were anomalies. After that, except for Trenton late in 1776, they had lost battle after battle against the powerful British army, supported by the best navy in the world.

So the Americans desperately needed allies. France, the mortal enemy of England, had money, military supplies, and trained troops. The French were anxious to settle scores for many defeats at the hands of the English, including the humiliation of being forced out of Canada. However, King Louis XVI and his ministers were reluctant to be drawn into a war allied with the unproven American rebels, who were likely to be defeated, leaving France with no allies to face England's wrath. They needed proof that supporting the Americans was worthy of their investment. Without a solid victory, proof that the Americans had a reasonable chance to defeat the British, assistance from France was out of the question.

Saratoga was that needed proof. France entered the war as an American ally shortly after news of Saratoga reached Paris in late 1777.

Some historians have listed Saratoga as one of the world's most decisive military battles. As a direct result of the battle, France provided desperately needed guns, cannons, powder, tents, uniforms, food, troops, money, and, most important, a surrogate navy that proved to be the decisive factor in the final victory at Yorktown in 1781. All of this and more flowed from the victory at Saratoga.

The battle at Quebec was the beginning of the eventual crowning success at Saratoga. Many of the expedition's soldiers who had been imprisoned at Quebec, including Daniel Morgan, Henry Dearborn, and many others were there. During the battle, both were at the head of now-veteran regiments heavily filled with Quebec men who had been paroled and released by the British. As events were to unfold, this parole was a grievous British mistake.

And, of course, Benedict Arnold was there as well, heroically leading the troops. It was Arnold and many of the Quebec veterans who led the final wild charge on Bemis Heights at Saratoga that collapsed the British right flank and sealed the fate of "Gentleman Johnny" Burgoyne and his army. His dejected army—of about 6,000 soldiers—surrendered lock, stock, and barrel several days later.

All the Quebec veterans, alive or dead, were there. In the end, Quebec's capture would not have been decisive to the outcome of the war, as it could not have remained in American hands. What did matter is that Arnold and his brave soldiers survived, learned, and fought well on another day.

The footsteps of the Expedition to Quebec began in Cambridge. They ended not at the walls of Quebec, but on the fields of Saratoga.

CANOEING

along the Expedition's Route

Introduction

From Gardinerstown, present-day Pittston, northward along the Kennebec and Dead Rivers to the Height of Land at the Canadian border, the expedition followed a water route using the rivers and several small ponds to transport men and many tons of supplies. Four to six men were assigned to each of the army's 220 bateaux. The men not in the bateaux would bushwhack along the roadless shore line, occasionally helping to haul boats through a stretch of fast water or at portages. From the Height of Land northward, along the shore of lac Mégantic, and then during the descent of the Chaudière River to Quebec, almost all the men were on foot.

Retracing the route of the expedition by car will be the means of travel for most readers. But to trace a portion of the original route via water will greatly enhance the experience of following in the footsteps of the Quebec expedition. A very few souls have actually paddled and poled the entire water route from tidewater at Augusta to tidewater at Quebec. Such an endeavor is much too involved for most of us. In places, the water route is very technical and even dangerous, particularly on the Chaudière River.

But there is no reason we cannot sample the best water sections the route has to offer. Traveling by water will also be fun and full of the enjoyment of Maine's natural beauty. If you have access to a canoe or kayak or can rent one en route, try a section or more of these waterways. You will be greatly rewarded. While paddling on a misty morning or quiet evening, you may hear the men of the expedition shouting to each other as they struggled along the rivers with their bateaux.

We have selected five canoe trips on different sections of the expedition's route. Each is quite unlike the others. Most of them should be traversed in the opposite direction from that traveled by the expedition. It is simply more fun to glide easily downstream than struggle upstream for miles against a strong current.

Each trip is a wonderful outdoor adventure in which, with luck, there will be an opportunity to spy eagles, blue heron, osprey, moose, deer, beaver, and other wildlife around each bend in the river. If you love to fish, try your luck for a three-foot sea sturgeon in the Lower Kennebec or a rainbow trout in the Chain of Ponds. None of these trips requires technical white-water canoeing skills. They are mostly flat-water or Class I fast-water conditions. Four of the five trips can be completed in a half-day or full day, according to how leisurely you travel or how much exploring you wish to do. The other one is a two-day lake trip.

From south to north, they are:

1. ***Fort to Fort,*** *Winslow to Augusta, eighteen miles, one day.*
2. ***Middle Kennebec****, Solon to North Anson, eight miles, with an option to extend it to Madison, fourteen miles total; a half-day or full day.*
3. ***Upper Kennebec****, The Forks to Caratunk, ten miles, half-day.*
4. ***Flagstaff Lake****, Eustis to Bog Brook, twenty-two miles, two days.*
5. ***Chain of Ponds****, Height of Land, five miles, half-day.*

There is a possible sixth trip, but it is not detailed here. This is the Upper Dead River (North Branch) from the Chain of Ponds, twenty-five miles down to Flagstaff Lake. This is an outstanding trip, but it is not described here because it has stretches of Class 2 or Class 3 white water, depending on conditions, and includes some portaging. It is usually done as a two-day trip. It would require a good degree of canoeing skill. For a detailed description of this trip, consult the Appalachian Mountain Club's Maine River Guide.

Yet another possible trip would be to canoe the Lake Megantic swamp, following the Arnold River down to the lake. It would give an intimate feeling of what the men experienced as they slogged through this huge swamp. The Arnold River can be accessed from the Canadian Route 161 bridge north of Woburn. Do not confuse this crossing with the other crossing, south of Woburn, nearer the United States border. Your canoe can be launched just north of the above-mentioned bridge. The river—at this point a small stream—is deep enough to canoe without scraping paint. If you follow the meandering river all the way to the lake, it will take about two to three hours. Pay careful attention to the location of the main channel, as there are several confusing side channels. We recommend that you obtain a topographical map of this area to better guide yourself.

Happy paddling!

Canoe Trip 1. Fort to Fort

In 1754, the long, bloody French and Indian Wars were nearing their climax after nearly a century of intermittent, vicious warfare. It was a turbulent time on the northern frontier of the American colonies. The vulnerable, scattered, farming settlements huddled along the coast and rivers in the Province of Maine, then a part of the Commonwealth of Massachusetts, had been attacked and pillaged many times during the previous century.

There had been ominous rumors of a French army, with their hated Indian allies, gathering in Canada, poised to swoop down through the Chaudière and Kennebec Valleys to ravage the English settlements. To counter this threat, as well as to promote the settlement of inland Maine, the

Massachusetts authorities decided to build fortifications on part of the expected route of invasion, the Kennebec River.

In the summer of 1754, a large force of soldiers and carpenters moved up the river to Cushnoc, now Augusta, at the head of navigation. Here they built a fort and supply depot, which was named Fort Western. They then moved eighteen miles upriver to a strategic point at the confluence of the Kennebec and Sebasticook Rivers. Here they built a second fort, similar in design, naming it Fort Halifax. Luckily, no attack materialized. A few years after the end of the war in 1763, the garrisons were withdrawn, but the forts remained.

In 1837, the first of a series of dams for mill power was built just above Fort Western. This raised the river approximately twenty feet and formed a seventeen-mile-long pool almost reaching to Waterville-Winslow. The dam submerged all the rapids and fast water under a long lake. It substantially changed the ecology of the river and considerably altered its appearance from that experienced by the men of the expedition. The real river was hidden for 162 years. In 1999, after a ten-year battle, state and federal agencies gave permission for the removal of the Edwards Dam in Augusta, with the object of restoring the river to its former nature.

Over the next several years, the river began its recovery. Sea-run fish began moving past the old dam site, reaching spawning and feeding areas along the river up to Ticonic Falls in Waterville. By 2000, eagles, ospreys and blue herons had returned to feed on the more numerous fish in the recovering river.

So today you can canoe downriver between the two forts just as it was done during the 1700s. Even going downstream, it still is an all-day trip, taking from five to seven hours. You need to spot a car at the take-out point at the boat landing next to Fort Western in Augusta. Take plenty of water and a lunch.

Begin at **Fort Halifax Park** *in Winslow, reached from US Route 201. Here is the preserved original wooden blockhouse, believed to be the oldest in the United States. Carry your canoe through the park to the point at the confluence of the two rivers. Look upstream and you will see the old Waterville-Winslow bridge and a large red-brick mill complex on the west shore. The mill marks the site of the portage trail used by the expedition to get around Ticonic Falls, which is just beyond the bridge.*

After launching, a strong current will propel the canoe all the way to Augusta. Civilization almost immediately begins to drop away. The new Waterville-Winslow high bridge is passed in about a half-mile. Below this, only an occasional house on the high hills is seen until you reach Augusta. The river enters a deep valley.

Messalonskee Stream enters on the west (right) shore at about a mile. Below this, you enter the first set of rips, **Petty's Rapids**, *which is best descended on the west (right) side. "Petty's" is probably a misspelling of "Pattee," the name of a prominent early settler in Winslow. A pond there is named for him. These are easy Class I rapids, as are all on this trip except for Six Mile Falls.*

A mile farther down, a second fast water, **Carter's Rips**, *is passed, also best descended on the west side. A short distance below,* **Six Mile Falls** *is encountered. According to water conditions, this may be a more difficult Class 2 rapid. It, too, is best negotiated along the west shore. We suggest you land and scout the rapid before attempting to run it. Arnold and several companies camped here on their first night out after leaving Fort Western.*

Watch for eagles and other fishing birds along this next stretch. About a half a mile below Six Mile Falls, you will encounter a two-mile section of fast, shoaly water that is best negotiated on the east (left) side. Soon you pass under a high power line, which alerts you to look for the Sidney boat landing. This is on the west shore, and it is clearly marked by a concrete boat ramp. As this marks the halfway point, it is a good place to stop and rest. Putting in or taking out here will shorten the trip. It is nine miles farther to Augusta.

Three miles below the landing, you will begin to see an extensive line of huge, wooden, rock-filled piers along the east shore. Prior to 1973, they anchored a log boom to divert logs floated downriver to a paper mill in Augusta. The river was used for log driving for more than two centuries. After the mid-1970s, log driving was prohibited on Maine rivers. Logs were found to be harmful to the river's environment. Give the river a few more years to work its ways on these piers, and they will magically disappear.

Just below the row of piers, an island on the east shore is encountered. Below it, there is a gradual right-hand bend in the river at another short rapid called **Bacon's Rips**. *It is easily navigated on the east side. Below, you will spy the church steeples of Augusta in the distance. A mile below Bacon's Rips is the last fast water, named* **Babcock's Rapids**. *Below this point, civilization begins to encroach upon the wildness of the river in the form of several industrial establishments on the east shore. A new, high bridge was under construction here beginning in 2002. A large paper mill is passed as the bridges in Augusta come into sight. This mill marks the location of the former Edwards Dam.*

Near the railroad trestle, the last rip, **Coon's Rapids**, *is now more of a single fast drop because of the change in the river brought about by the construction of the railroad bridge. It is experienced only at low tides. At high tides, you will note only a fast current. Below the railroad bridge is the upper edge of tidewater on the river.*

Fort Western is located on a high bank on the east shore just past the small Father Curran automobile bridge. The Augusta boat landing, the take-out point, is just below the fort. The boat landing is the exact spot where the expedition's bateaux were packed and loaded for the upriver journey.

If you have not already done so, plan to visit Fort Western. It is well worth the time spent. For five days, the men of the expedition used it for their staging area.

Canoe Trip 2. The Middle Kennebec

The Middle Kennebec has been heavily altered since the time of the expedition's ascent of the river. The construction of dams at Skowhegan, Madison (Norridgewock Falls), Solon, and the huge Wyman Station Dam above Bingham have transformed it from a free-flowing upland river into a series of placid pools. Although the dams may have been needed, they came with a cost: the loss of one of the most vibrant and varied river ecologies in the northeastern United States. Long sections of the river that the army knew are now under the backup pools of these dams. Towns, roads, bridges, and all the other trappings of civilization have added to the river's transformation. Fortunately, there are a few stretches of the unaltered river that are still free-flowing and much as they were in 1775.

This downriver trip samples the best of the remaining unaltered sections in the middle part of the Kennebec. It can be done as a half-day trip from Solon to North Anson, a distance of seven miles, or as a longer, thirteen-mile, all-day trip to Madison, the site of Norridgewock Falls. This latter section, although scenic and well worth the effort, passes over part of the backwater behind the dam at Madison. The section with the least intrusion of civilization is the first seven miles to North Anson.

The river valley here teems with waterfowl, wildlife, and even supports a few eagles. Fishing along this section is reputed to be quite good. The water is clear and relatively clean, a most welcome change from the conditions farther south. The Kennebec has formed a series of beautiful islands here, several of which are protected by the Maine Nature Conservancy. Some of them are farmed because of their fertile soil.

The expedition went up this section in early October. A number of the journal writers, including Arnold, commented that the land here was very fine. The hardwood trees must have been at peak color, adding to the beauty of the land. Halfway between Solon and Madison, a large tributary, the Carrabassett River, enters from the west. In 1775, this was known as Six Mile Stream, as its mouth was that distance above Norridgewock Falls.

Those who do not have a canoe may rent one from the proprietors of the Evergreens Campground at the put-in point. The campground also has kayaks and tubes for rent. It can provide a car shuttle to the take-out point of your choice. The campground is located in Solon near the Solon-Emden bridge over the Kennebec on Route US 201A. The Evergreens is beautifully situated on an historic site; many of the expedition's companies camped here. Artifacts uncovered indicate Native Americans had camped and lived here for thousands of years. Across the river are Native American petroglyphs along the river's edge. If you are camping, there is no charge to use the launching facilities. Noncampers are charged a small fee to launch canoes. Information about this campground is contained in the Travel Guide section entitled "Skowhegan to The Forks" and in the Appendix. Although the best put-in point is located at the Evergreens, some people choose to put in just below Caratunk Falls, a mile upstream. The take-out point for the half-day trip is located at a landing on Madison Street in North Anson. To reach this point, when you spot your car go south for eight miles on Route US 201A from the bridge next to the Evergreens. As you approach the center of North Anson, watch for the Methodist Church on the left (east) side of the highway. Turn left there onto Madison Street and proceed eastward. In 0.5mi., the road becomes gravel. At one mile, you will see a landing on the right on the shore of the Carrabassett River. It is a half a mile downstream to its confluence with the Kennebec. Cars may be left at this landing.

If you decide to undertake the longer, thirteen-mile trip downstream to Madison, a car may be spotted at the public boat landing on the east side of the river in the town of Madison at a point a half-mile above the dam. From the main street in Madison, turn north onto Madison Avenue and proceed for 0.4mi. Watch on the left for a prominent sign to the landing. Turn here and follow a gravel road for 0.3mi. to the landing.

Let's begin our canoe trip at the Evergreens Campground. After launching, let the current sweep you downstream away from civilization into a beautiful maze of islands formed by the ever-at-work river. To see wildlife, coast downstream slowly and quietly. You may choose any of the channels weaving around the islands. You will be transported into another world, for there are few signs of civilization hereabouts.

To get a feeling for the effort the expedition's men had to put forth, turn your canoe around and paddle upstream for a few minutes. You have a light, maneuverable canoe. They had clumsy, heavy, wooden bateaux that rode deep in the water. If the water was low, many of the men had to get out and wade in the cold, swift water, dragging the bateaux upstream.

Speaking of water levels, remember the critical fact that the water level you are experiencing as you descend the river is considerably higher than in October, 1775. The dams of today maintain a relatively steady flow to feed the generation of electricity.

After six and a half miles, the river takes a long, gradual dogleg right, around a point. Look for an old, granite bridge abutment in the middle of the river. If you intend to take out in North Anson, stay close to the right (west) bank of the river. Several channels bearing left (south) confuse the route. As you follow the curve of the river, gradually turning west, the current diminishes when you enter the mouth of the Carrabassett River. After paddling up this river about a half-mile, you will reach the landing on the right (north) shore. A faded red paint splotch on a tree marks it. It is 1.1mi. west on the road from the landing for North Anson. Improvements are scheduled to this landing.

The full-day trip continues south down the river. (To follow this route, do not use the description above leading into the Carrabassett.) The current on the Kennebec soon becomes less perceptible as you reach the backwater of the dam at Madison. A half-mile downstream, after passing Savage Island, pass on the right the south mouth of the Carrabassett River.

About a mile and half from the north mouth of the Carrabassett, the Kennebec sweeps abruptly left to form a mile-long loop, nearly doubling back on itself. Since the construction of the Madison Dam, the river has formed several short-cut channels within this loop. The longest, most easterly loop is the original course of the river. At the narrow neck formed by the loop, some of the expedition's men portaged forty rods across to shortcut their trip.

Below this point, the river passes through farmland that uses the fertile intervales located along this section. The main highway, US 201A, soon comes close to the west shore as the towns of Madison and Anson are approached. Large pylons that were used during log-driving days dot the river here. The boat landing, which is the take-out point on the left (east) shore, is a half a mile above the dam. There are a boat ramp and a dock here.

Canoe Trip 3. The Upper Kennebec

North of Devil's (Caratunk) Falls, in present-day Solon, the men of the expedition had to battle an increasingly swift and shallowing Kennebec River. As they approached the Great Carrying Place, the watercourse became continuously fast and shallow. Today, the dam at Solon (Williams Station) and the huge Wyman Station Dam just north of Bingham have transformed this section of the Kennebec into two lakes covering most of the old river.

The trip recommended here is not actually on the route of the expedition. It is located just north of the point where the Great Carrying Place began. But this voyage will give you a very close approximation of the character of the river when the men experienced it in 1775. It will be a fun downstream journey through a beautiful, mountainous river valley. The highway, Route US 201, parallels the river closely, but the rest of the deep valley is untouched, with only a few homes or camps visible.

This trip does not require white-water expertise and is mostly Class I fast water. It is ten miles in length. Since the current is swift, only an easy half-day paddle will be required, although it can be extended to a full day if you wish to stop and explore along the way. The route intersects the famous Appalachian Trail's ford of the Kennebec in Caratunk. You could land the canoe or kayak at the crossing and hike along the trail westward, following beautiful Pierce Pond Stream for some distance. There are many fine waterfalls and swimming pools along the stream.

The starting point for this trip is The Forks, a small village on US 201, approximately thirteen miles above the point where the expedition left the river. The takeout point is the Caratunk Boat Landing on upper Wyman Lake, a mile below where the river becomes a lake. The trip will take a minimum of three to four hours of easy paddling, if there are no stops.

A dam above The Forks, Harris Station, which is on the East Branch of the Kennebec, almost daily opens its gates to provide water releases for the extensive white-water rafting conducted in the Kennebec River Gorge north of The Forks. This is one of the best white-water river stretches in the eastern United States. The releases also provide water for downriver power generation. These releases reach the main river at The Forks about noon, so the afternoon has the best water for a canoe trip. You will need to be alert to rapid rises in water levels. This rise in water levels changes the dynamics of canoeing the river. In the morning, the river is sometimes low and will take a little more maneuvering around exposed gravel bars and rocks.

Canoes may be rented from the many white-water outfitters in and around The Forks. These same outfitters will also help you, for a fee, to spot your car at the takeout in Caratunk.

To begin, drive north up US 201 to The Forks. Ancient Native Americans, including the Red Paint People, camped and lived here for thousands of years. After you have made arrangements to have your car spotted, drive to a landing on the East Branch located on a gravel side road that turns off US 201 just north of the bridge over the East Branch. Follow this road for several hundred yards to a point where you can launch your canoe.

The trip begins in fast water. Paddle downstream under the US 201 bridge. Three hundred yards farther will bring you to the actual forks of the Kennebec, where the Dead River enters on the right. You are now on the main stem of the Kennebec. The deep valley is quite striking, even with its proximity to human works such as the highway. There are no roads or camps on the west shore.

Eagles and other large birds are often seen here. Moose and deer frequently come down to the river shore for a drink. As you float easily down the fast river, try to imagine the men of the expedition straining with their clumsy bateaux as they worked their way upstream against this kind of current. Try turning your canoe upstream and paddle against the current for a few minutes. Then you will understand why they left the river to portage over the Great Carrying Place, to avoid mile after mile of these conditions and worse.

At about seven miles downstream, Holly Brook is passed on the left (east) shore. At eight miles, the Appalachian Trail ford is reached. You will recognize it when Pierce Pond Stream enters the river (west side), causing a large, rocky outwash at its mouth. The trail is located on the river's shore just above the mouth. On the west (right) shore, the trail follows the stream valley uphill three miles to Pierce Pond and then continues on to Georgia, two thousand miles south.

Just below the mouth of Pierce Pond Stream, the water current slackens, and the river disappears into the upper end of Wyman Lake. The take-out landing is located on the east (left) shore, about a mile south, and it has a picnic and rest area.

Canoe Trip 4. Flagstaff Lake

This is a flat-water, two-day trip, twenty-two miles in length. Flagstaff Lake is an impoundment created when the gates of the Long Falls Dam were closed in 1950. It covers all of the Middle Dead River and much of its valley from the dam to a point westward near the village of Eustis. What was once an upland farming valley, with three small villages, is now a vast, shallow lake. The Dead River formerly meandered across the valley's floor and, of course, was the pathway for the expedition.

The army reached the east side of the valley at Bog Brook and then followed the Dead River's quiet waters upstream to a fork near the present town of Stratton. From this fork, the route to Canada followed the North Branch through the Boundary Mountains.

One thing has not changed. Dominating the entire valley and lake is the magnificent, fourteen-mile-long Bigelow Mountain Range. The range consists of six peaks, two of them four-thousand-footers. They separate the lake and the wild border country from the coastal plain. The men of the expedition admired the mountain's grandeur as much as we do today.

This canoe trip over the lake is through a semi-wilderness, thus making it a fine adventure. It parallels the Bigelow Range, which was protected from development by the establishment of the Bigelow Preserve. In 1976, the people of Maine, after a hard-fought referendum battle, chose state preservation over development of this great mountain range into a ski resort. The mountain is named in honor of Major Timothy Bigelow, an officer in Greene's division and a Worcester, Massachusetts, patriot. The Appalachian Trail follows along much of its crest.

Because most of the lake is protected by state and electric-utility ownership, its shore is undeveloped, with only a few camps visible. The fishing is poor, as the lake is substantially drawn down in the fall of each year.

This is a nontechnical canoeing trip because it is on flat water. But the lake is five miles across at its widest point and twenty-two miles long, and a wind can blow up huge whitecaps. While canoeing the lake, be aware of possibly dangerous conditions caused by the wind. Of some interest are large piles of dry-ki (lake driftwood) along its shoreline. When the lake was created, it covered forests lands that had to be cut prior to the flooding. The stumps and roots over time have broken loose and popped to the surface. They are then blown to shore in piles, where the sun bleaches the wood to its unique gray color. These piles are collected by entrepreneurs who fashion them into decorative mantelpieces and other artistic displays for sale all over the country.

There are several ways to canoe the lake. We recommend traversing it west to east to take advantage of the prevailing westerlies. Your muscles will be most appreciative if you choose this route. Canoeing the lake will require you to spot a car at the east end or to make arrangements to be picked up. We recommend launching at the Cathedral Pines Campground on Route 27 in Eustis, three miles north of Stratton. This campground is on the shore of the upper end of the lake, not far from where the water resumes its identity as a river. The campground has a public landing. It is also a good place to camp in preparation for the trip. Inquiries can be made here to obtain assistance in shuttling your car to the other end.

The best take-out point is at a beach accessed by a branch of the Long Falls Dam Road. This is locally called the Bog Brook Landing, and it is located at the southeast corner of the lake. To reach this point from Eustis, you must drive south on Route 27 to Kingfield, east via Route 16 to North New Portland, and then north up the Long Falls Dam Road through Lexington Plantation. When you approach the Bigelow Preserve and the southeast corner of the lake, look for preserve signs at a left turn onto a gravel road. This important turn is marked by a group of mailboxes on the right-hand side of the highway. After traveling approximately a half-mile, you will reach a fork. Bear right and in a quarter of a mile reach the south end of the lake at Bog Brook Cove, where you can leave your car. The road ends at the beach. Consult local maps such as those in DeLorme's Maine Atlas & Gazetteer to help you find this location. It will require four hours round-trip to shuttle your car to this place.

There are several public sites to camp overnight on the lake. The best is an island near the narrows that divides the lake. This is Hurricane Island, halfway down the lake. There are several state-maintained campsites on the island. The views of the Bigelow Range are outstanding.

A second campsite farther east is located at Round Barn Cove, on the south shore, four miles southeast of Hurricane Island. Safford Brook enters the lake near this cove. The state Department of Conservation maintains the numerous campsites here. This campground also can be accessed by auto over a narrow, rough, gravel road from Bog Brook and the Long Falls Dam Road.

Both camping areas have no resident campsite caretaker and are visited by rangers sporadically. The sites are available purely on a first-come basis, but they are free. In the Conservation Department terminology, these are "primitive" campsites.

The Safford Brook Trail starts on the gravel road access to the Round Barn Campground. This trail heads south and uphill into a sag between Bigelow's Avery Peak and Little Bigelow Mountain. Here it intersects the Appalachian Trail. The AT can then be followed up to Avery, the east summit. This is an all-day hike of about seven miles round trip. Thus, you may wish to consider a combined canoe and hiking trip to the summit of Bigelow, if you are willing to extend your canoeing trip to three or more days. Views from the summit are wonderful, providing a panoramic vista of the wild country the expedition passed through all the way north to the Canadian border. For those who wish to continue hiking on Bigelow, there are campsites and lean-tos at points along the range. The state has combination map-guides to the Bigelow Preserve. Contact:

Maine Bureau of Parks and Lands
P.O. Box 327
Farmington, ME 04938
(207) 778-8231

We also recommend consulting the pertinent federal topographical maps. Most sporting goods stores in Maine, such as L.L. Bean in Freeport, carry them.

Canoe Trip 5. The Chain of Ponds

This is a great half-day trip through the wild Chain of Ponds near the Height of Land and the Canadian border. The expedition reached these ponds on Oct. 25 and 26, 1775, after a very difficult ascent of the North Branch of the Dead River. When the men dragged themselves to the ponds, they were cold, wet, exhausted, and very hungry. They crossed the ponds in snow squalls, adding yet another layer of misery.

The Chain of Ponds is still relatively wild country, with quite similar conditions to those existing in 1775, although Route 27 parallels the ponds, and sometimes a logging truck's noisy engine will echo through the narrow valley. There are a few camps along the ponds' shores, and there is a campground at the northwest end. High mountains hem in both sides of the Chain, with craggy cliffs extending down to the water's edge in several places. The State of Maine has been actively buying land along the Chain to preserve its natural features. It is a lovely experience gliding over the clear, dark waters in a canoe, surrounded by high mountains on all sides. The local trout fishing is quite good.

The Chain is a string of five ponds connected by narrow thoroughfares, totaling five miles in length. It can be canoed equally as well in either direction, although the prevailing wind is usually from northwest to southeast. It can be done as a round trip, but spotting a car at the finish is not difficult. Purists who wish to traverse it in the same manner as the expedition should start at the southeast end at the outlet dam where the North Branch begins. This is reached by a narrow gravel road leaving Route 27 at 17.9mi. north of the center of Stratton or two miles north of Route 27's crossing of the North Branch. It is an obscure road, and you must have an eagle's eyes to catch it. It is about 200 yards along this road to the dam, where you can off-load your canoe.

After launching your canoe, glide slowly along the very beautiful ponds. The expedition's men, upon reaching the Chain where the current dam is located, rowed against a wicked head wind to the Chain's northwest end. Many men whose bateaux had been smashed had to join the men on foot and thrash along the rocky, snow-covered shoreline as best they could. Try to imagine bushwhacking along this shore in half-starved condition in ragged and wet clothes! Your trip up the Chain will be somewhat easier.

Toward the northwest end of the Chain, you will reach Natanis Pond, the largest. At its northwest end is a narrow peninsula that divides Natanis and the last of the Chain, Round Pond. Here is located the **Natanis Point Campground**, *a fine place to camp while in the area. It has a full range of facilities, and it has an excellent sand beach for swimming. The campground proprietor may be hired to spot cars. Canoes may be rented here as well. A small fee is charged to launch or take out canoes if you are not staying at the campground or are using your own canoe.*

Natanis Point was important to the expedition. It was where the eight-mile portage over the Height of Land began. Some men carried their bateaux over the Height, but most did not, abandoning their boats along the trail. Some followed Horseshoe Stream upstream from Round Pond, continuing the water route as far as Arnold Pond farther west, nearer the Height of Land. Natanis Point is also an historic campsite for Native Americans who for thousands of years used this site while traveling between the Atlantic coast and the St. Lawrence River. On the point is the grave of the Indian woman named Natanis. She has no known relationship to the 1775 Natanis, a man involved with the expedition. A trapper, she was murdered at the Chain of Ponds in the mid-nineteenth century.

As an extension to the trip or as a separate trip, you can cross Round Pond, find the mouth of Horseshoe Stream, and follow this beautiful, serpentine watercourse farther along the route of the expedition. For a mile or so, it is deep enough to canoe easily. Wildlife abounds along the stream. You will have to pull the canoe over several beaver dams when the stream narrows and becomes shallower. As it shallows to a few inches, you will have to "frog it" (wade the stream) by pulling your canoe over the gravel streambed in spots. This takes time and is not recommended for most canoes, as most bottoms will pay a price. You may leave a trail of paint the same color as your canoe.

If you plan to travel all the way to the last pond, you will have two portages of about a quarter-mile each over unmarked trails to reach Arnold Pond, the end of the water route. We highly recommend that you study and use topo maps of the area to guide you through this very confusing country. It is hard work to follow this part of the route! Only strong parties should attempt it. If you continue this way, you must cross, in order, Horseshoe Pond, Mud Pond, and finally Arnold Pond, which is one of the sources of the Kennebec. Arnold Pond lies only a half a mile from the Canadian border. It is much easier to use Route 27, which parallels Horseshoe Stream and the three ponds.

Chain of Ponds.

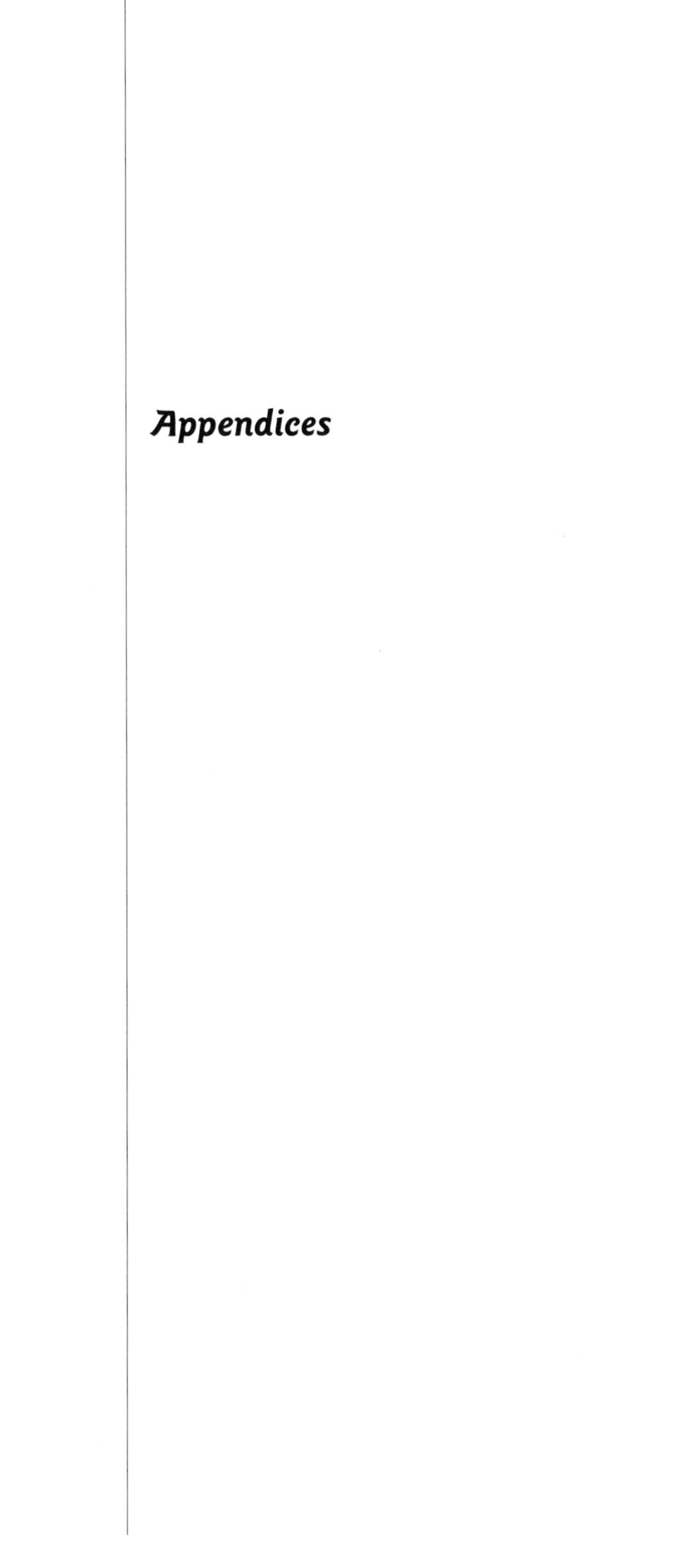

Appendices

Campgrounds along the Route

Listed in this section are campgrounds that could be used by travelers following the route of the expedition. There are many other campgrounds that could be listed. We are limiting this list to those most relevant to the expedition and its route. There are several easily found World Wide Web sites that contain listings of most campgrounds in Maine and Quebec Province. These may be referred to in order to expand the limited number of campgrounds here.

Most campgrounds are quite busy and sometimes full during July and August, so making reservations well in advance is essential to avoid disappointment.

There are no State of Maine or provincial campgrounds or parks with overnight sites along the route, but the Bigelow Preserve near Stratton, Maine, is adjacent to the route. The preserve does have some limited overnight, drive-in camping, but most sites in the preserve are reached by backpacking, including sites along the Appalachian Trail. The Maine Bureau of Parks and Lands Home Page describes these facilities and others nearby. Contact www.state.me.us/doc/prkslnds/park/htm, then click on "Public Reserved Lands."

Bath-Popham, Lower Kennebec River

There are no campgrounds along the Lower Kennebec River. There is a fine, full-service facility about six miles from Popham, located right on the ocean near Small Point. This is reached by following Routes 209 and 216 to the end of the peninsula. It has a fine sand beach and many excellent sites on both the ocean and an estuary. It has extensive hiking trails and possibilities for many outdoor activities.

Hermit Island
Small Point, ME 04562
(207) 443-2101
www.hermitisland.co

Solon-Bingham, Upper Kennebec River

In Solon, on the east shore of the Kennebec, is a fine campground, The Evergreens, located on one of the actual campsites used by the expedition. Several companies camped here. It is about a mile below Caratunk Falls (Devil's Falls). The site is also an old Native American campsite dating back thousands of years. Many artifacts have been discovered here. It is an excellent place from which to explore the entire Upper Kennebec River Valley and the Great Carrying Place. It has facilities for tents and RVs, a small restaurant, and some small cabins for rent. This is also the launch site for Canoe Trip 2. Canoes may be rented here.

Evergreens Campground
Route 201A
Solon, ME 04979
(207) 643-2324
www.kynd.com/evrgrncp

Stratton-Eustis

The Cathedral Pines Campground is near the head of Flagstaff Lake at the point where the North Branch of the Dead River resumes its course northwest into the Boundary Mountains. It is a good base from which to explore the entire Dead River country. The expedition's route is adjacent to the campground. All normal campground amenities are available here. It is beautifully situated within a huge grove of magnificent red pine. Located three miles north of Stratton on Route 27, it is open May 15 to October 1. This campground is also the launch site of Canoe Trip 4.

Cathedral Pines Campground
HC 72, Box 80
Eustis, ME 04936
(207) 246-3491

Chain of Ponds

The Natanis Point Campground may be the most beautiful along the entire route of the expedition. Located on the Chain of Ponds in wild country near the United States-Canada border, it is situated on a prominent peninsula dividing two of the ponds. High, majestic mountains surround the ponds. The campground is located on an old Native American campsite used for thousands of years. The men of the expedition also camped here. It marks the beginning of the long, eight-mile portage over the Height of Land. It has facilities for both RVs and tenters. Canoes may be rented here. It is the put-in or take-out point for Canoe Trip 5.

Natanis Point Campground
HC 73, Box 270
Eustis, ME 04936
(207) 297-2694
www.natanis@tdstelme.net

Lake Megantic (lac Mégantic)

There are four campgrounds on or near the lake. The largest, which offers all services and facilities including rustic camping, is located at the northwest corner of the lake less than two miles from downtown Lac-Mégantic. It has more than two hundred sites and many activities, including swimming in the lake. Like all campgrounds in Canada, July and August are very busy, so it would be wise to make reservations.

Baie des Sables
505, route 263 sud
Lac-Mégantic, Quebec, Canada G6B 2S5
(819) 583–3965
www.campingquebec.com/baiedessables

There is an excellent information center about a mile out of town on Route 161 (west). It can give you more information about the area.

St-Georges

Six kilometers north of St-George on Route 173 is a campground with facilities for both RVs and tenters. It is a large facility with full services.
Camping la Roche d'or
Route 173, Notre-Dame-des-Pins
Beauce, Quebec, Canada G0M 1K0
1-800-463-2240
www.quebecweb.com/larochedor

Lévis

Near the end of our journey, the city of Lévis lies on the south shore of the St. Lawrence River directly opposite Quebec City. There are at least four campgrounds in or near Lévis. They all claim to be within twelve minutes of the Lévis-Quebec ferry, which you may use to cross the river. As do most campgrounds in the province, they tend to cater more to RVs than to tenters. It is outside the scope of this book to list the individual campgrounds, since management and services change frequently. They tend to be very busy during July and August, so advanced reservations are important. Your best bet is to get on the web and contact the Lévis Tourist Information Bureau for an updated list:
Bureau d'Information Touristique de Lévis
Gate Intermodale de Lévis
5995 rue St-Laurent
Lévis, Quebec, Canada G6V 4E2
(418) 838-6026
www.ville.levis.qc.ca

We will just mention one campground that does cater to both tenters and RVs. It also has an excellent web site. It is listed in the Lévis Tourist Information Bureau's site listed above.
Camping Transit
Saint-Joseph-de-la-Pointe-de-Levy
Quebec, Canada G6V 6N4
(419) 838-0948
Email: flo@oricom.ca

Points of Interest along the Route of the Expedition

Below is a summary, for planning purposes, of major points of interest along the route of the expedition. They are arranged in geographical order from Cambridge to Quebec City. All relate directly to the expedition. They are explained in detail within the Travel Guide sections. There are, of course, a multitude of other interesting things to see or do along the route that are not directly related to the expedition. We suggest the reader use the Internet to check with local Chambers of Commerce for more detail.

Cambridge to Newburyport

*The **Longfellow House,** Washington's headquarters in Cambridge, where Arnold departed to begin the expedition.*
***Cambridge Common** in Cambridge, where most of the men of the expedition camped as they prepared for the march to Quebec.*
***Nathaniel Tracy House** in Newburyport, Arnold's headquarters for three days while preparations for the sea leg of the journey were completed.*
***Newburyport waterfront,** where the army boarded ships to be transported up the coast and into the Kennebec River.*
*The **Old South Church,** where many of the officers and men listened to a sermon by the expedition's chaplain, the Rev. Samuel Spring.*

Popham to Augusta

***Popham,** at the mouth of the Kennebec River. Fort Popham, a Civil-War-era fortification, is a major tourist site here.*
***The Chopps,** a narrow point in the Kennebec through which the fleet had to pass to reach Merrymeeting Bay before further ascent up the river. Several ships grounded in the shallow bay. The Chopps is in present-day Woolwich.*
***Swan Island,** where Henry Dearborn, Aaron Burr, and other officers stayed overnight while ascending the river. Several of the houses of that time are still standing. It is reached from Richmond.*
***Colburn House** in Pittston, which Arnold used as his headquarters for three days and where the bateaux were built in a nearby shipyard. Now it is the home of the Arnold Expedition Historical Society.*
***Fort Western** in Augusta, the assembly point for the expedition. This was the last significant settlement before the troops struck into the wilderness.*

Augusta to Caratunk

***Fort Halifax** in Winslow, where many of the men camped as they prepared for their first major portage.*
***Ticonic Falls** at the present Waterville-Winslow Bridge. This was the expedition's first portage.*
***Skowhegan Falls** in that town, which was the second*

major portage. The soldiers used the island between the falls as their portage route.

Norridgewock Falls *at Anson-Madison, where the expedition spent several days repairing their leaking bateaux while portaging the mile around the falls. Arnold spent five days here.*

The Evergreens, *now a private campground by the US Route 201A bridge in Solon, where many of the expedition's men camped overnight.*

Caratunk (Devil's) Falls *in Solon, the fourth portage on the Kennebec River.*

The Great Carrying Place *near Caratunk, a thirteen-mile portage between the Kennebec and Dead Rivers. The three Carry Ponds were part of the portage. This carry can only be followed on foot, using part of the Appalachian Trail (see Carry Ponds Side Trip).*

Stratton to Lake Megantic (Lac-Mégantic)

Bigelow Mountain, *named after Major Timothy Bigelow, located near Stratton. It offers fine hiking along the Appalachian Trail and provides great views of the expedition's route.*

Cathedral Pines, *near the point on the Dead River where the army was hit by a hurricane. This was also about where Lieutenant Colonel Enos and three companies, comprising the rear division, retreated downriver. It is in present-day Eustis.*

Ledge Falls, *one of the many portages along the North Branch of the Dead River. It is reached from Route 27.*

Shadagee Falls, *Camp Disaster, also reached from Route 27. This was the point where the hurricane flooded the river and the expedition lost seven bateaux with their cargos of precious food supplies.*

Sarampus Falls, *the last falls on the Dead River. It is now a small drop next to Route 27 at a picnic area.*

Natanis Point, *Chain of Ponds, where the men of the expedition began the eight-mile portage over the Height of Land to the Arnold River in Canada.*

Beautiful Meadow, *Arnold River, in Woburn, Quebec. This meadow has been transformed by commercial development. It was located along the banks of the Arnold River just north of the Route 161 bridge. It marked the end of the Height of Land portage.*

Lake Megantic swamp. *Route 161 skirts these swamps to the south and east before reaching the east shore of the lake. This swamp is not easily observed from the road and can be reached only by boat from either the Route 161 bridge or from the lake.*

Lake Megantic (Lac-Mégantic) to Lévis

The **outlet of Lake Megantic,** *in the center of the city of that name, is the beginning of the Chaudière River. The army followed along its course to the present town of Scott, near Ste-Marie.*

St-Ludger. *From this town northward, the highway follows the Chaudière Valley to Scott and is almost the exact route followed by the army. Most of the men were on foot.*

Grand Falls of the Chaudière. *Three miles south of Route 204's junction with Route 173 lie these falls. A short distance above, the starving men were saved when they met a relief party sent by Arnold with supplies and cattle.*

St-Georges, *at that time called Sartigan, the location of the first French settlement reached by the army. Arnold was able to obtain and store supplies here.*

Ste-Marie. *Here, Arnold called a halt to the march to allow stragglers to catch up and to rest and reorganize. He made his headquarters at the fine Taschereau Manor near the Chaudière River.*

Quebec City

Wolfe's Cove *is the point on the St. Lawrence where the expedition landed during the early morning of Nov. 14, 1775, avoiding two anchored British men-of-war. It is located three miles upstream from the ferry terminal and below the Plains of Abraham.*

Plains of Abraham. *Located just west of the walled city, this was where the army first confronted the enemy. Later, American artillery batteries were mounted on the plains.*

City walls. *Although they have been rebuilt and strengthened since 1775, a walk along these fortified walls will give the visitor a clear idea of what the American army was up against.*

Artillery Park. *Located near the St. John Gate (Porte St-Jean), it was the military center of the city. Many of the captured American soldiers were imprisoned here.*

First and Second Barricades. *In the Lower Town, their locations are marked by plaques. During the attack, the men of the expedition were caught between these two barricades, surrounded, and forced to surrender.*

Site of General Montgomery's death. *In the Lower Town, west of the ferry terminal, is the place where General Richard Montgomery and several of his chief officers fell during the attack on the snowy night of Dec. 31, 1775. A plaque on the cliffs marks this spot.*

Time Line of the Expedition to Quebec

This time line is given to help the reader understand the movement of the expedition. The four divisions and scouting contingents were at many different locations on a given day. For instance, when Arnold's party reached Sartigan, the first French settlement, on the first day of November, the rest of the army was located all along the Chaudière River route fifty miles back to Lake Megantic. As you follow the various contingents of the expedition, refer to this time line to sort out this sometimes-confusing picture of their positions in the line of march. The dates here are taken mainly from Benedict Arnold's journal.

September 11, 1775
The first troops leave Cambridge, Massachusetts, on the march to Newburyport.

September 15
Arnold leaves General Washington's headquarters in Cambridge. He travels by horse and arrives in Newburyport that evening.

September 16
The final contingent of troops arrives in Newburyport.

September 18
The entire army of 1,100 soldiers embarks on eleven coastal vessels and awaits good weather and favorable winds.

September 19
All vessels leave Newburyport during the morning and bear northward along the coast. At approximately midnight, the vessels heave to at the mouth of the Kennebec River in Maine.

September 20
The fleet enters the Kennebec and proceeds upriver, anchoring for the night at Georgetown.

September 21
The fleet continues up the river through Merrymeeting Bay. Some vessels reach the Colburn shipyard in Pittston. Others are grounded in the mud flats of the bay.

September 22
The troops disembark from the vessels and reload supplies, equipment, and arms into the waiting bateaux, which are then dispatched up the river to Fort Western, the assembly point.

September 23
The army continues to shuttle men and equipment to Fort Western. The men continue preparations for striking out into the wilderness. Arnold arrives at Fort Western.

September 24
Arnold dispatches Lieutenant Steele and six men upriver to scout the route over the Height of Land. He also dispatches Lieutenant Church and seven men with a surveyor and a guide to scout and mark the route over the Great Carrying Place from the Kennebec to the Dead River. The army continues preparations for the departure of the expedition upriver.

September 25
Captain Morgan with the three rifle companies forming the First Division depart from Fort Western with orders to proceed to the Great Carrying Place, there to cut a portage trail for themselves and succeeding divisions.

September 26
Lieutenant Colonel Greene, leading the Second Division, proceeds upriver with three companies.

September 27
The Third Division, consisting of four companies, leaves Fort Western under Major Meigs. Sick and injured men are sent back downriver on the last of the departing transports.

September 28
Most of the remaining troops move up from the Colburn shipyard to Fort Western. Lieutenant Colonel Enos remains at Colburn's awaiting completion of the final bateaux.

September 29
Arnold departs Fort Western, leaving Enos to collect the last men and provisions. They proceed the following day. Scott's and McCobb's companies leave the fort. Arnold camps this night on the river at Six Mile Falls, south of Fort Halifax.

September 30
Arnold proceeds upriver to Ticonic Falls, where he finds Dearborn's and Goodrich's companies portaging around the falls in what is now Waterville. Arnold hires a team to portage his canoe and baggage about five miles upstream to avoid a section of rips in the river.

October 1
Arnold proceeds up the river through a number of rapids and fast water. He reaches Skowhegan Falls and portages over on a rocky island dividing the falls. He proceeds upriver five miles farther and lodges at the Widow Warren's house in the present town of Norridgewock.

October 2
Arnold proceeds upriver to Norridgewock Falls (at present, between Madison and Anson), where he overtakes Morgan's lead division, which had just completed the portage around the falls. He camps here for the next several days as he oversees the long portage.

October 3
Arnold stays at Norridgewock Falls to direct Thayer's and Hubbards's companies over the portage. The bateaux at this point are very leaky, and repairs are made. Some provisions are already spoiled. The First Division proceeds upriver toward the Great Carrying Place.

October 4
Greene's Second Division completes repairs and proceeds upriver. Meigs's Third Division arrives and begins repairs and portaging. Colburn and some of his carpenters arrive to help on the repairs to the leaky bateaux.

October 6
Meigs's division departs upriver. Enos and the Fourth Division arrive at the falls and begin the carry.

October 8
Enos's division continues to sort bad provisions and carry equipment over the portage. Arnold portages his equipment and canoe to the end of the carry. A heavy rain keeps him here.

October 9
Arnold leaves Norridgewock Falls and continues upstream, portaging over the neck of a serpentine bend in the river. He passes Six Mile Stream (now the Carrabassett River) and camps with McCobb's company on one of the many islands in the river, two miles south of Caratunk Falls.

October 10
Arnold reaches Caratunk Falls (at the present Williams Dam in Solon), which Arnold describes as about a fifteen-foot sheer drop. After a short carry, his party proceeds ten miles farther through very swift water to a point north of present-day Bingham.

October 11
Arnold's party heads upriver and reaches the mouth of Carrying Place Stream, which marks the beginning of the Great Carry to the Dead River. Arnold catches up with Morgan's and Greene's lead divisions, who are portaging to the first of the three Carry Ponds. Church reports the Great Carry is about thirteen miles across.

October 12
To supervise portaging, Arnold camps near the west shore of the first pond. He orders a log cabin be built to house sick men who are to be sent back downriver. He dispatches Lieutenants Steele and Church north to the Height of Land to cut a portage trail.

October 13
Arnold reports that this day parts of two divisions have reached the Dead River. He writes dispatches to Washington and to "certain men in Quebec."

October 14
Arnold completes the second portage to Middle Carry Pond and continues over the third portage to the east shore of West Carry Pond. He comments on the beauty of the pond and of the "forked mountain" (Bigelow Mountain) in the distance.

October 16
Arnold and his party cross a horrible, mile-wide bog in knee-deep mud, finally reaching Bog Brook, which marks the end of the Great Carrying Place. This leads in about a mile to the Dead River. They then proceed rapidly up the relatively placid, winding river almost eighteen miles farther and camp with Greene's Division near the present town of Stratton. While portaging Hurricane Falls, he passes Morgan's division, which has temporarily fallen into second place. He comments on an Indian hut on a prominent point, the lodge of Natanis.

October 17
At Greene's Camp, Arnold dispatches Major Bigelow to take men to the rear division to bring up provisions, as Greene's companies are found to be short of food. Morgan's division passes and resumes the lead. The weather turns bad, and a steady rain commences—to last for five days.

October 18
Goodrich's and Dearborn's companies pass Arnold's encampment. Meigs's companies arrive at dark. Arnold gives orders to begin making cartridges for the muskets.

October 19
Arnold proceeds up the North Branch of the Dead River to a falls requiring a short portage, now known as Black Cat Rapids, near the town of Eustis. He camps here. Steady rain falls all day and even harder during the night.

October 20
Arnold remains in camp while Meigs's division comes up and portages the falls, then continues on. It rains very hard all this day.

October 21
Arnold's party proceeds upriver in a steady rain, portaging around four falls, and camps upstream of Ledge Falls early in the evening. Because of rain-saturated wood, they have a hard time getting a fire going to dry out their clothes. About 4 a.m., the roar of the river, which according to Arnold's estimate rose nine feet during the night, awakens them. They have to abandon their camp and retreat to higher ground.

October 22
The storm, a full-blown hurricane, continues, and the raging river makes it dangerous to proceed. Arnold and his men spend most of the day trying to dry their clothing and equipment. Arnold writes that the provisions are almost exhausted.

October 23
The army continues to flounder against the floodwaters of the Dead River. When they reach a large tributary of the North Branch (Alder Stream), part of the detachment on foot mistakenly follows it for several miles. A major setback occurs when seven bateaux are overturned and destroyed in the raging water, all provisions being lost. The two lead divisions and Arnold camp here, naming it Camp Disaster.

October 24
Arnold and the officers present have a council of war and decide to send back twenty-six sick or injured men with fifteen days' provisions. The water is still at flood stage, and it rains most of the day. Captain Hanchet and fifty men are dispatched ahead to attempt to reach the French settlements to send back food. Arnold's party continues upstream and camps a mile south of the first of the Chain of Ponds.

October 25
Arnold and the two lead divisions finally reach the Chain of Ponds. They row up the five connected ponds against a heavy headwind and snow squalls.

They reach the end of the ponds and enter narrow Horseshoe Stream. They push on one and a half miles and camp, not knowing if they are on the correct route.

Meanwhile, down the Dead River near the present town of Eustis, another council of war is taking place. It includes Greene, Enos, and their officers. Enos and his three company captains say they will not continue and decide to return to Cambridge.

October 26

Arnold proceeds up Horseshoe Stream, reaching a series of small ponds with portages between each. His party then continues over the Height of Land through a low gap, camping that night with some of Captain Hanchet's men.

October 27

Arnold completes the one remaining mile of the portage, reaching a beautiful meadow next to what is now the Arnold River, in present-day Woburn, Quebec. When his baggage and boats come up, the river is followed north toward Lake Megantic. His party emerges from a swamp onto the lake, row about two miles to a prominent point, and camp at an Indian bark hut. Captain Hanchet and his fifty men attempt to follow along the river on foot and are caught in the swamp. They have to wade in cold water for more than two miles until they come out near the edge of the lake. Upon hearing their cries, Arnold sends his remaining bateaux to ferry them across to his campsite

October 28

Arnold's party rows the remaining twelve miles to the north end of Lake Megantic. Its outlet is the beginning of the Chaudière River. Arnold's group begins its descent of the river. After going down continuous rapids for twenty miles, they overturn three of their bateaux.

October 29

Arnold's party continues down a rocky and widening river for twenty-nine miles. His birch-bark canoe hits a rock and is lost. Back at the "Beautiful Meadow," the rest of the army breaks into two groups, one descending along the Arnold River into the swamp, the other trying to skirt the swamp to the east. Most of the bateaux have been abandoned upon receiving Arnold's orders, so most of the army is on foot.

October 30

Arnold's party continues down the Chaudière, reaching a large falls that they portage with their two remaining bateaux. They meet two friendly Indians who help them. They soon reach the junction of the River des Loups and, a short distance below, the first French habitation at Sartigan, present-day St-Georges.

October 31

Arnold immediately sends back supplies and food to the starving troops straggling down the Chaudière from Lake Megantic.

November 1

Arnold continues to collect and store supplies and food for his army. He also lays plans for the last push to Quebec City. For the next four days, detachments straggle into the French villages. Arnold continues downriver as far as Ste-Marie.

November 6

Arnold continues to procure supplies for his troops and to prepare for the final march on Quebec. He is able to gather about forty canoes and other craft.

November 7

Late in the afternoon, the army begins its final march. Under the cover of darkness, they proceed as far as St-Henri and send out scouts.

November 8

Arnold's advance detachments arrive at Caldwell's Mill on the south shore of the St. Lawrence west of Lévis. During the next several days, more troops arrive from Ste-Marie.

November 13

Two British warships are anchored in the St. Lawrence to prevent the American army from crossing. Arnold and the men make final preparations for crossing, bringing to the mill the hidden canoes and boats. Arnold decides to cross this night.

November 14

Over 400 men are ferried across the St. Lawrence to Wolfe's Cove, three miles above Quebec, silently passing around the two British warships. At Wolfe's Cove below the Plains of Abraham, Arnold organizes his troops. After ascending to the plains, they find the gates to the city closed and guarded. The army begins a siege. After several days, most of the army retires to a small village upriver, Point-aux-Trembles.

December 1

General Richard Montgomery arrives at Point-aux-Trembles to join Arnold. He assumes command. He brings about 300 men with him and some light artillery. Arnold has 675 soldiers, some in poor condition. During the next four weeks, they mount continuing pressure on the city's defenders with mortars and small-caliber cannons. The British bombard the Americans with cannon fire.

December 31, 1775

The attack on Quebec begins after dark in a blinding snowstorm. General Montgomery attacks under the cliffs of Cap Diamant and is killed by a lucky cannon blast on a narrow road. Leaderless, his contingent retreats. Arnold leads an attack on the Lower Town through the suburb of St-Roch.

After overcoming the first barrier, he is shot in the leg and carried off to a hospital. Captain Morgan assumes command and penetrates farther into the Lower Town. But the troops are unable to overcome a second barrier and, as dawn breaks, they are cut off and surrounded in the narrow streets. Nearly 400 men are captured. After the attack, the remainder of the army stays at Point-aux-Trembles until spring, when a large British relief force arrives at Quebec, requiring the American army to retreat.

Note to Educators

As a former educator, the author hopes that teachers will consider the material in this book useful to expand the classroom experience. Classroom use of the book would complement the usual Maine history curriculum, but the best educational experience would occur if a class followed a section of the route as a field trip.

However, there are limits on expedition-related field trips. Most trips can take place only within the very tight time constraints of the daily class schedule. That would mean a limit of six to seven hours, at most, to manage such a trip. A Saturday trip could add a little more time, but not much.

And, to make the trip meaningful, the travel time should be limited to about an hour each way to reach and return from a part of the expedition's route. This would place a distance limit of approximately sixty miles from the school to a given site along the expedition's route. If your school is within this rough driving zone, and you are able to twist your superintendent's budget arm, it may be possible to plan one or a series of field trips. Below are listed some trips that could work. The educational value of such a trip will depend on the students' receptivity to the experience, and the teacher can best judge that.

Each trip should contain a fun element as well as an educational component. Kids need to be out and actively "doing" something, as every teacher knows so well. Museum-type trips work only in small, well-planned doses. The younger the student, the more important this suggestion becomes.

1. Newburyport, Massachusetts

Use the city's walking tour, which will take in the Boardwalk on the waterfront, the Maritime Museum, the Tracy House, the Old South Church, the Green, and much more. The architecture of the old three-story homes is wonderful. The Chamber of Commerce and the staff at the library (Tracy House) can help you organize this trip.

2. Popham to Bath, Maine

In addition to a fifteen-mile drive along the beautiful lower Kennebec River, this will include exploring Fort Popham, a short hike up to Fort Baldwin, and, possibly, a stop for lunch at Popham Beach State Park. The site of the old Popham Colony of 1607 can be included. An excellent trip!

3. Maine Marine Museum, Bath

There is so much to see and explore here, it will require a full day trip. Make arrangements with the museum coordinator, as the museum has special programs for students. It can be combined with a boat trip up the Kennebec, if time allows.

4. Swan Island near Richmond

This trip will require coordination with the Maine Department of Inland Fisheries and Wildlife because it involves a short ferry ride to reach the island. A guided tour can be arranged to view the historic and wildlife-management sites. A campground halfway down the island will provide a picnic spot. This is a great educational site.

5. Old Fort Western, Augusta

This museum is possibly the best in Maine in depicting colonial life. It has excellent educational programs for students of different ages, including demonstrations of weaving and spinning, musket and cannon firings, plus numerous other displays. Contact the museum's director for details. Nearby, in the State Capitol complex, is the Maine State Museum, with many historical exhibits.

6. Waterville to Skowhegan

This is a twenty-mile trip up the expedition's route along the middle Kennebec River. Include a stop at Fort Halifax in Winslow and the fine L.C. Bates Museum in Hinkley. A good picnic spot is Coburn Park in Skowhegan.

Any material within this book may be reproduced without special permission, up to twenty pages, if intended for educational purposes.

There are two main sources for much of the material in this book. The definitive authority for the expedition is Justin H. Smith's *Arnold's March from Cambridge to Quebec,* published in 1903 by G. P. Putnam & Sons, New York. A 1989 paperback reprint by Heritage Books is, unfortunately, also out of print, but, like other out-of-print volumes mentioned here, they may be found in many libraries or used-book establishments. Smith's book is a scholarly and meticulous reconstruction of events surrounding the expedition. Smith wrote at a time when there were no accurate topographic maps of the route. Also, sections of the route were still quite wild. For instance, the Chain of Ponds country at that time did not even have a road passing through it. The book is heavily footnoted and draws copiously from the expedition journal writers' own words. It may be too detailed and scholarly for many readers, but it delves several layers deeper into the expedition's history than does this book.

Kenneth Roberts, the famous American historical novelist and writer for *The Saturday Evening Post,* wrote two excellent novels in the 1930s about the northern campaign of the American Revolution. *Arundel* chronicles the Expedition to Quebec and its defeat. *Rabble in Arms,* a sequel, weaves a wonderful story around the events of the subsequent American defeats at Valcour Island and Ticonderoga, and it ends with the monumental American victory at Saratoga. Doubleday originally published them, but Down East Books now has them in paperbacks. These constitute great reading and are highly recommenced. We suggest reading at least *Arundel* before undertaking a serious retracing of the expedition's journey. This book will give the reader an appreciation for what the men experienced in a way that only a great novelist can.

While Roberts was undertaking his careful research before writing *Arundel,* he began an effort to locate and compile all the known journals of the expedition. Doubleday published this important compilation as *March to Quebec* in 1938. It, too, is out of print. At the time it was published, there were forty-six men who were known to have written accounts of the journey. Their journals comprise a rich, first-hand history. Since the publication of *March to Quebec,* several other journals have come to light. They should be printed in book form within several years.

Other useful sources of information about the expedition are:

Arnold, Isaac N. *The Life of Benedict Arnold: His Patriotism and His Treason.* Chicago: 1880.

Boatner, Mark M., III. *Encyclopedia of the American Revlution.* Mechanicsburg, Penn.: Stackpole Books, 1994.

Codman, John. *Arnold's Expedition to Quebec.* New York: 1901.

Gardner, John. *The Dory Book.* Mystic Conn.: Mystic Seaport Museum, 1987. This volume details the history and construction of bateaux.

Martin, James Kirby, *Benedict Arnold, Revolutionary Hero: An American Warrior Reconsidered.* New York: New York University Press, 1997.

There are many other biographies on the life of Benedict Arnold that contain limited information about the expedition's journey. These may be found in any large library.

ABOUT THE AUTHOR

Stephen Clark lives in the small Maine town of Shapleigh. A native of Maine, he has spent a good part of his life exploring its ponds, lakes, rivers, and mountains as an avid hiker, canoeist, camper, and guide to youth groups.

A former businessman, teacher, and coach, he has been associated most of his life with the care and protection of the Appalachian Trail. He is past president of the Maine Appalachian Trail Club and past vice chairman of the national Appalachian Trail Conference. A life-long conservationist, he has been an officer of several environmental organizations.

For fifteen years, he has been editor of *Guide to the Appalachian Trail in Maine.* He also is the author of *Katahdin: A Guide to Baxter Park and Katahdin,* currently in its fifth edition. He has written numerous articles about the mountains and rivers of Maine.

As a young man, he became fascinated with the story of the famous 1775 expedition to capture Quebec. He has walked and canoed the route several times. *Following Their Footsteps* results from his recognition that there were no guides to help the modern traveler enjoy this historic trail.

Maps to
Following Their Footsteps

A section of twenty maps of the route of the Expedition to Quebec

Map 1. Cambridge Walking Tour

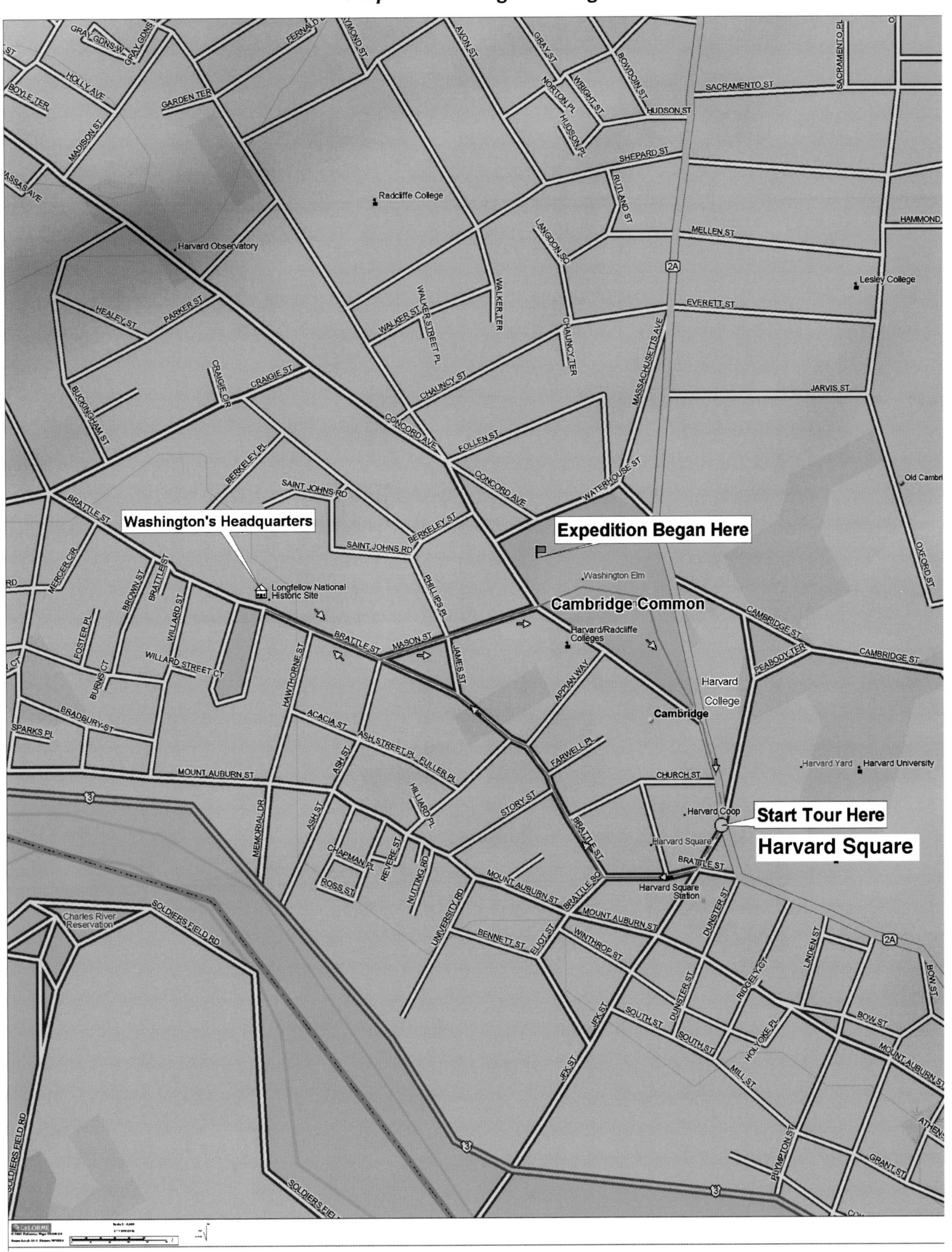

Map 2. Newburyport

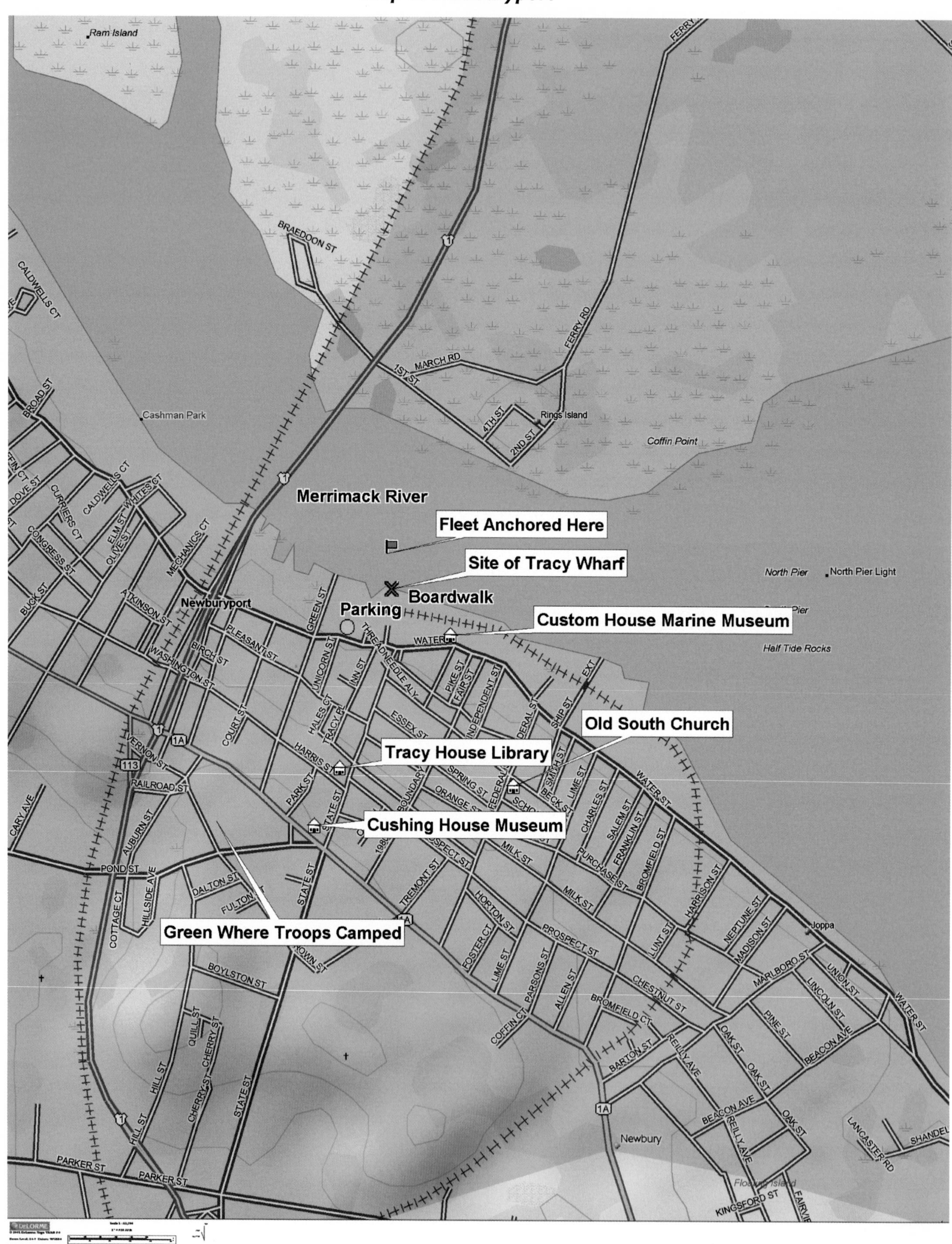

Map 3. Mouth of the Kennebec River

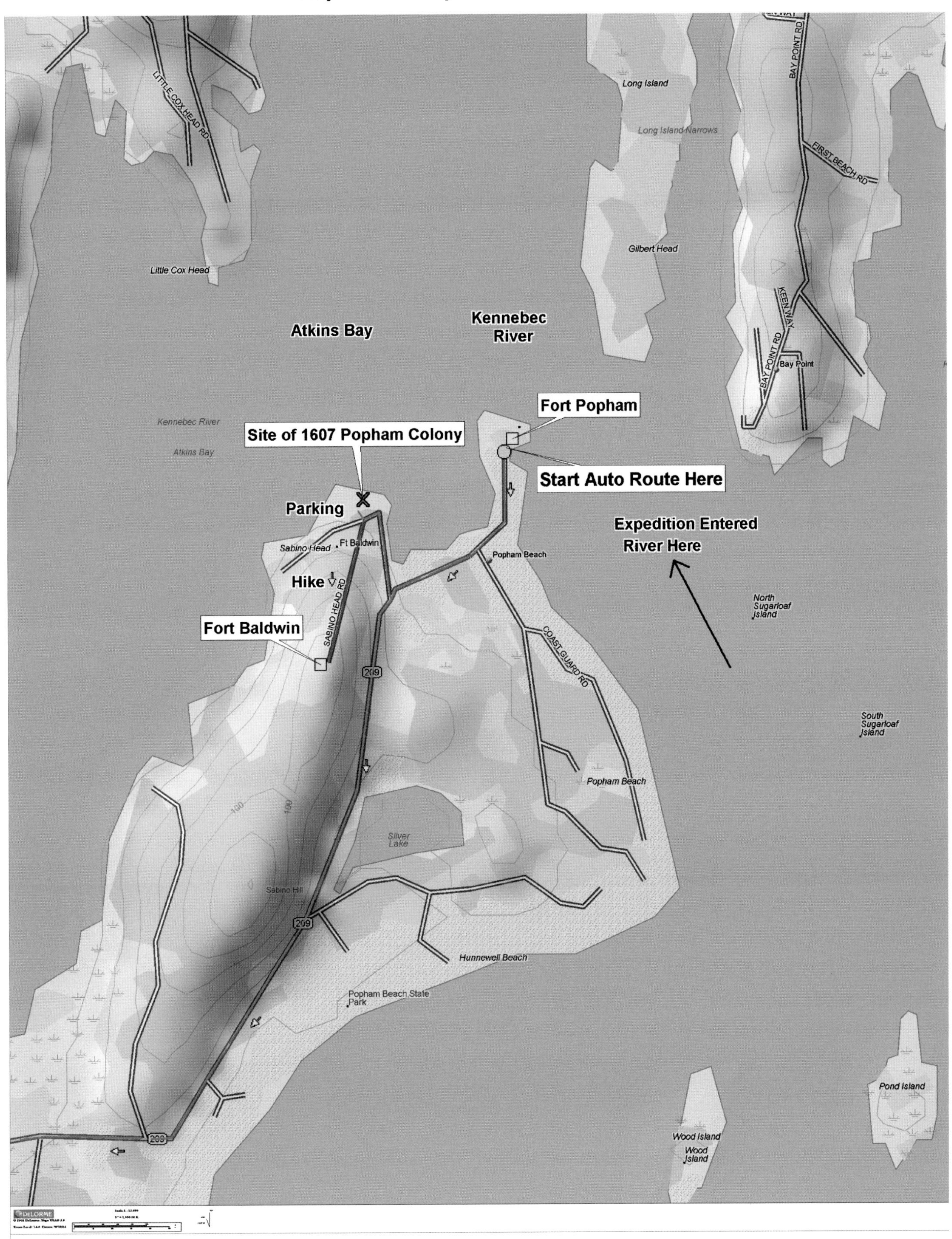

Map 4. Popham to Bath

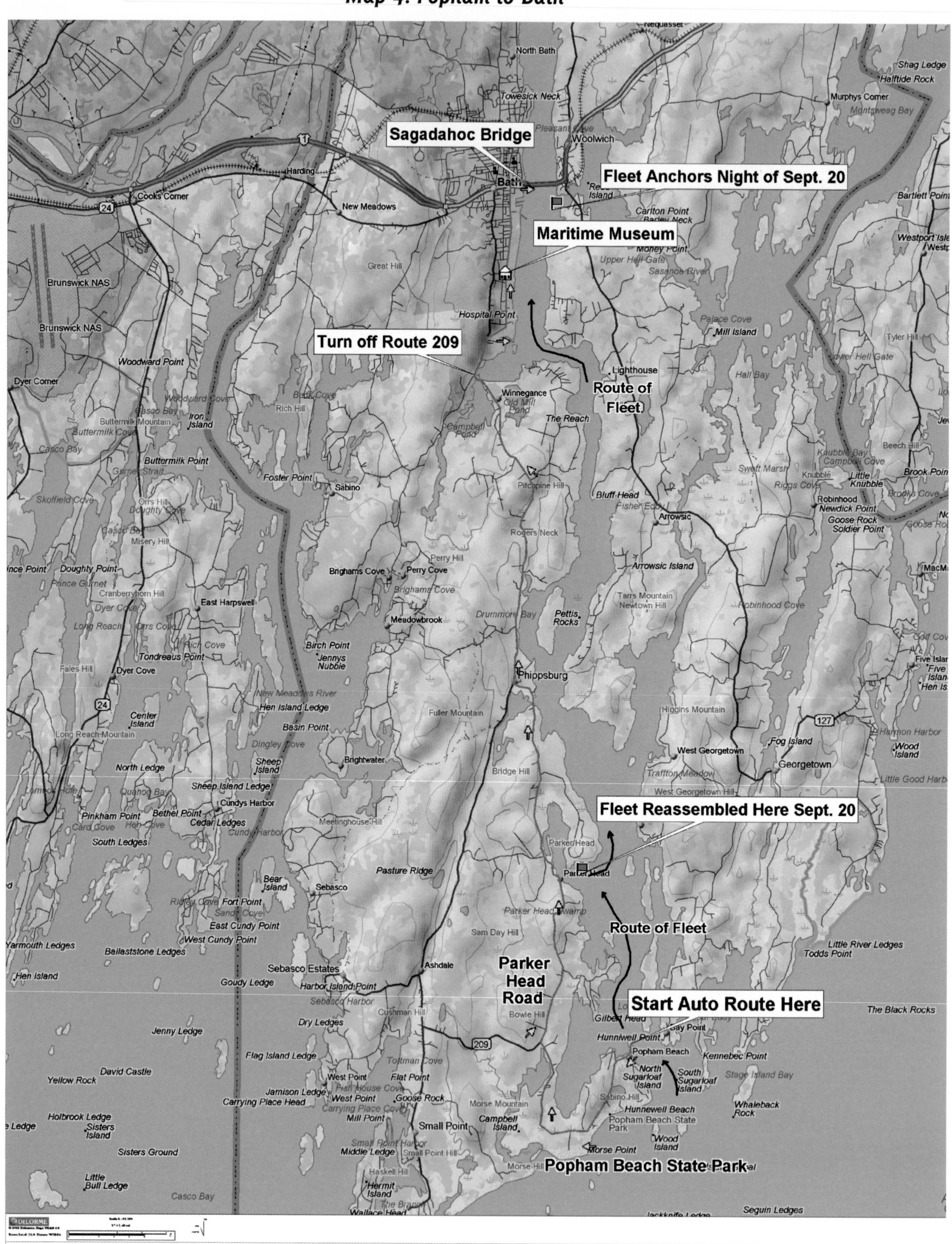

Map 5. Bath to Richmond

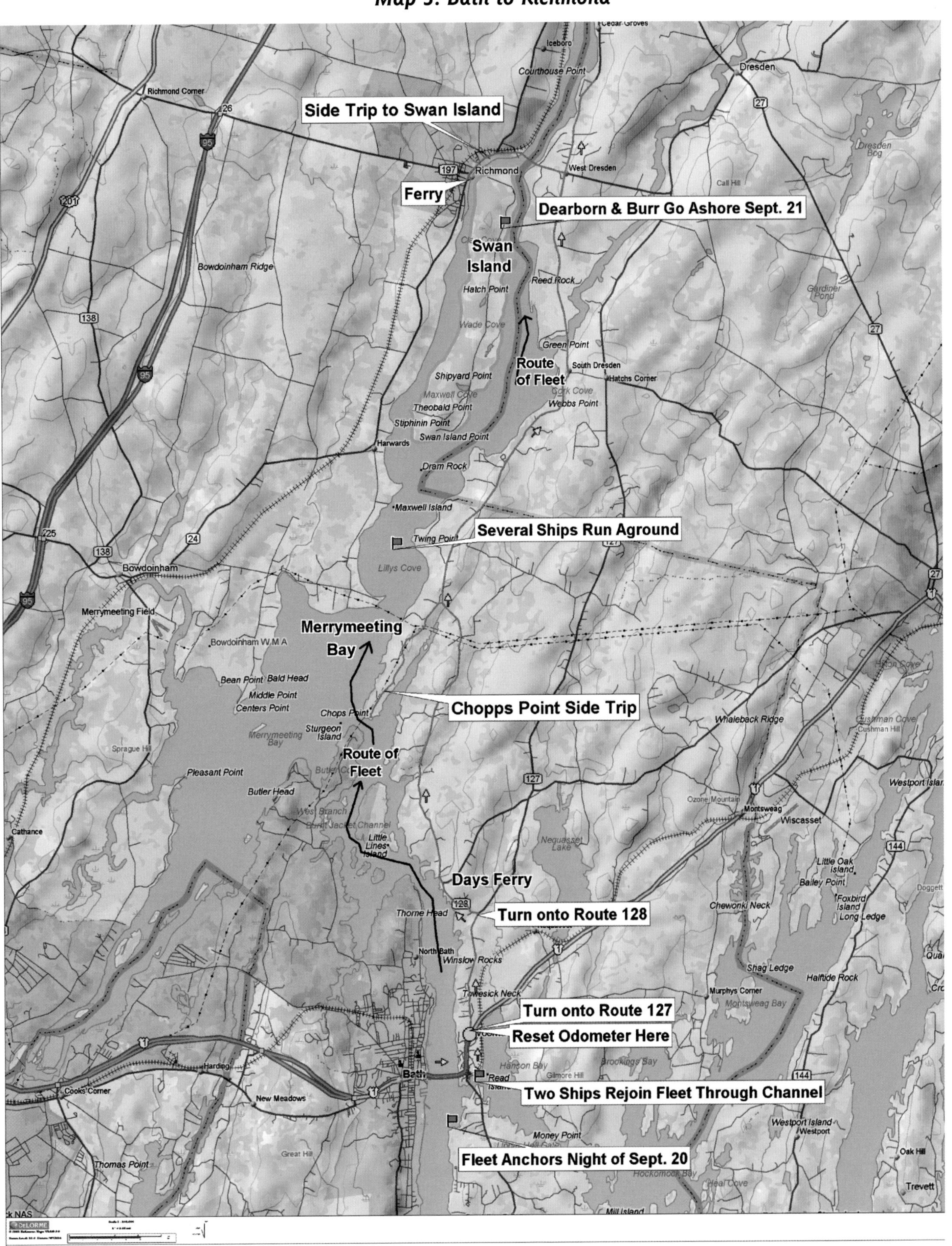

Map 6. Richmond to Hallowell

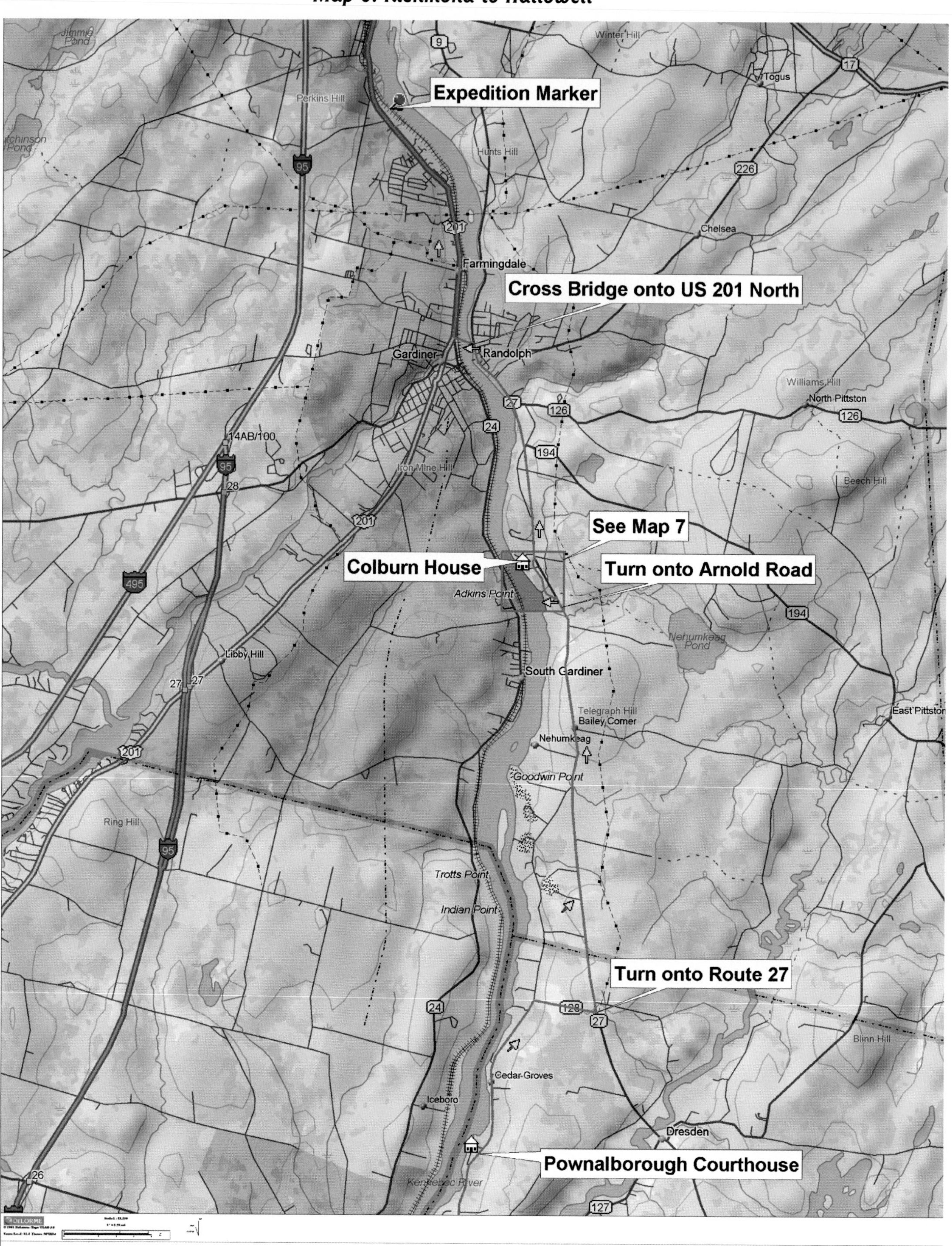

Map 7. Colburn House and Shipyard

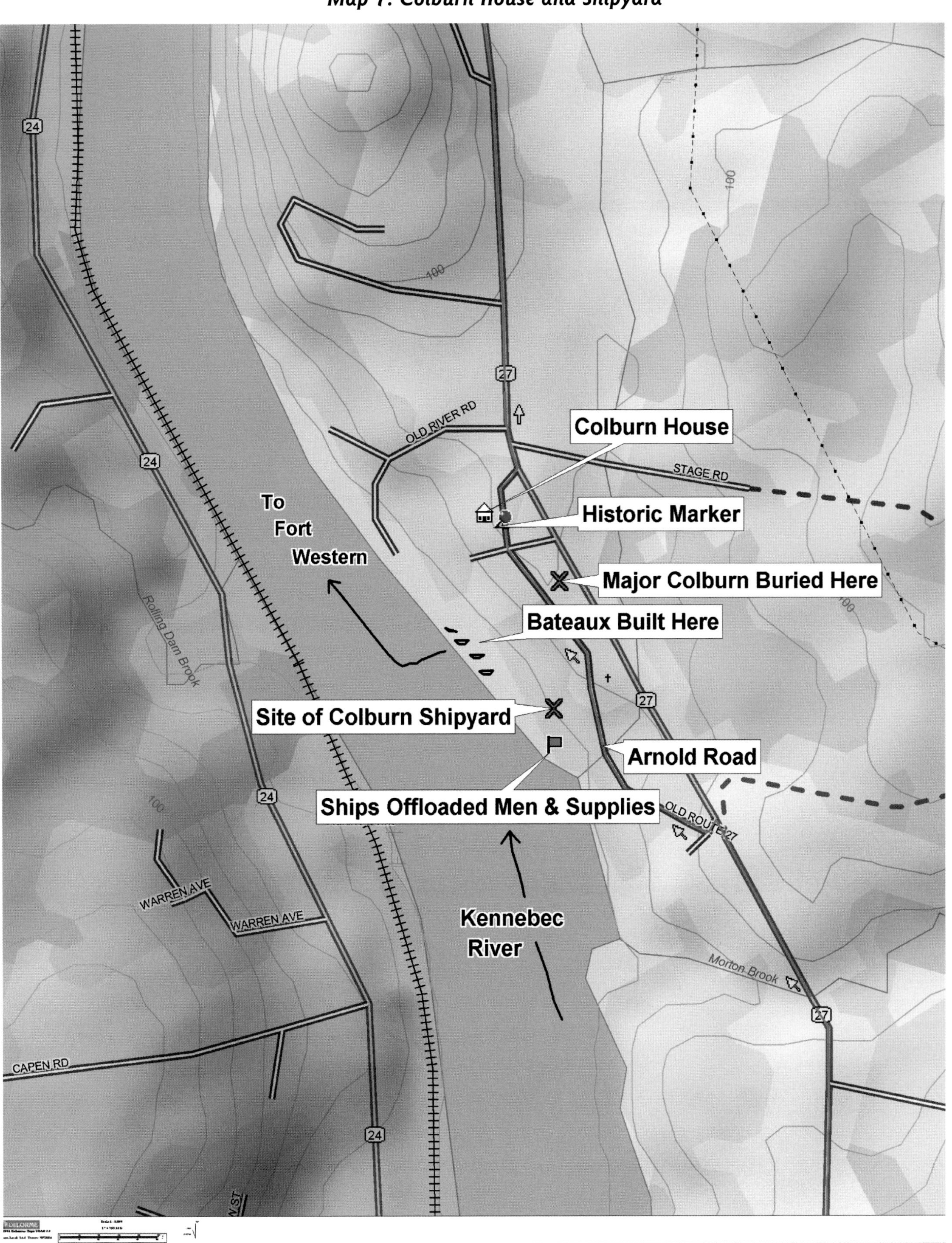

Map 8. Fort Western, Augusta

Map 9. Waterville-Winslow, First Portage for Expedition

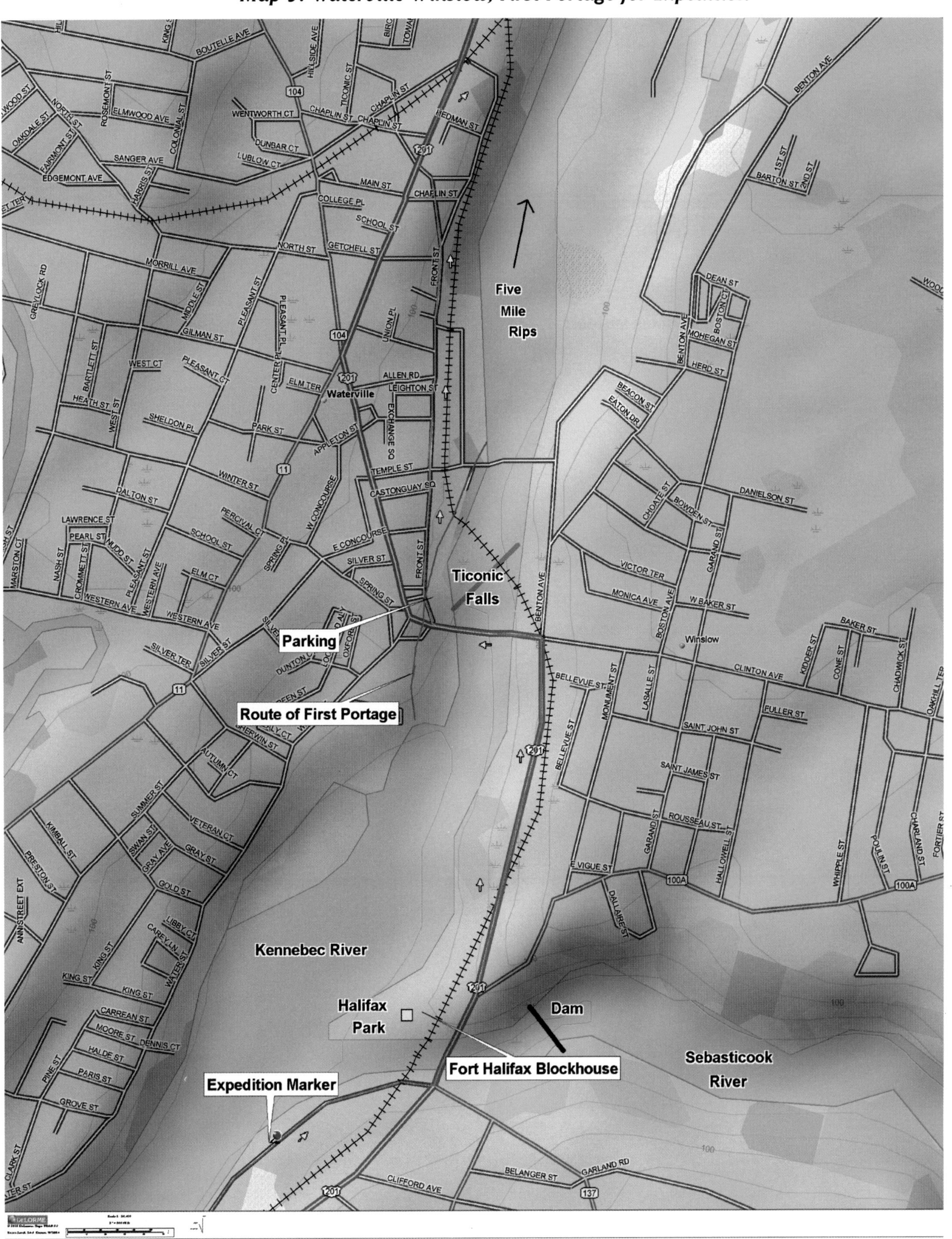

Map 10. Fairfield to Hinckley

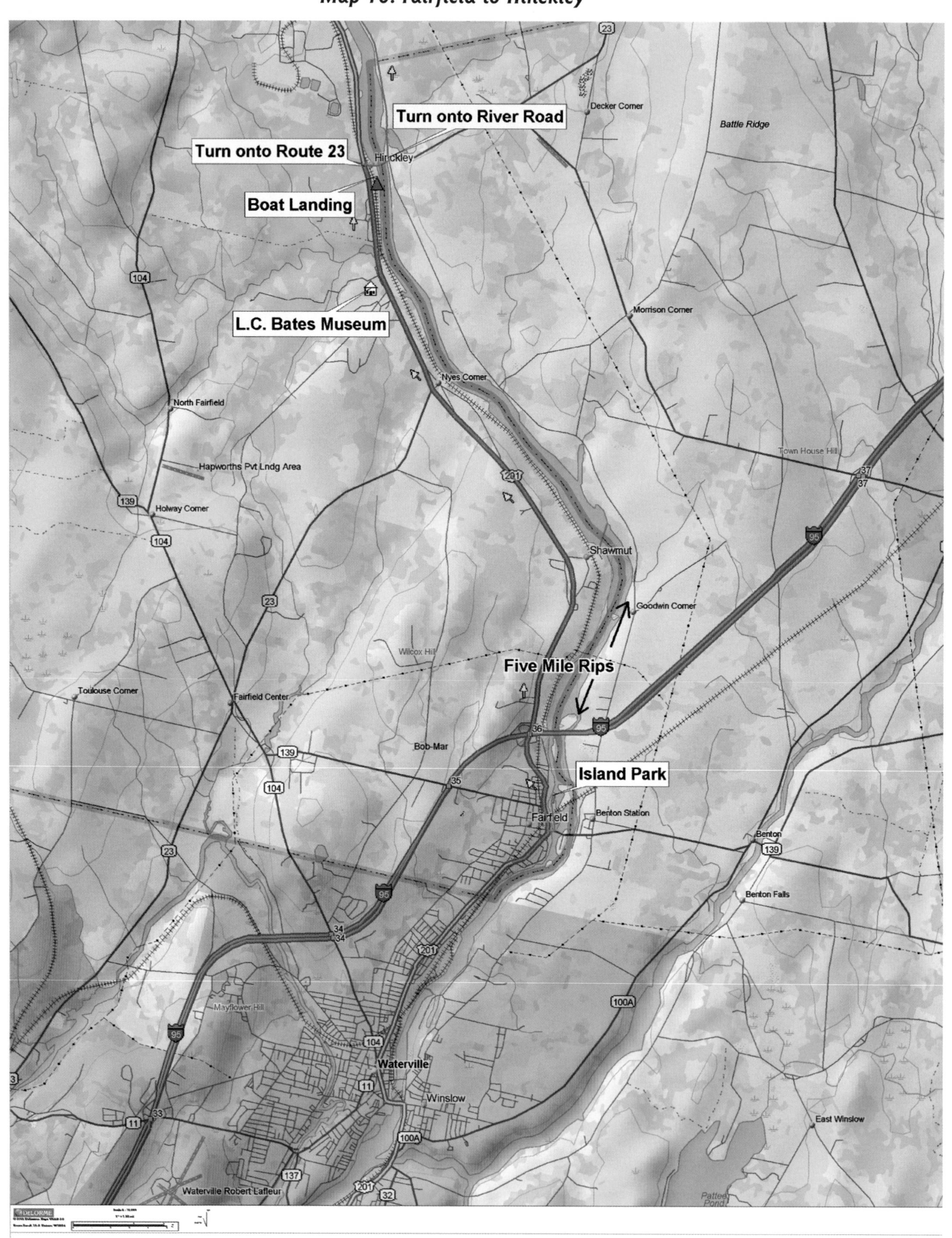

Map 11. Skowhegan, Second Major Portage

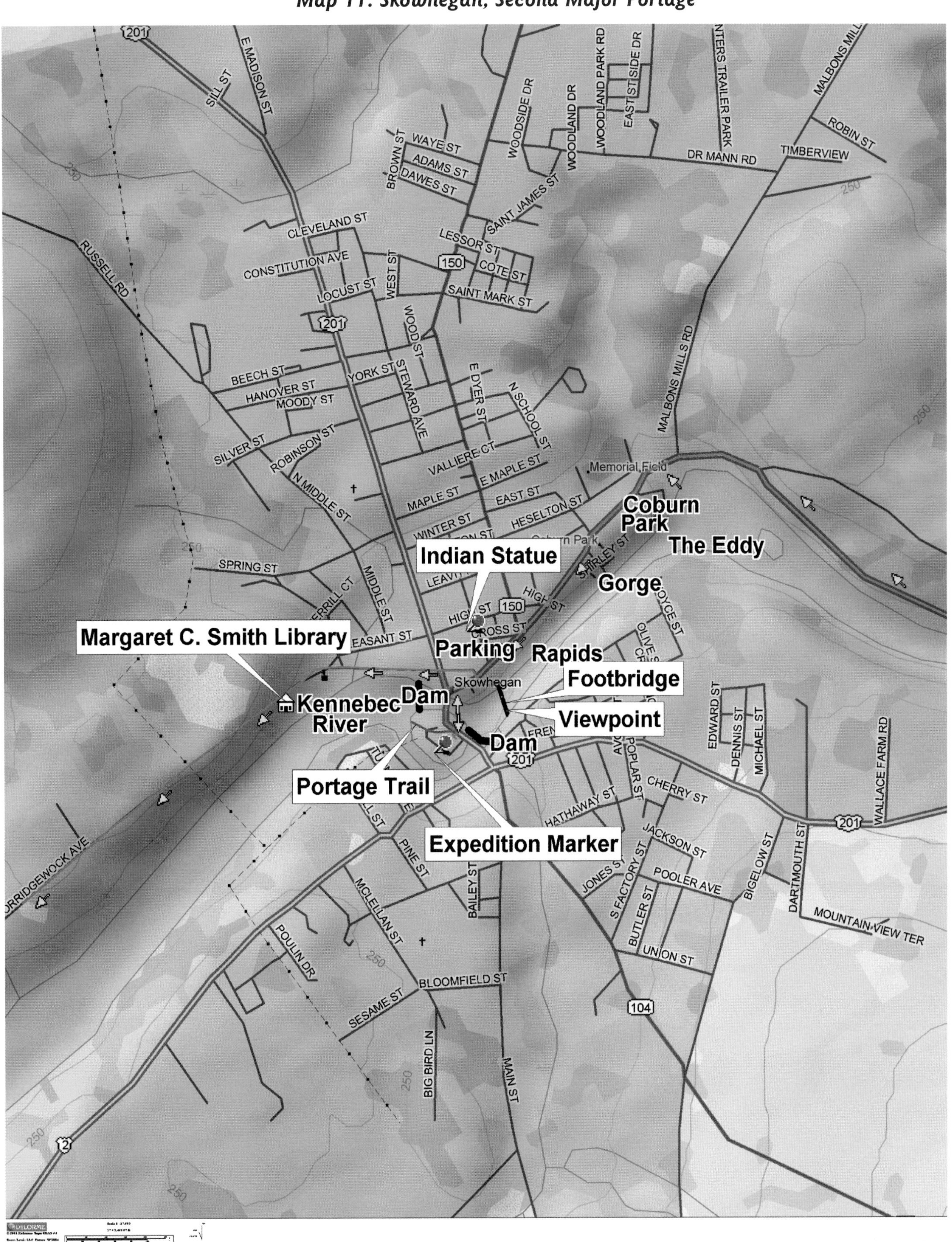

Map 12. Skowhegan to North Anson

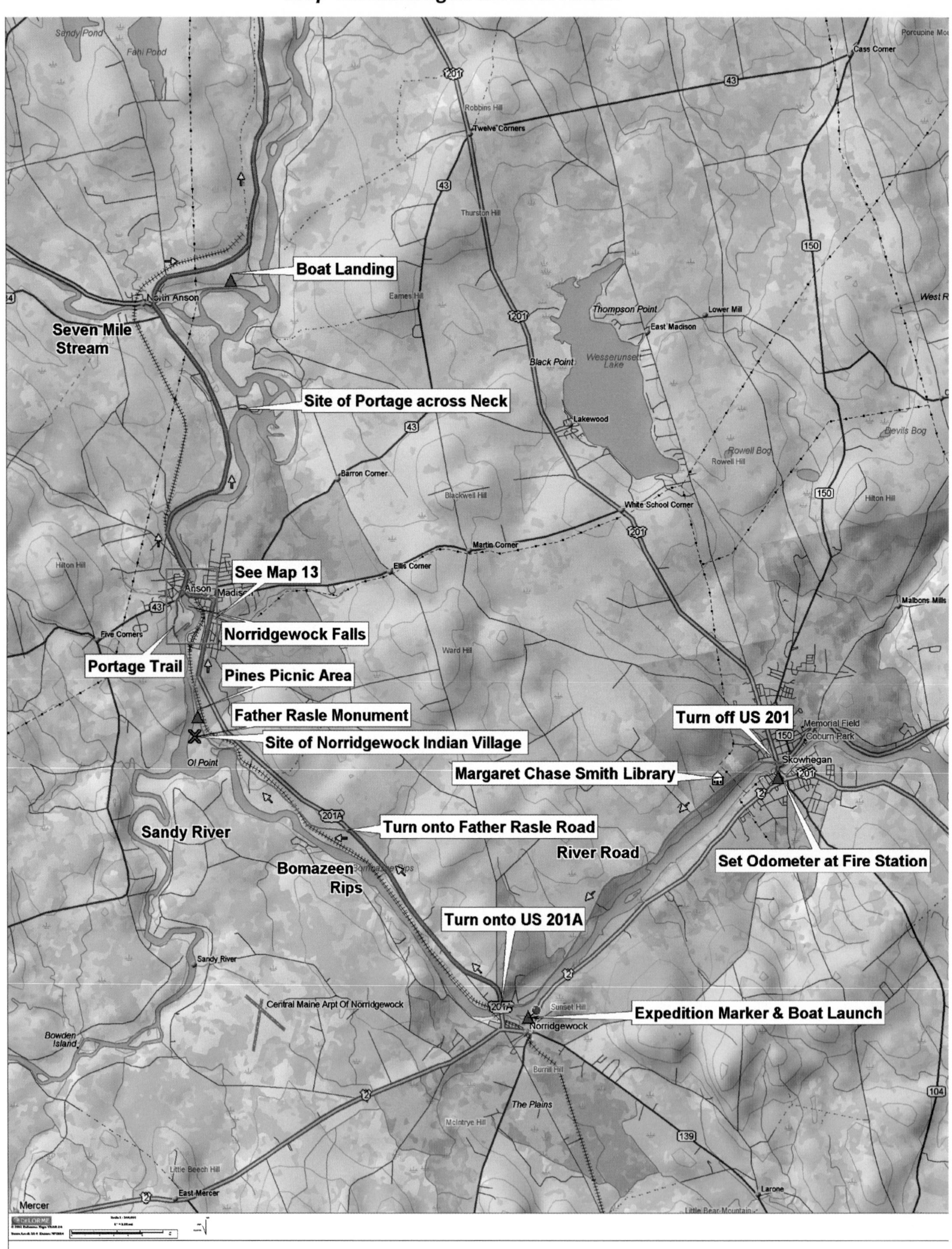

Map 13. Norridgewock Falls, Third Portage

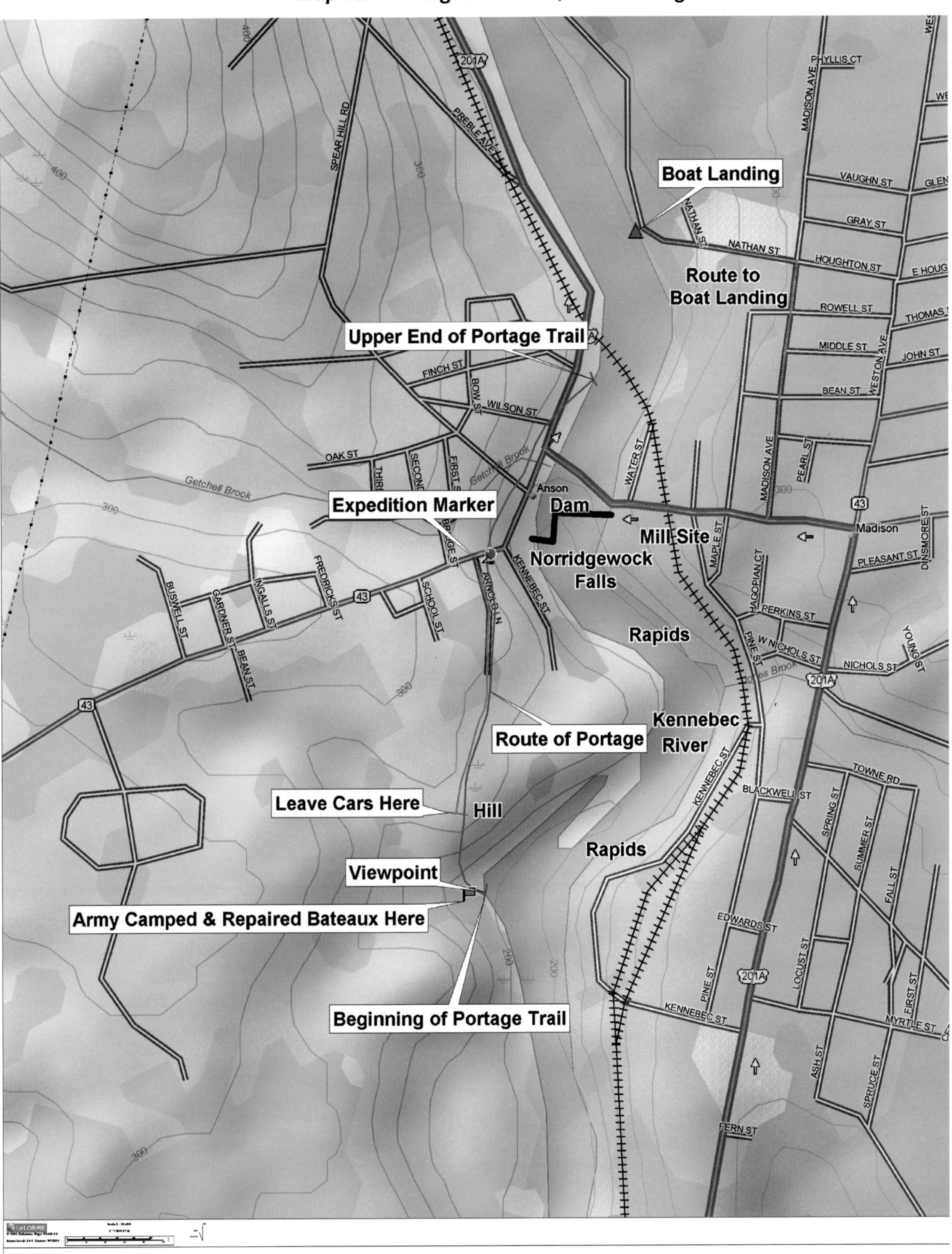

Map 14. Solon, Caratunk Falls, Fourth Portage

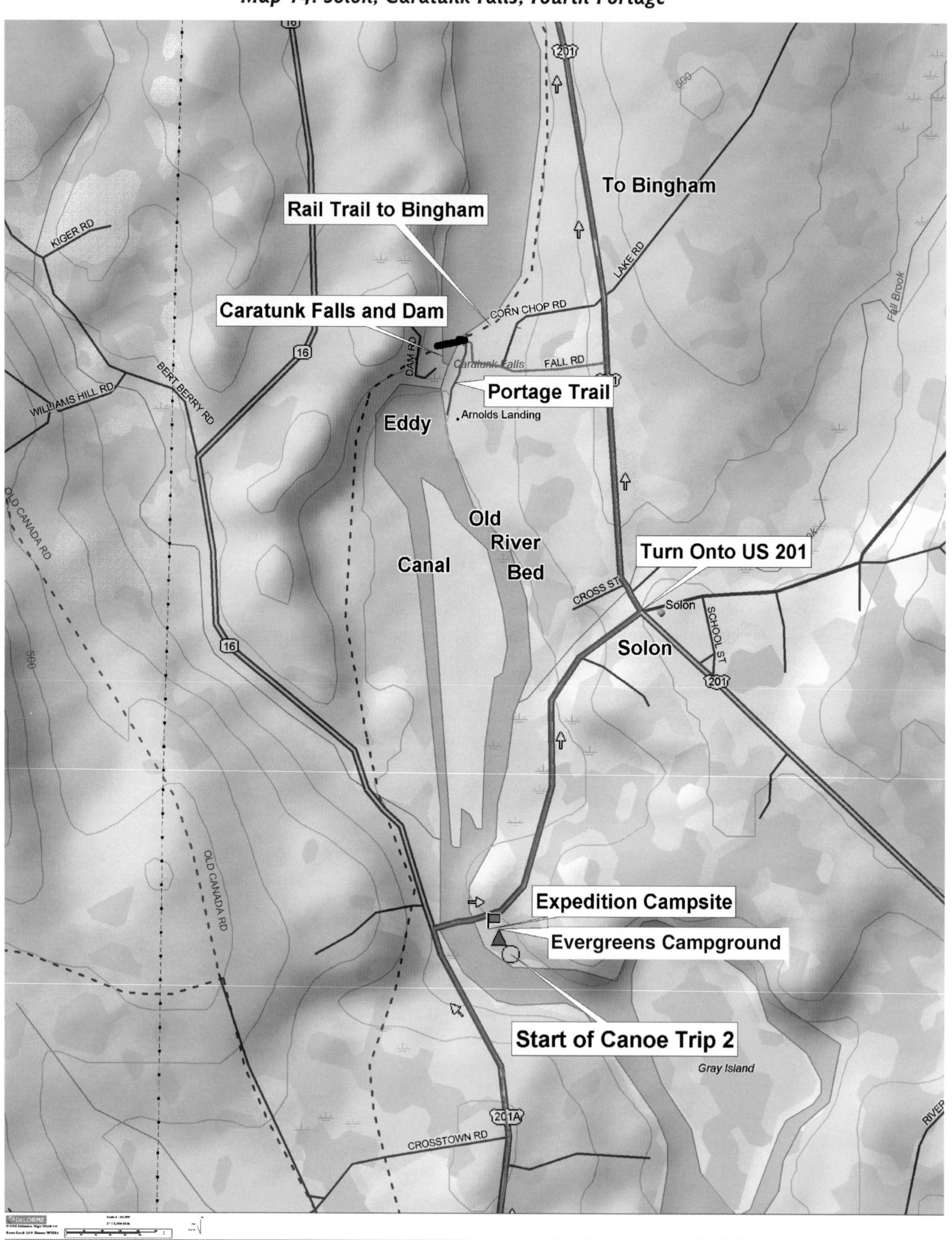

Map 15. Bingham to Caratunk

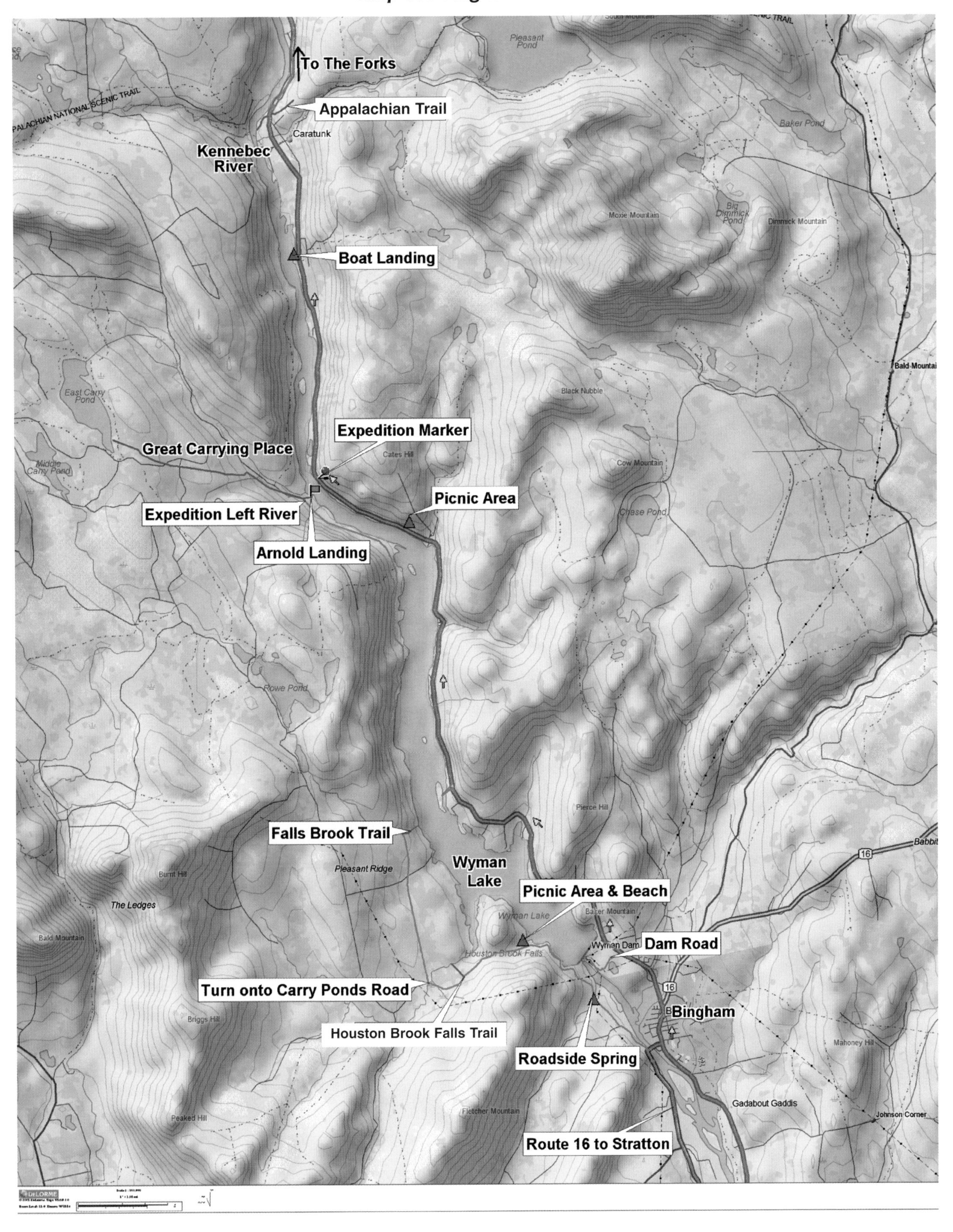

Map 16. Carry Ponds

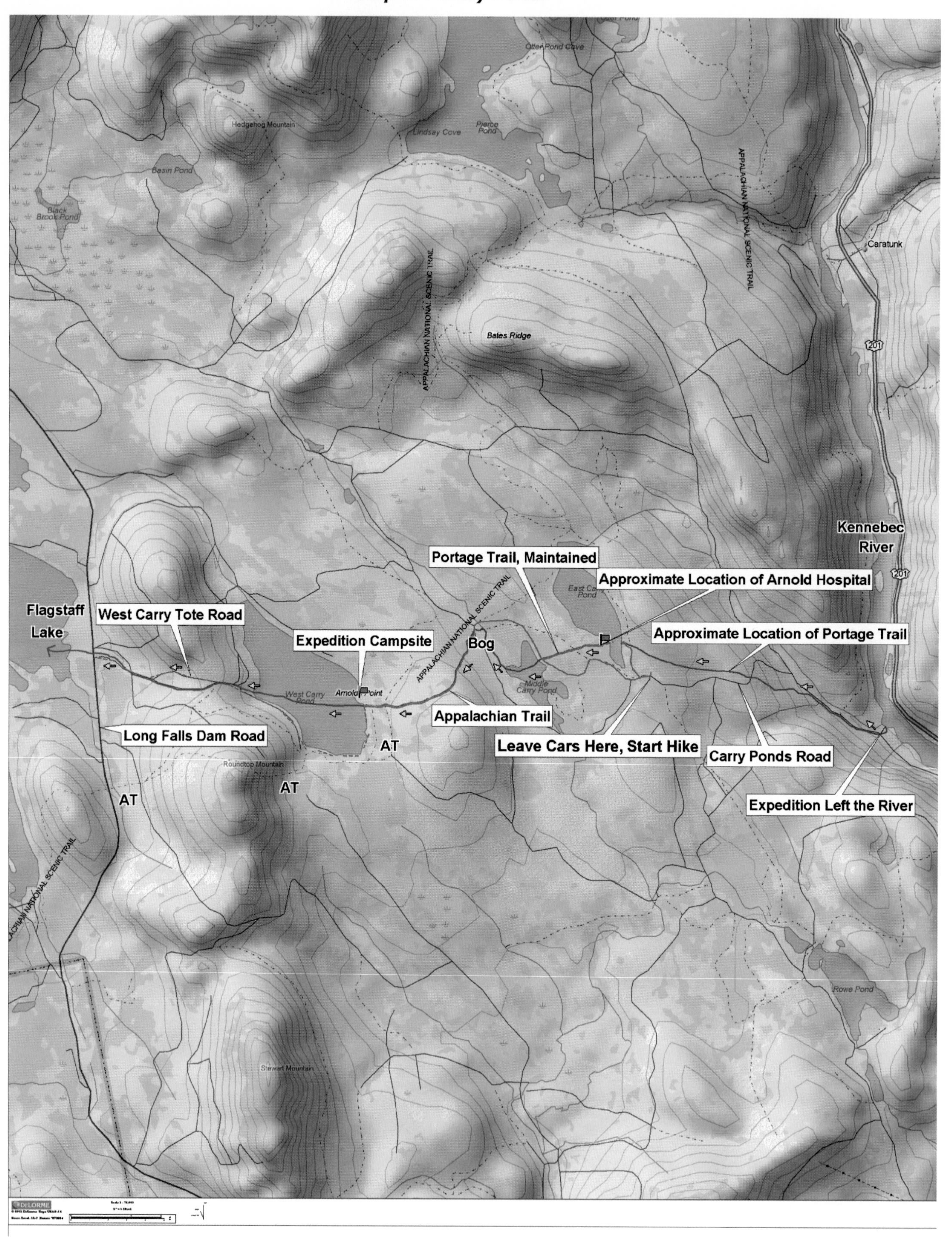

Map 17. Stratton to Chain of Ponds

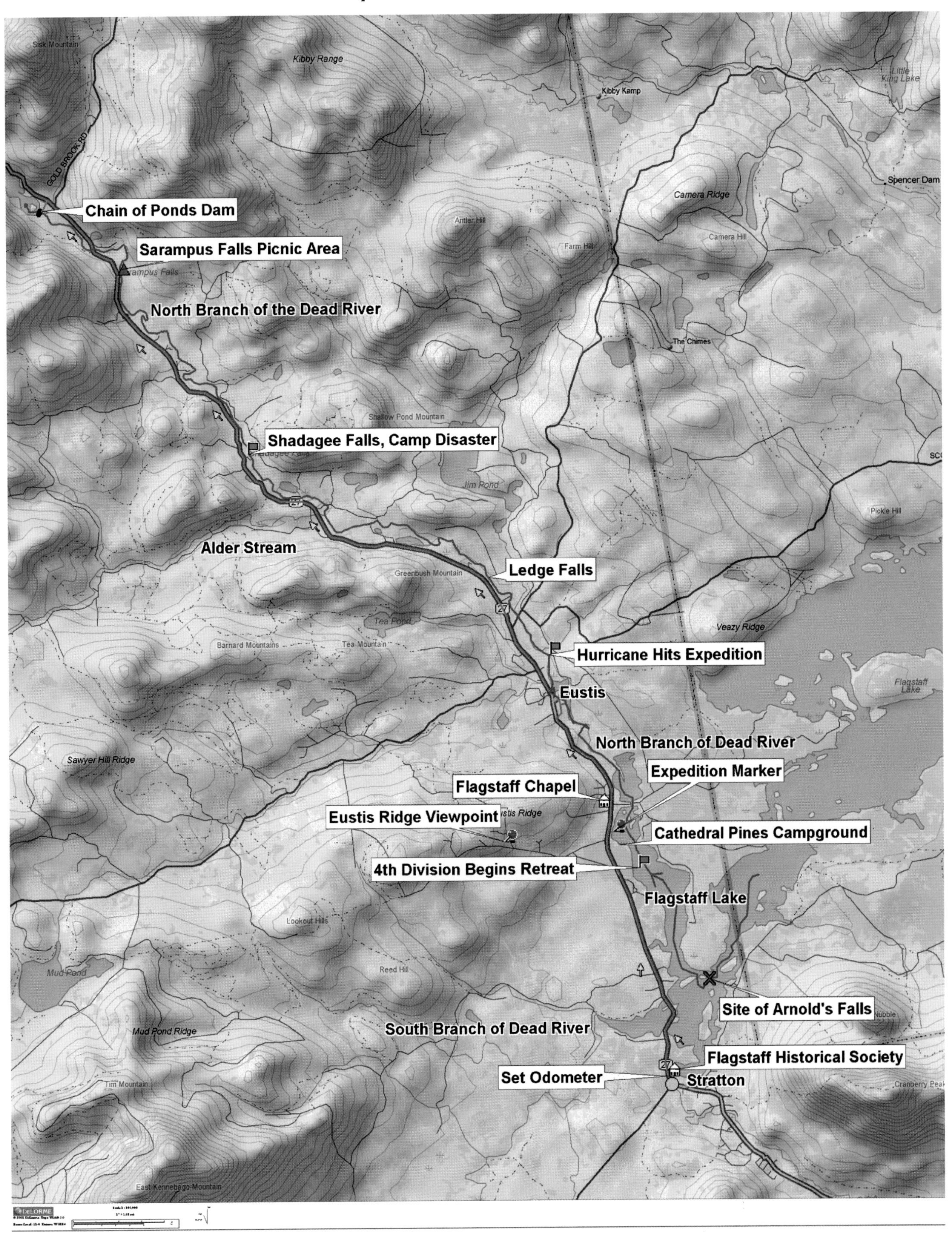

Map 18. Eustis Village

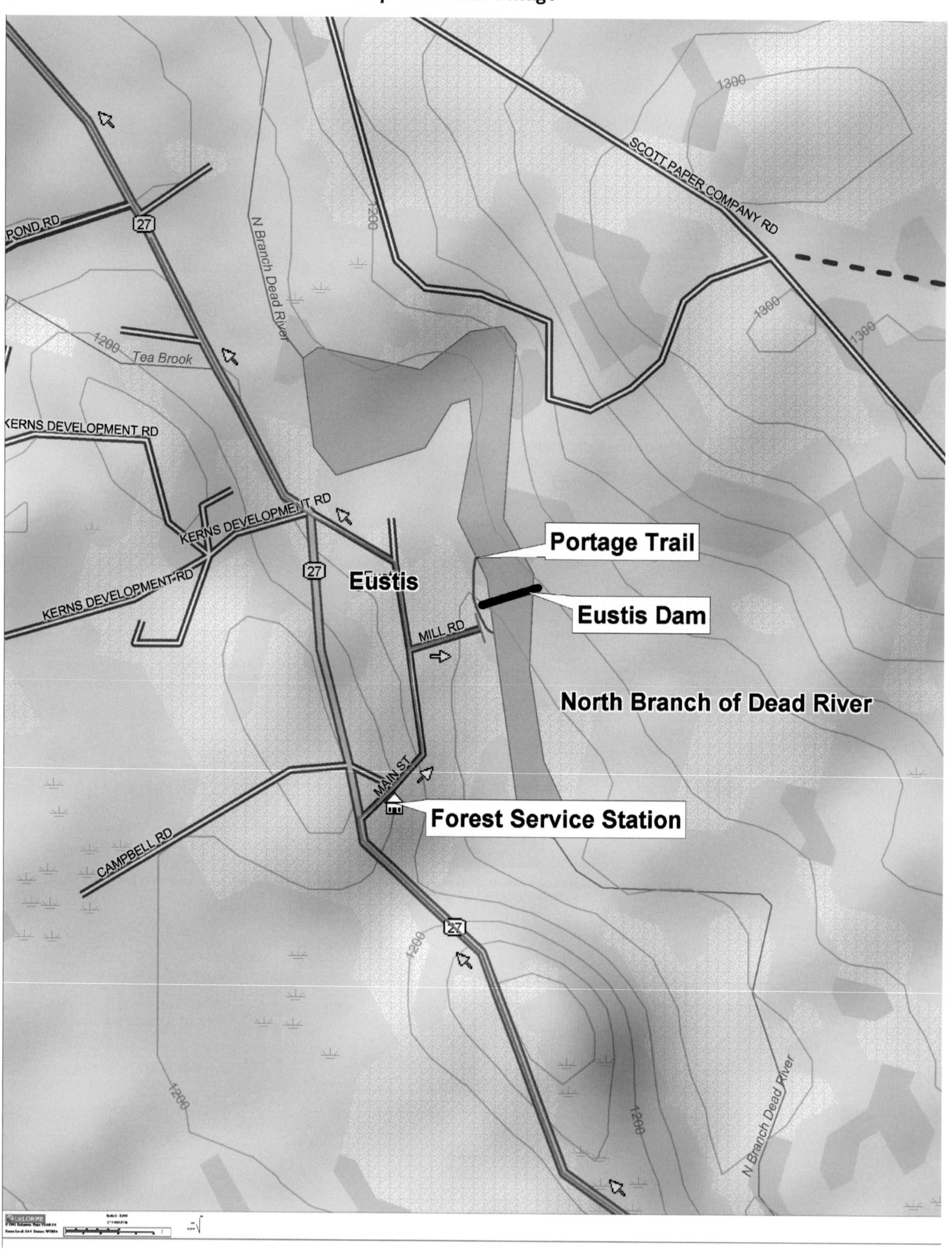

Map 19. Chain of Ponds to Canadian Border

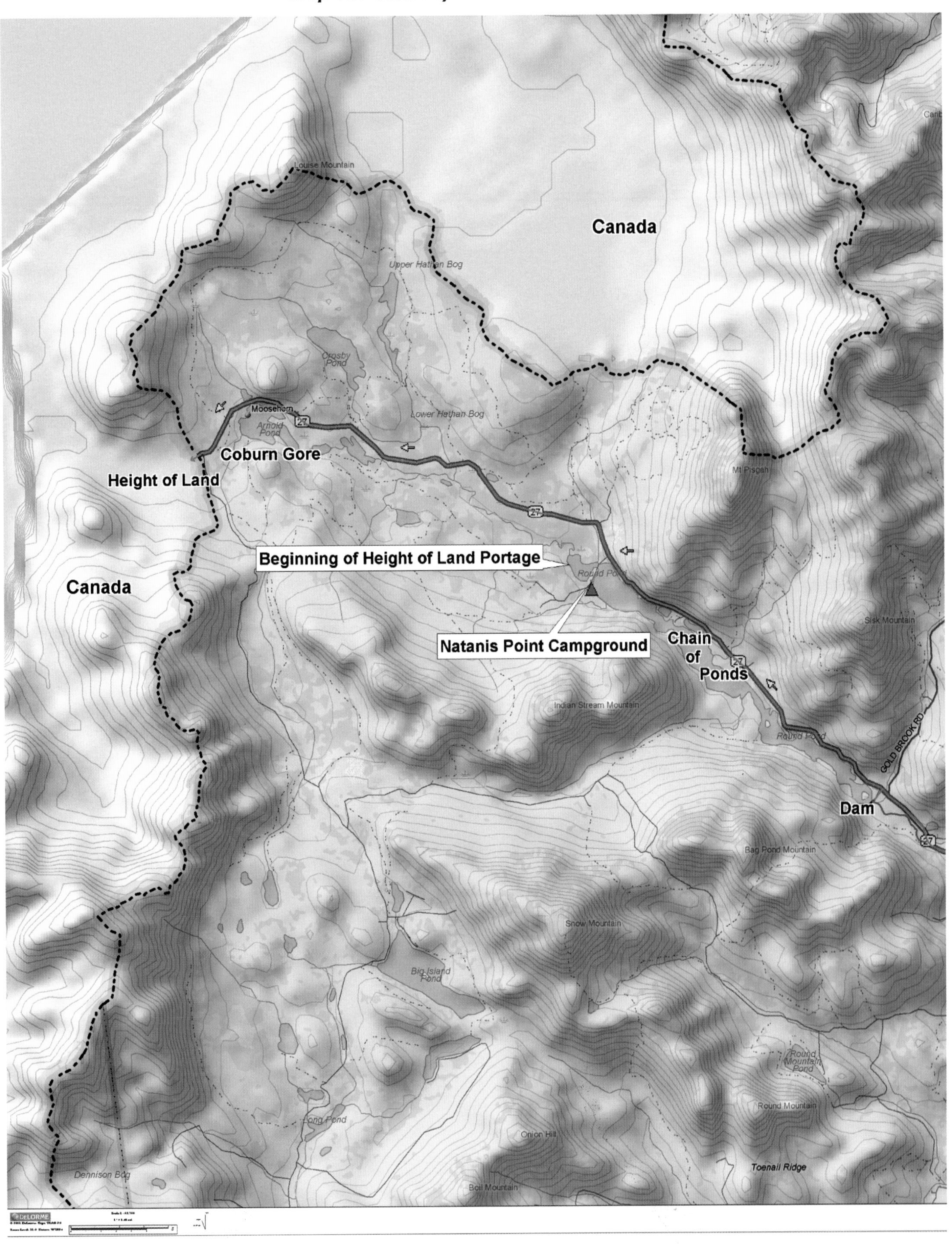

Map 20. Portage Route over Height of Land

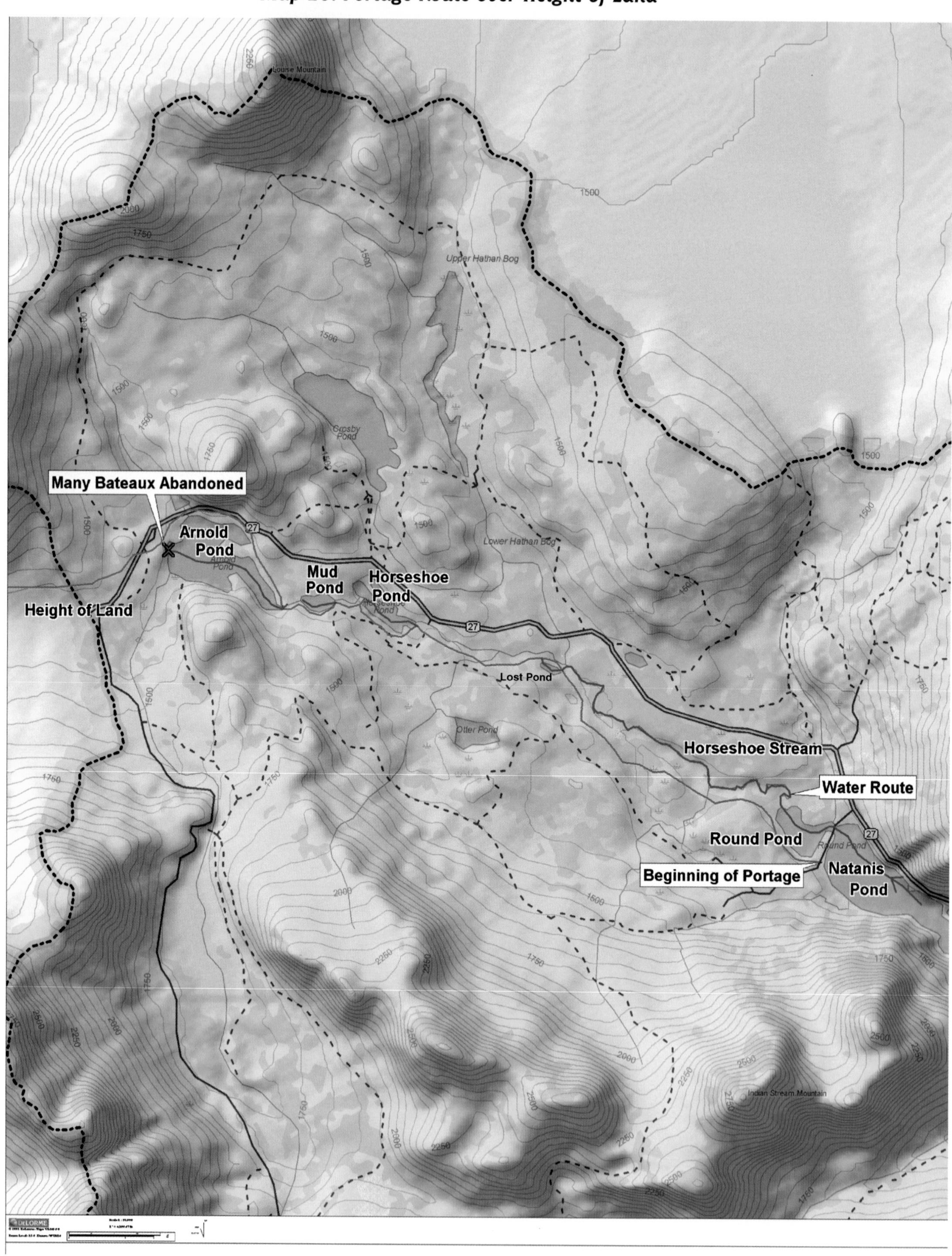

Cambridge Common, Massachusetts

Fort Popham, Kennebec River, Maine

Colburn House, Pittston, Maine

Fort Western, Augusta, Maine

Wyman Lake, Maine, near the Great Carrying Place

Flagstaff Memorial Chapel, Eustis, Maine

Ledge Falls, North Branch, Dead River

Lower Town, Quebec City